THE NEW MIDDLE AGES

BONNIE WHEELER, *Series Editor*

The New Middle Ages presents transdisciplinary studies of medieval cultures. It includes both scholarly monographs and essay collections.

PUBLISHED BY PALGRAVE MACMILLIAN:

Women in the Medieval Islamic World:
Power, Patronage, and Piety
    edited by Gavin R. G. Hambly

The Ethics of Nature in the Middle Ages:
On Boccaccio's Poetaphysics
    by Gregory B. Stone

Presence and Presentation:
Women in the Chinese Literati Tradition
    by Sherry J. Mou

The Lost Love Letters of Heloise and Abelard:
Perceptions of Dialogue in Twelfth-Century France
    by Constant J. Mews

Understanding Scholastic Thought with Foucault
    by Philipp W. Rosemann

For Her Good Estate:
The Life of Elizabeth de Burgh
    by Frances Underhill

Constructions of Widowhood and Virginity
in the Middle Ages
    edited by Cindy L. Carlson
    and Angela Jane Weisl

Motherhood and Mothering
in Anglo-Saxon England
    by Mary Dockray-Miller

Listening to Heloise:
The Voice of a Twelfth-Century Woman
    edited by Bonnie Wheeler

The Postcolonial Middle Ages
    edited by Jeffrey Jerome Cohen

Chaucer's Pardoner and Gender Theory:
Bodies of Discourse
    by Robert S. Sturges

Engaging Words: The Culture of Reading
in the Later Middle Ages
    by Laurel Amtower

Crossing the Bridge: Comparative Essays
on Medieval European and Heian Japanese
Women Writers
    edited by Barbara Stevenson and
    Cynthia Ho

Robes and Honor:
The Medieval World of Investiture
    edited by Stewart Gordon

Representing Rape in Medieval
and Early Modern Literature
    edited by Elizabeth Robertson
    and Christine M. Rose

Same Sex Love and Desire Among Women
in the Middle Ages
    edited by Francesca Canadé Sautman
    and Pamela Sheingorn

Listen Daughter: The Speculum Virginum
and the Formation of Religious Women
in the Middle Ages
    edited by Constant J. Mews

Science, The Singular, and the Question
of Theology
    by Richard A. Lee, Jr.

Gender in Debate from the Early Middle Ages
to the Renaissance
    edited by Thelma S. Fenster
    and Clare A. Lees

Malory's Morte Darthur:
Remaking Arthurian Tradition
    by Catherine Batt

The Vernacular Spirit: Essays on Medieval Religious Literature
edited by Renate Blumenfeld-Kosinski, Duncan Robertson, and Nancy Bradley Warren

Popular Piety and Art in the Late Middle Ages
by Kathleen Kamerick

Absent Narratives, Manuscript Textuality, and Literary Structure in Late Medieval England
by Elizabeth Scala

Creating Community with Food and Drink in Merovingian Gaul
by Bonnie Effros

CREATING COMMUNITY WITH FOOD AND DRINK IN MEROVINGIAN GAUL

Bonnie Effros

CREATING COMMUNITY WITH FOOD AND DRINK IN MEROVINGIAN GAUL
Copyright © Bonnie Effros, 2002.
All rights reserved. No part of this book may be used or reproduced in any manner whatsoever without written permission except in the case of brief quotations embodied in critical articles or reviews.

Cover Photo Credit
Detail of the marriage at Cana taken from the late antique or Carolingian ivory, the Andrews Diptych, depicting the miracles of Christ. Photograph reproduced with permission of the Victoria & Albert Museum, London.

First published 2002 by
PALGRAVE MACMILLAN™
175 Fifth Avenue, New York, N.Y. 10010 and
Houndmills, Basingstoke, Hampshire, England RG21 6XS.
Companies and representatives throughout the world.

PALGRAVE MACMILLAN is the global academic imprint of the Palgrave Macmillan division of St. Martin's Press, LLC and of Palgrave Macmillan Ltd. Macmillan® is a registered trademark in the United States, United Kingdom and other countries. Palgrave is a registered trademark in the European Union and other countries.

ISBN 978-0-312-22736-4

Library of Congress Cataloging-in-Publication Data
Effros, Bonnie, 1965-
Creating community with food and drink in Merovingian Gaul / by Bonnie Effros.
    p. cm.—(New Middle Ages)
  Includes bibliographical references and index.
  ISBN 978-0-312-22736-4
  1. Merovingians—Food—Social aspects. 2. Dinners and dining—France—History. 3. Fasts and feasts—France—History. 4. Civilization, Medieval. 5. France—Social life and customs. I. Title. II. New Middle Ages (Palgrave (Firm))

GT2853.F7 E34 2002
306.4'0944—dc21   2002025396

A catalogue record for this book is available from the British Library.

Design by Letra Libre, Inc.

First edition: December 2002
10 9 8 7 6 5 4 3 2 1

In memory of Shifra Stone Kupperman

"Per pietatis opus, per qui pius imperat astris,
per quod mater amat, frater et ipse cupit,
ut, dum nos escam capimus, quodcumque loquaris:
quod si tu facias, bis satiabor ego."

—*Venantius Fortunatus,* De convivio

CONTENTS

Series Editor's Foreword		xi
Abbreviations		xiii
Acknowledgments		xv
Introduction		1
1.	The Ritual Significance of Feasting in the Formation of Christian Communities	9
2.	Food, Drink, and the Expression of Clerical Identity	25
3.	Gender and Authority: Feasting and Fasting in Early Medieval Monasteries for Women	39
4.	Food as a Source of Healing and Power	55
5.	Funerary Feasting in Early Medieval Gaul and Neighboring Regions	69
Epilogue		93
Notes		97
Select Bibliography		145
Index		169

SERIES EDITOR'S FOREWORD

The New Middle Ages contributes to lively transdisciplinary conversations in medieval cultural studies through its scholarly monographs and essay collections. This series provides new work in a contemporary idiom about precise (if often diverse) practices, expressions, and ideologies in the Middle Ages. In this monograph, *Creating Community with Food and Drink in Merovingian Gaul,* Bonnie Effros invites readers to consider the varied uses of feasting and fasting as means of evoking material abundance, self-control, and spiritual efficacy in Christian communities as they evolved. Her study gives great particularity to (and in some cases challenges) the argument that Christianity absorbed or overlaid its predecessors' most ingrained private and social habits. In Merovingian communities, Christian religious power flowed from one hierarchy to another through gift exchanges of food and drink, and each element of this exchange required clerical intervention, since rites of purification were exclusive manifests of the clergy and the wonder-working saint. Early medieval religious power, Effros demonstrates, was embedded in and enhanced by the efficacy of these exclusionary material practices. The fasting associated with ascetic cloistered women was a visible, mandated signal of their holiness, yet even here the nurturing hospitality of food and drink—of *convivia*—by female monastic houses adroitly cemented their alliances, proclaimed their Christian status, and amplified their power. In case after case, Effros shows us how early medieval religious communities of women as well as men could eat their cake and have it too. Effros binds the techniques of the archeologist who deciphers material culture to the strategies of the wide-ranging social and political historian in her effort to show us how cultures propagate their beliefs and status systems through what we might call the discourse of the gut. *Creating Community* gives us a remarkable recipe for cultural formation in the liminal period of Christianization in early medieval Gaul.

Bonnie Wheeler
Southern Methodist University

ABBREVIATIONS

AA	Auctores antiquissimi
AFAM	Association française d'archéologie mérovingienne
AK	*Archäologisches Korrespondenzblatt*
AM	*Archéologie médiévale*
Annales ESC	*Annales: Économies, sociétés, civilisations*
BAR	British Archaeological Reports
CBA	Council for British Archaeology
CCSL	Corpus christianorum, series latina
CNRS	Centre nationale de la recherche scientifique
CSEL	Corpus scriptorum ecclesiasticorum latinorum
EME	*Early Medieval Europe*
FS	*Frühmittelalterliche Studien*
HJ	*Historisches Jahrbuch*
MGH	Monumenta Germaniae historica
PL	Patrologia latina
SC	Sources chrétiennes
SRG	Scriptores rerum Germanicarum in usum scholarum
SRM	Scriptores rerum Merovingicarum
TRW	Transformation of the Roman World

ACKNOWLEDGMENTS

Growing up in a household fairly observant of the laws of Kashrut, I learned from a young age the importance of food rituals even when they seemed strangely out of context in southern California during the 1970s. My mother followed a strict regime of maintaining separate cooking vessels, dishes, and utensils for meat and milk, a lesson which was reinforced during visits to my Orthodox grandparents in Brooklyn. Since our attendance at synagogue was rather infrequent, the preparation and sharing of holiday meals often seemed the strongest, if not the most memorable, marker of our religious identity. Particularly notable was the enormous dedication of my mother to readying the household for Passover, when she cleared the kitchen, brought out separate dishware used at this time of year only, and rid the pantry of items containing leaven. The offending foodstuffs banished to the garage were "sold" to the rabbi for the length of the holiday. Although my experience was certainly far from unique, I was deeply impressed by the number of traditions to which my mother faithfully adhered, even when they seemed far from logical to me. Moreover, the practical effects of Kashrut on our lives were clear. These food regulations determined not only where and what one could eat, but in general terms the company one kept in eating; more religious friends were restricted to a small number of kosher restaurants and butcher shops distant from the Los Angeles suburbs where we lived.

The message about Kashrut in my family was far from a unified one, however, and the rules were subject to willful bending once outside of the house. My father, who had received a more liberal upbringing than my mother, encouraged us to partake in all sorts of "forbidden" foods. Much in the tradition of many assimilated Jews from New York, I have fond memories of visits to Chinese restaurants and the many delicacies we sampled there. Food laws, while to a certain degree fluid and mutable in my family, nonetheless remained a constant reminder of the frontier between participating in mainstream American life and maintaining an identity as a member of the Jewish faith. Despite having grown to adulthood without retaining these observances, my fascination with the

xvi CREATING COMMUNITY WITH FOOD AND DRINK

multiple rituals attached to the breaking of bread has continued. Working in a field normally devoid of direct links with my own background, my study of the early Middle Ages gained a personal connection when I unexpectedly came across certain food prohibitions in the penitential literature that rang very familiarly to my ears. Wondering why of all things aspects of this long abandoned facet of Old Testament prescriptions played a brief role in the early Middle Ages both in Ireland and on the Continent, I decided to explore what needs such traditions possibly fulfilled in Merovingian-period communities.

My decision to measure the bonds created by food and drink were from the beginning inspired by the work of Mary Douglas and Caroline Walker Bynum, but would have never been formulated without the infectious enthusiasm of Kandace Keithley, then a colleague at the University of Alberta studying women and food on the North American frontiers. Over the meals we shared, we spoke of the undervalued contribution of food preparation to the shaping of human societies. The broader outline of this book was conceptualized during a number of stimulating encounters between 1995 and 1998 with colleagues in Group One of the Transformation of the Roman World (TRW) project sponsored by the European Science Foundation. I thank Palgrave for permission to submit an early version of chapter one to *The Construction of Communities in the Early Middle Ages: Texts, Resources and Artifacts,* edited by Richard Corradini, Max Diesenberger, and Helmut Reimitz, TRW (Leiden: E. J. Brill, forthcoming). Despite the numerous potential topics that could be covered if one used feasting, or other sorts of activities based around food, as a lens through which to view the early Middle Ages, I limited the format of the work to an introduction and five essays on related themes. This exploratory approach was devised in order to avoid any pretense of having completed a comprehensive assessment of early medieval feasting and fasting.

On account of the nature of the surviving written evidence from Merovingian Gaul, I was faced with a number of methodological challenges. From the start, I decided that this work would not address the practical aspects of what was being eaten in the early Middle Ages or how food and drink were grown, prepared, or distributed in rural and urban communities. Besides the limited information provided by written sources and the amount of archaeological research currently underway or still to be done on this subject, these questions had already been addressed elsewhere more capably than I could have undertaken myself.[1] My intention lay instead in exploring the symbolism invested in the rituals associated with the provision and consumption of nourishment. However, because most of the sources I was using to discuss the role of food and drink in Merovingian society were written by monks, nuns, or bishops, they presented foremost

ACKNOWLEDGMENTS xvii

the landscape as seen through the eyes of an aristocratic, clerical minority. Moreover, much of the material presented by these authors was directed at creating ideals of behavior, whether by lauding the feats of holy men and women or by castigating what they perceived as unacceptable behavior. The bearing of these texts on reality was thus not altogether clear. Their perspective permeated the texts to such a great degree that I became convinced that only their limited world view could be presented with any accuracy. The attitudes of women and even lay elites, by contrast, could only be discerned indirectly, and thus far less completely, than their male or religious contemporaries. Consequently, I selected the subject matter of the chapters so as to heighten recognition of the objectives of clerics in recording descriptions of or controlling food and drink rituals. This approach has resulted in a very different sort of work than would have emerged from evidence for a later period in the same regions.

This book was written intermittently amidst a variety of other obligations during the past five years. Early chapters were composed in the fall of 1997 during a semester's residency at the Camargo Foundation in Cassis, France, and in the summer of 1998 with a Berkshire Summer Fellowship at the Mary Ingraham Bunting Institute at Radcliffe College. A consecutive series of Summer Research Fellowships from Southern Illinois University at Edwardsville between 1998 and 2001 were dedicated in part to the composition of various chapters and their revision. The last part of the research and writing was completed during my tenure of a Sylvan C. Coleman and Pamela Coleman Memorial Fund Fellowship at The Metropolitan Museum of Art and Title F leave from the State University of New York at Binghamton in 2001–2002. All of these grants provided much needed financial support or equally necessary workspace and library access, and allowed me more than stolen moments to devote to the project; they also fostered stimulating interchanges with colleagues and made possible attendance at international conferences to present the work-in-progress. I am grateful for the support of Peter Barnet, Carole Frick, Melanie Holcomb, Marcie Karp, Ellen Nore, Don Quataert, and Leslie Levene during my fellowship year.

Although I am doubtless omitting people to whom credit is due in this short space, I would like to begin by thanking Walter Pohl whose invitation to join Group One of the TRW and whose ensuing friendship and encouragement made this book possible. Frans Theuws, Matthias Hardt, and Jörg Jarnut likewise encouraged me to pursue this project and helped shape its conception; a number of spirited conversations with Hans-Werner Goetz about the role of gender in early medieval society likewise firmed my resolve to work on this topic. Isabel Moreira read and thoughtfully critiqued the entire manuscript, and Nina Caputo and Eric Ruckh provided

xviii   CREATING COMMUNITY WITH FOOD AND DRINK

helpful criticism of various chapters-in-progress. Patrick Périn and Chantal Dulos at the Musée des antiquités nationales de Saint-Germain-en-Laye and Paul Williamson at the Victoria & Albert Museum generously assisted me in procuring photographs for chapter five and the cover. I am grateful to Frederick Paxton for providing an enormously helpful bibliography on early medieval healing; Amancio Isla and Christian Lohmer for tracking down a number of important pieces to which I did not otherwise have access; Barbara Altmann for her comments on two early chapters; and Sarah Davies Cordova for a series of inspiring meals and hikes along the calanques of Cassis in 1997. I wish to thank Richard Rouse, Peter Brown, Patrick Geary, and Guy Halsall for unhesitatingly supporting the various fellowship applications that made this project possible. Lyn O'Conor-Ferguson organized Publications Day at the Bunting Institute where I met my future editors, and she allowed me to use surplus office space in 1999; Nicole Bériou very kindly made available housing while I was in Paris. Michael Flamini at Palgrave and Bonnie Wheeler have been patient and supportive editors despite the many unanticipated delays that prevented me from finishing the book in a more timely fashion.

As always, I have had the encouragement and hospitality of my family and friends throughout the process of writing and revising, and the moves that have interrupted it. These include Gail and Richard Effros, Michelle Effros, Jim Effros, Dorothea and Roland Stevens, Mitch Hart, Wulf Kansteiner and Sonja Wolf, Dick Trexler, Roberta Shapiro, Lori Weintrob, Jonathan Blitz, Tom Head, Dianne Golden, Grace Benveniste, Peter Pozefsky, Martin Taylor, Rita and Ed Effros, Jane and Steven Hochman, Marcia and Manuel Cohen, Bea and Joe (ז״ל) Katel, George and Debbie Hensley, and Barbara Goldoftas. With this book, I honor the memory of my great, great grandmother and (Hebrew) namesake Shifra Stone Kupperman, who brought her knowledge of cooking, canning, and distilling from Rovno, Ukraine, and fed generations of her family after their arrival in Hartford, Connecticut, in the early 1920s.

INTRODUCTION

In piecing together the history of Gaul during the relative turmoil of the final years of the Roman empire and the formation of the Germanic kingdoms, scholars have long devoted attention to the expression and enforcement of political and military authority. Whether written from a legal perspective or with a more holistic outlook, most of these discussions of the transformations occurring in such distant societies have focused on the workings of governing bodies, interactions among elites, the politics of ethnic identity, or the role of religious institutions.[1] Yet, due to the nature of surviving primary sources, these important studies have frequently omitted reference to the activities of the majority of the population who did not often occupy legal positions of authority. While some of these gaps have been unavoidable since they reflect the historical and archaeological evidence, such as with respect to most aspects of peasant and slave life, others are far less easily explained.[2] Fairly typical, for instance, is the absence of a discussion of the influence yielded by high status women who did occasionally receive attention in the chronicles of Gregory of Tours (d. 533), Fredegar (d. circa 660), and the anonymous author of the *Liber historiae Francorum* (circa 727). Despite significant social and legal obstacles, several notable Merovingian queens managed to manipulate unstable situations, such as the lack of an adult heir to the throne, so as to enhance their own standing and political power.[3]

Aside from the many historical works that have neglected to integrate evidence of contributions to early medieval society made by those other than elite men, some scholars have concentrated too heavily on accounting for women's failure to achieve more than temporary advances in powerful circles in Gaul and other parts of Western Europe.[4] Instead of assessing how they achieved some of their goals, early medieval, like modern historians, have cast a disparaging eye upon the few contemporary female leaders who successfully harnessed political or military might.[5] The remainder of early medieval women have not fared much better in the historical literature as their existence has been seen as marginal at best.[6] In brief, women have been described mainly in relation to their

2   CREATING COMMUNITY WITH FOOD AND DRINK

male counterparts, and their shortcomings characterized as the effects of conforming to existence in a man's world.[7] Scholars have thus relegated women and other marginalized groups to a more passive role than they likely played.

Yet, as is clear from a number of recent works, formal networks of authority do not constitute the only possible paradigm by which to interpret the workings of late antique and early medieval society.[8] By limiting the vocabulary of authority to solely political institutions, scholars have overlooked other sources of power, including the economic, military, and ideological bases that contributed to a complex social system.[9] Although the juxtaposition in this discussion of formal and informal authority is in and of itself problematic, since these categories imply a level of organization that did not exist in early medieval Gaul,[10] they help emphasize that most institutions sanctioned and described by the secular and religious leadership excluded nearly all women and peasants.[11] Nonetheless, their absence from these cannot be used to construe that they made no contribution to early medieval society: this transitional period conversely allowed for a high level of plurality and social interaction.[12] While the activities of groups such as peasants and slaves, who are nearly universally neglected in the surviving early medieval evidence, will be very difficult to reconstruct, other sectors of the population are somewhat more realistically assessed. Particularly in the case of elite women, who are vastly under-represented in sources describing contemporary institutions,[13] alternative means need to be established for viewing how power relations might be coordinated outside formal venues of political authority. In order to render more accurately accounts of early medieval women's contributions to social organization, for instance, networks of ritual exchange must receive increased attention as central facets of medieval power.[14]

Rather than suggesting that women were passive participants in communities over which they had no influence, fleeting glimpses of their activities and emotions in contemporary sources indicate that their actions and networks were complex.[15] Studies of the implications of gender difference have proved particularly important, for instance, in works of hagiography. Even while not armed in the traditional sense, the fury of a young girl such as Gertrude of Nivelles (d. 659) might be portrayed by her hagiographer as gaining the cooperation of a monarch in her favor rather than representing an outrageous affront.[16] Despite the constructed nature of saints' *Lives* promoting the holiness of their subjects from an early age, more lies beneath the surface than immediately evident. At least some elite women were able to assert their will in order to achieve their desired goals. By pursuing more ascetic avenues, for instance, some Christian women managed to earn the grudging respect of their peers and superiors and thereby achieved influential positions that did not preclude political power. Entering the political arena directly as a female player, by contrast, was a more dangerous ambition, since women were likely to create many enemies in the exercise of authority.

In the case of early medieval Gaul, the sources are almost exclusively composed from a male, clerical perspective and focus on urban populations where clerical powers were strongest. Moreover, we lack the counterbalance of the reactions of their congregants to these directives.[17] The task of broadening our reading of texts beyond family history and local stories pertinent to clerical authors is thus rendered difficult.[18] Searching for a means by which to reconstruct the fabric of early medieval society can be exceedingly frustrating. Yet, what may often seem to be incidental information may in fact be carefully placed scenes in canonical and hagiographical texts. These shed light on at least some of the objectives and audience of the authors.[19] Descriptions of festivals may likewise give insight into what communities celebrated and thus valued. Such sources help to identify where some of the possibilities existed for building relationships between individuals or groups.

Many early medieval accounts, and especially hagiographical ones, described feasting or abstention from the consumption of food and drink. Not only did these rituals serve to legitimize power relations,[20] but they greatly expand our understanding of how individuals might coopt or reject dominant social norms to their advantage, and thereby adopt the most effective strategies to reach their objectives. Besides their practical ends in nourishing the human body, eating and drinking were highly symbolic acts and might be manipulated to a variety of purposes.[21] Although most forms of food aside from the Eucharist were not considered holy in and of themselves, bread, wine, water, and oil not only constituted dietary substances but also operated as liturgical symbols.[22] Fish, too, played a role in recalling events in the Gospels and evoking the daily relevance of the life of Christ.[23] Despite the fact that their value was ephemeral due to their perishable qualities, their entry into exchange represented a link in a larger, more powerful chain of reciprocal gift-giving that might last a single lifespan or the course of generations.[24] And, in some cases, the expenditure of valuable foodstuffs at events such as funerary meals did not have a primarily utilitarian purpose, but rather enhanced the status of the families who could afford to suffer the loss of these foodstuffs so publicly.[25]

The organization of foodways and the display of consumption of—or abstention from—food and drink thus shed considerable light onto Christian communities' hierarchies and value systems.[26] They also allow us to lessen distinctions such as between Gallo-Romans and Franks, or between rural and town inhabitants. Although their diets varied in considerable ways,[27] all

4 CREATING COMMUNITY WITH FOOD AND DRINK

had traditions incorporating food and drink. Shared meals therefore provided an important symbolic language through which assimilation or competition between various groups might occur. In addition to the symbolic roles of foodstuffs, they served practical ends. Alongside their role in gift-giving, food and drink represented edible commodities, subject to the vagaries of production, distribution, and trade or sale in the marketplace.[28]

Clerical descriptions of the preparation, distribution, and consumption of food and drink provide insight into their perception of existing networks of power within and between lay and religious communities in the early Middle Ages.[29] While clerical authors were rarely interested in writing about the logistics of acquiring ingredients, brewing, or cooking, perhaps because they were considered manual and hence less valued activities, church foundations constituted important centers of economic activity, including the production of food, and clerics recognized its real worth in addition to its symbolic value.[30] In their historical and hagiographical writing, however, they focused on their main interest: under what circumstances and under whose authority the foodstuffs, including the Eucharistic wine and wafer, might be consumed.[31] They appear to have been concerned, for instance, with which individuals might seek to wield authority over public and private exchanges of food and drink or how lay men and women might use such influential positions to gain followers. They also recognized that the sharing of meals could bring greater unity among disparate groups of people.

While traditional approaches toward the ritual applications of feasting and fasting have often pejoratively linked such activities to primitivism in antiquity and the early Middle Ages,[32] that is, other than in the context of banquet scenes in a lord or king's hall, the relationships which they sustained represent an important structural component of early medieval society. This under-utilized methodological tool may bear fruit for our understanding of power relationships as well as in discerning what sort of gift-giving was considered effective by at least the elite members of Christian communities who are best documented in surviving sources. Even if we cannot determine the banquets' precise value as commodities, in part because so much of the production side of the equation is missing, the symbolic importance of the transactions may be marked by the influence they had on subsequent exchanges between the parties involved.[33]

Hence, the uses of feasting were diverse in the early Middle Ages. Just as they might foster unity, foodways could also contribute to the establishment of the distinctiveness of one group in a larger community. Similar to the use of clothing to distinguish ethnic parties in a particular conflict,[34] the display of food and drink in a variety of ritual contexts could serve an analogous role. In some hagiographical accounts, for instance, clerical authors depicted

INTRODUCTION 5

alleged pagans, or more likely Christians presumably performing traditional rites, as challenging the will of bishops and abbots. As will be discussed in the first chapter, clerics' reactions to these illicit celebrations in the countryside, and the speed with which they shut them down despite being outnumbered, illustrated their claims on the distance to which their authority reached even outside of town walls.[35] Prescriptions for both religious communities and lay congregations as to what might be eaten, with whom, and in conjunction with what rituals thus became central to their ability to define what it meant to be Christian. Distinctions between purity and pollution, such as between Catholics and heretics or Jews or between urban and rural populations, created order and thereby drew important boundaries between those who obeyed God's command and those who did not.[36]

Fasting, too, could play an important role in delineating a hierarchy of Christians before God. In the late sixth and early seventh century, a system of private penance emerged that equated individual sin with a corresponding need for atonement. By abstaining from all nourishment but bread and water for specified periods of time that reflected their transgressions, Christians thereby gained the benefit of God's indulgence on a daily basis.[37] They might thus be reintegrated into the community of the faithful. Fasting also represented a means of attaining purity and thus indicated preparedness for baptism, the Mass, and visionary experiences.[38] Since penitential prescriptions altered the lifestyles of those who adhered to them, they helped establish beyond the rite of baptism expected norms of behavior for the Christian faithful.

In chapter two, attention shifts to the manner in which customs regulating food and drink were highly relevant to the ability of clerics, who did not possess the right to bear arms, to further social, religious, and political agendas. Typically, scholars have not taken altogether seriously the relationships formed in large part through rites of hospitality, since they do not view them as having possessed the strength of military loyalties. Hans-Werner Goetz has, for instance, suggested the tenuous nature of the ties thereby established:

> It is widely assumed that there was a common obligation to receive strangers and pilgrims as guests, but it is more likely that hospitality was considered a virtue rather than a duty, except for charges of hospitality towards one's own lord. Once a guest was accommodated under one's roof, however, the host was responsible for his protection. Nevertheless, hospitality merely created temporary bonds.[39]

Yet, in both secular and religious contexts, symbolic exchanges of weaponry, precious objects, and food were vital to the formation and sustenance of

6   CREATING COMMUNITY WITH FOOD AND DRINK

friendship (*amicitia*) and thereby elite power.[40] As attested in the writings of Gregory of Tours and other early medieval historians, plunder, banquets, and massed treasures along with impressive requisite eating and drinking vessels were a standard element of the Merovingian political scene.[41] A bishop's sanction or even sponsorship of feasting therefore might earn him the patronage of a powerful nobleman or monarch. Conversely, his refusal to participate or his miraculous ability to stop the festivities, might publicly demonstrate his loyalty to a power greater than that of the king or duke. These accounts helped redefine the effective expression of masculinity among early medieval clerics.

More specifically, the means by which hospitality was offered or denied provides evidence of important mechanisms at the heart of Christian and non-Christian communities. As has been noted by Annette Weiner, the ability to give generously and publicly without seeming to suffer loss is a means of demonstrating the abundance of possessions in one's control: the giver thus gains the dominant position over individuals who are now in his or her debt.[42] While this sort of influence may not be measured in quantitative terms in the early Middle Ages, such favors were unlikely either quickly forgotten or of little consequence. As noted in chapter three, the sponsorship of banquets allowed an abbess, for instance, to distinguish enemies from those whom she currently held in high esteem. Although certain early medieval bishops like Caesarius of Arles recognized the burden of such practices and therefore sought to restrict women's means to establish such ties of patronage by limiting their ability to provision lay elites and even ecclesiastical leaders with feasts (*convivia*), their endeavors were unsuccessful in the long term.[43] Participation in these powerful networks, which contrasted with the efforts of ascetic nuns to deny themselves similarly pleasurable meals, was recognized as too critical to the prosperity and protection of women's monastic houses to be abandoned definitively.

Discussions of food and drink in chapter four also provide important insight into clerics' understanding of what sorts of traditions were necessary and appropriate for the health and welfare of the population. They also reveal how they sought to regulate them. Popular medical healing in Gaul had long been associated with the use of herbs, amulets, and a variety of other cures of the sort described by Pliny the Elder.[44] Some of these rituals underwent superficial transformations making them more acceptable to the leaders of Christian communities. The source of healing had changed, as illustrated by the cure of a paralyzed girl named Sigrada, who was healed through a vision in which the saint Anstrude anointed her with holy oil and blessed her by motioning the sign of the cross.[45] Yet many lay healers remained true to existing oral traditions and retained their folkloric roots. Because they represented competition for saints' shrines, these types of

INTRODUCTION

cures were regularly condemned by clerics as superstitious or magical vestiges of paganism.[46] Although physicians fared better than folk healers in the writings of clerics, and were in some cases valued for their skills, their handiwork was regularly characterized by religious authors as inferior to the miraculous cures effected by relics.[47]

By contrast, knowledge of the writings of ancient physicians, particularly the influential works of the second-century Roman author Galen, waned significantly in the West by the sixth century. Although some classical treatises had been preserved in Western monasteries, Byzantine libraries were far better stocked and their physicians better educated in Greek theoretical traditions. One exceptional case of the sharing of this knowledge with Western counterparts is a letter on diet composed by a Byzantine physician named Anthimus. He wrote this treatise during his exile from Constantinople in his capacity as an ambassador to the Franks on behalf of the Ostrogothic king. Addressed to the Merovingian king Theuderic some time after 511, Anthimus's *De observatione ciborum (On the Observance of Foods)* was largely borrowed from recipes and medical advice included in the works of Apicius and Galen. In his epistle, the ambassador described to his Frankish royal audience the foods and drinks most suited to maintaining physical health and well-being.[48] While we do not know whether the Frankish monarch took Anthimus' advice on diet, or whether any in his court actually read the treatise, this text merits study as the last of its kind known to have circulated in early medieval Gaul for the next several centuries.

Overshadowing such medical learning about food and drink in late antiquity and the early Middle Ages was the impact on healing of the custom of pilgrimage to the shrines of saints.[49] In the works of Caesarius of Arles, the bishop also emphasized the beneficial effects of liturgical rites such as anointing with holy oil.[50] Relics and blessed oil required faith of those who were ill in order for a cure to be effected. Consequently, some clerics viewed consultation with a doctor as a sign of a Christian's lack of faith in God and the miracles He worked through the saints.[51] Therefore, few clerical scholars were interested in copying ancient medical treatises either in part or in their entirety. These texts nonetheless continued to shape indirectly the attitudes of early medieval clerics in certain fields. We know, for example, that excerpts from medical manuscripts made their way into the writings of the Church Fathers on a variety of topics. They reinforced, for example, religious attitudes towards the benefits of curbing women's improper behavior through fasting;[52] this belief had an enormous impact on nuns' and other religious women's lives in the early Middle Ages.

While the various customs related to food and drink preserved by clerical authors may not be representative of the daily lives of most Christians

8   CREATING COMMUNITY WITH FOOD AND DRINK

in Merovingian Gaul, the rites celebrated in the context of burial were pertinent to the majority of the early medieval population.[53] Despite the limitations of clerical informants, archaeological remains of funerary feasting supplement our understanding of the rich inner workings of the lives of the inhabitants of Gaul during the Merovingian period. The fifth chapter of this work therefore focuses upon feasting in the context of early medieval funerary traditions, and the central role that it played in cementing all manner of social relations between living and deceased Christians.[54] Rather than being viewed as polluting, contact with the dead became a means of reaffirming kinship and celebrating the successful transition of the faithful into the next life. Although clerical authorities often spoke out against such rites as being tainted by their derivation from older pagan customs, archaeological remains of both cemeterial meals and the deposition of food and drink in individual graves demonstrate that these warnings do not appear to have had a significant effect prior to the sixth century.[55] Material evidence of active participation by Christians in the preparation and consumption of meals in cemeteries thus provides an opportunity to discuss the limits of clerical attempts to control the behavior of the faithful.

As noted at the start of this discussion, the nuances of texts addressing the topics of food and drink are often subtle and must be evaluated as fully as possible in the context of the situations in which they arose. Moreover, it is always useful to identify the projected audience of these works, among them saints' *Lives,* letter collections, or ecclesiastical or monastic prescriptions, as the identity of readers influenced the way in which clerical authors chose to frame their descriptions. Whether prescriptive works meant to curb the appetites of the faithful for certain unacceptable forms of feasting or saints' *Lives* intended to reinforce ascetic behavior, these sources reveal many of the important ways in which food and drink rituals shaped the lives of early medieval Christians in Gaul. While bishops were often the harshest critics of the excesses of feasting, they recognized the role it played in community building and in reinforcing identities and alliances. By prescribing certain types of behavior and seeking to control festivities that went beyond these limits, early medieval clerics essentially defined what it meant to be Christian on a daily basis and not just on the holiest days of the year.

CHAPTER 1

THE RITUAL SIGNIFICANCE
OF FEASTING IN THE FORMATION
OF CHRISTIAN COMMUNITIES

Saints and Sacrifices in Sixth-Century Gaul

As Jonas of Bobbio recounted in the sixth-century *Vita Columbani* 1.27, the Irish saint was greatly angered on one occasion when he encountered an Alemannic group making a profane offering of ale to the pagan god Woden. In response, the saint blew on the cask, which contained about twenty measures, and the vessel immediately fragmented, spilling the precious liquid in all directions. In his description of this confrontation, Jonas observed that the devil had been hiding in the barrel, conceivably because he knew that he might win over more souls by providing alcoholic refreshment to the local inhabitants. The miraculous demise of the cask containing the pagan sacrifice thus brought about the conversion of the awed pagans, and the holy man convinced even those who had earlier become Christians to give up their errant ways.[1] Likewise, in the *Vita Vedastis* 7, Jonas described how the saint had agreed to attend a feast of the Franks to which he had been invited. Although many there were Christians, Vaast observed nonetheless that they participated in pagan rites marked most conspicuously by a barrel of beer in the middle of the dwelling. In response, Vaast made the sign of the cross, thereby causing the vessel to shatter and the liquid to pour out upon the floor. Recognizing the inherent spiritual danger of such encounters, he justified his attack on the festivities as necessary for the salvation of all of those present.[2]

These hagiographical accounts and others have been the subject of a number of studies addressing Christian conversions in the Gallic countryside during the early Middle Ages.[3] In both of the above encounters, what was described as a pagan feast or *convivium* was effectively halted by the

10 CREATING COMMUNITY WITH FOOD AND DRINK

saint, and the participants were shown the error of their ways through the destruction of a container holding a sacrificial offering. A recent proposal has suggested that such miracles stories should be interpreted primarily as literary *topoi* derived from texts such as 2 Timothy 2.20–21, which enumerated the noble and ignoble uses of vessels, since paganism was by this time largely banished from even rural areas.[4] The message that they conveyed, however, must have reflected legitimate and contemporary concerns of the Merovingian clergy even if the language they used to describe such groups was exaggerated.[5] Although these encounters likely represented conflicts over ritual practice rather than doctrinal differences,[6] bishops and priests nonetheless desired to establish greater control over ceremonial exchange in Gaul. They therefore characterized as un-Christian those who continued to celebrate ancient rites in addition to Christian festivals.[7] While Donald Bullough has proposed that the deliberate squandering of precious foodstuffs may have been seen as more reprehensible than the sacrificial rite itself,[8] this legitimate quarrel with revelers was not the only one.

In fact, in a number of sixth-century texts, it is very difficult to deny the religious connotations of such festivities.[9] The penitential of Columbanus, for instance, expressed some of the difficulties in preventing lay Christians from participating in rites of this nature:

> But if any layman has eaten or drunk beside the temples, if he did it through ignorance, let him undertake forthwith never to do it again, and let him do penance forty days on bread and water. But if he did it in derision, that is, after the priest has declared to him that this was sacrilege, and if then he communicated at the table of demons, if it was only through the vice of greed that he did or repeated it, let him do penance for a hundred and twenty days on bread and water; but if he did it in worship of the demons or in honour of idols, let him do penance for three years.[10]

The severity of each prescribed punishment corresponded to the intentions of the participant as interpreted by the priest who heard his or her confession. The fear that Christians would return to customs resembling pagan practices after baptism, including ritual meals associated with sacrifices to idols was, moreover, not an isolated phenomenon. This concern mirrored Paul of Tarsus's sentiments in 1 Corinthians that for Christians, any meat was suspect because it may have been offered to idols in the market or by a friend before being presented as part of a meal; he hence urged caution in eating meat prepared by others.[11] Condemned by participants in the Council of Orléans (533) were thus the conscious as well as the unwitting consumption of animals that had died or been suffocated.[12] The Council of Clichy (626–627) likewise referred to those who still ate with

THE RITUAL SIGNIFICANCE OF FEASTING   11

"pagans" against the admonitions of clerics.[13] Seventh-century clerics such as Eligius of Noyon and Audouen of Rouen continued to face such challenges to their authority in rural regions.[14] What was at stake was not so much paganism as the desire to contain impurity and pollution within sharply demarcated boundaries, thereby highlighting what clerics understood to be within their prerogatives.[15]

As noted above, what also attracted the condemnations of clerics were alleged sacrifices and more general excess associated with these rites. Denunciations of unacceptable behavior, which were in part stereotypical, negative characterizations of pagan activities borrowed from texts circulated in Roman antiquity,[16] included singing, drinking, and unspecified lasciviousness;[17] in some instances, they referred even to the unruly conduct of Christians who chose to dance and jump before basilicas dedicated to the saints.[18] Indeed, ritual sacrifice and feasting became so problematic that at some points, sixth-century clerical admonitions against drunken dancing and offerings were reinforced by royal proclamation and papal directive.[19] In a letter dated September 597, Gregory I wrote to Queen Brunhild requesting that she monitor Christians in her kingdom more closely, so that they not return to pagan customs such as sacrifice.[20] There is good reason, nonetheless, to doubt that the intervention of secular officials in such affairs was any more effective than the ministrations of clerics among their congregants. Besides their inability to regulate the activities of isolated villages, lay leaders seem to have expressed ambivalence with respect to these objectives. Some may have even defended what were perceived as more innocuous ancient traditions. In one of the rare measures addressing such issues, the *Pactus legis salicae* 2.16 sanctioned punishment in the form of a fine for those who were witnessed stealing castrated boars, the kind customarily used in sacrificial rites and feasts.[21]

Miracles of the saints that disrupted rural celebrations were not intended, however, as straightforward lessons of the evils of excessive food and drink, for during this period pointed efforts were made to show cathedrals and monasteries as places of plenty. Although certainly there was consistent promotion of the benefits of abstinence from wine and meat, and bishops' palaces were often characterized as lacking the amenities of the king's hall,[22] these structures were not built with the primary intention of impressing the faithful with clerical austerity. In fact, numerous accounts survive attesting to the ability of holy men and women to provide for the faithful even when the contents of their cellars were insufficient to do so without miraculous intervention. The ability to give without suffering loss allowed the wonderworking saint to earn the status of patron,[23] much in the way that lords were expected to provide banquets for their followers, and in the manner that Christians imagined the lavish spreads of pagan feasts.[24]

12 CREATING COMMUNITY WITH FOOD AND DRINK

Just as evergetism, the voluntary and lavish sponsorship of civic activities in the late Roman world, was used to heighten the prestige of the aristocracy,[25] food and drink miracles enabled basilicas and monasteries to
compete with non-clerical forms of patronage and display.[26] In this fashion, the fifth-century Abbot Lupicinus was able to use the proceeds from
a treasure hoard he had uncovered to finance the *convivia* of the brethren
in his house.[27] Even if such acts did not always earn abbots positive ac-
claim, they nonetheless fulfilled important needs for their monastic institutions. Such close affinities between religious and secular uses of food and
drink did not signify "pagan survivals" as argued by Karl Hauck, but rather
demonstrated that food and drink rituals were fully integrated into Christian custom.[28]

The main examples of extreme ascetic behavior, conversely, were usually presented in hagiographical descriptions of late antique and early medieval holy men and women who avoided contact with worldly pleasures.
Having its roots in various pagan philosophical movements such as the
Cynics, the rejection of meat and other luxury foods and drink was taken
up in the second and third centuries by highly devout Christians in the
Mediterranean East.[29] Ritual abstinence was practiced extensively by the
desert saints and early cenobitic communities to distinguish monastic practitioners from more lukewarm converts to Christianity and above all from
pagans.[30] Although such rigidly abstemious diets were less common in the
West and actually discouraged by late antique bishops such as Irenaeus of
Lyons and Augustine of Hippo,[31] a number of hagiographers in Gaul continued to use such Eastern precedents as models for holy behavior. In the
late sixth century, Venantius Fortunatus noted, for instance, that the former
queen and monastic founder Radegund abstained from pure wine, mead,
and beer along with most sorts of food.[32] Yet, even here, the accuracy of
such descriptions was not altogether straightforward, since Fortunatus dedicated many poems to Radegund and the first abbess of her foundation,
Agnes, that alluded to their generous gifts of food.[33] Accounts of the ascetic achievements of the desert saints, while transmitted to Gaul by such
disparate sources as Cassian and Columbanus,[34] were evidently not promoted among the general faithful. Indeed, these ideals were more prof-
itably directed at the residents of monastic houses who had already
committed themselves to a religious vocation and were presumably more
disposed to exhibiting such behavior.

With the rise of the celebration of Rogations in the fifth century, public fasting first came to play a central role in bringing together Christian
communities in Gaul. Originally instituted in the city of Vienne under
Bishop Mamertus, these ceremonies incorporated prayer, almsgiving, and
fasting with processions in times of hardship and at certain seasonal inter-

vals.[35] And as their practice proved effective in uniting the community, it prompted other bishops to follow suit. At the Council of Orléans in 511 and the Council of Lyons in 567–570, clerics regularized these events in their jurisdictions and specified that Rogations should occur during the period prior to Ascension and the Kalends of November.[36] Such public displays of contrition served to solidify urban inhabitants' sentiments regarding the need for repentance to win God's favor. Voluntary fasting, unlike purely liturgical ceremonies conducted by clerics, allowed all faithful Christians to make a contribution to community well-being.

By contrast, the circulation of penitential literature, first in monastic communities and then among the laity from the late sixth century, allowed clerics to transmit to the faithful a stricter model of abstention from most sorts of food and drink than that involved in Rogations processions. Rather than focusing on communal well-being at certain times of the year, these manuals conveyed through prescribed amounts of fasting the continuous need for personal atonement for sins committed during one's lifetime.[37] In this fashion, rather than waiting for the Last Judgment, the penitent cyclically performed penance to purge himself or herself of debts incurred by sinning.[38] On such lists of penalties, punishments for most violations deprived penitents of the right to consume many kinds of nourishment, particularly meat, animal grease, oil, eggs, and wine, and restricted them to bread and water.[39] Instead of constituting an effort to impose on lay Christians the type of ascetic behavior heretofore practiced by holy men and women, these rites were seen as urgent preparatory measures necessary for the sinner's reintegration into the community of the faithful.[40] By alluding to the Eucharist as well as representing a self-conscious rejection of sociability,[41] the penitentials' temporary restrictions on consumption limited the repentant to bread and water and thus excluded them from important community interactions. Penitence was also intended to lessen the purgatorial horrors faced at death that played an increasingly vivid role in the Christian imagination from the sixth century onward.[42] Because such steps were self-administered, however, they did not constitute effective tools for modifying the habits of those on the fringes of Christian society. With no means of directly enforcing fasting, little incentive for cooperation with the clergy existed among those who were already hostile to their demands.

Saints and the Provisioning of Plenty

Consumption in and of itself therefore does not seem to have concerned Columbanus and Vaast when they encountered feasting. The aforementioned interruptions by saints of what were portrayed as pagan rituals in

14 CREATING COMMUNITY WITH FOOD AND DRINK

hagiographical accounts would be better described as Christian efforts to disrupt and redirect indigenous customs related to food and drink in Gaul.[43] By alleging that Columbanus and Vaast asserted themselves in this manner, Jonas identified deep-rooted differences between the beneficiaries but not the basic actions of traditional Gallo-Roman or Germanic ritual practices and Christian ritual practices. In essence, the saints proved to their opponents who were reluctant to give up such rites that profane offerings were demonic activities, powerless unless cleansed of ungodly associations. However, their words did not constitute a rejection of or a desire to eradicate *convivia* altogether. The *Canones hibernenses,* circulating on the continent by the eighth century, indicated that it was all Christians' obligation to provide hospitality. They likened this necessity to Lot's welcome of the angels that had freed him from the destruction visited upon the remaining inhabitants of Sodom and Gomorrah.[44]

The saints, who lived and worked within the context of the same social landscape as the general population, did not even conceive of undermining feasting rites since they had long represented one of the major components of gift exchange and thus fictive kinship in Gaul. During the late Roman empire, for instance, emperors had bestowed food on cities based not on their poverty and need but their status. These bequests reinforced the image of the imperial figure as a benefactor of the powerful.[45] In Gaul, where clerical and lay culture had never been separated by a great divide, saints might employ food and drink to similar ends, albeit in rather different situations.[46] Indeed, holy men and women in the early Middle Ages were widely known to engineer highly positive encounters with perishable goods, even in the most mundane of circumstances. Hagiographical works testified that many saints, in imitation of the life of Jesus as recounted in the Gospels, provided the faithful with abundant nourishment from the vessels in their possession. These practices did not give evidence of a "slipping of standards" from early Christianity,[47] since such an interpretation overlooks the influential place of food and drink in the Roman empire at the foundation of patron-client relationships. It is more useful to suggest that the extreme asceticism of the desert saints was not the only model of appropriate behavior for early medieval nuns, monks, and clerics. Early medieval feasting in the proper context celebrated the miraculous bounty of God, and may have had connections to ancient Christian eucharistic meals that included a far wider variety of foods than bread and wine, such as cheese, milk, honey, salt, fruits, vegetables, and fish.[48]

Although discouraged in some instances due to their implied association with pagan activities, rituals involving the consumption of food and drink had enormous significance in Christian custom.[49] Clerics simply asked that they occur only in suitable circumstances. In the seventh-century penitential attributed to Theodore of Canterbury, for instance, vomiting due to drunkenness was an act punishable among both clerics and lay persons; those who did so after joyfully celebrating the Lord's birthday, Easter, or a feast day following long abstinence or illness, however, were exempt from these provisions as long as they did not violate any other restrictions.[50] Although viewed with more suspicion than official church celebrations, rites such as the funerary meal, which in some communities incorporated the celebration of the Eucharist, reinforced the bonds between the living and the dead. This was true in early medieval Gaul as had been the case in late antique communities.[51] The ritualization of historical events, the most pertinent in miracle accounts of plenty being the multiplication of loaves and fishes at Cana and the Last Supper, thus enabled the same actions in many different places to recall these deeds. Their reenactment made it possible to overcome some of the divisiveness in Christian communities caused by distance and time.[52] Readers of saints' *Lives* were thereby encouraged to envision interactions involving food and drink provided by the saint as a manifestation of divinely sponsored gift exchange.

A few examples serve to illustrate this point more concisely. According to her anonymous sixth-century biographer, Genovefa supplied refreshment to the builders of Saint-Denis by praying and making the sign of the cross over the large drinking vessel at her disposal. Due to her efficacious actions, sufficient liquid appeared to slake their thirst.[53] Rather than being portrayed as a sorceress engaged in *maleficium,* as was the fate of other early medieval women who possessed similar abilities, Genovefa's actions were ultimately perceived at least by her supporters as miraculous.[54] This particular miracle type has been characterized by Giselle de Nie as the spontaneous generation of wine or blessed oil *ex nihilo,* a theme found among sixth-century authors such as Gregory of Tours, Venantius Fortunatus, and Gregory the Great.[55] An earlier instance of this phenomenon was recounted circa 406 by Sulpicius Severus with respect to the deeds of Saint Martin, among which he included the blessing of a glass ampule of oil that was able to replenish itself miraculously.[56] Genovefa, too, possessed an empty ampule of oil that filled spontaneously so that she might save a possessed man.[57] Such mysteries were indeed interpreted as the product of divine creativity and were witnessed by clerical authors well into the Carolingian period.

In eighth- and ninth-century texts describing, among others, Merovingian saints, vessels blessed by the holy also provided the faithful with plenty. Nonetheless, by this time, the saints' participation in rendering wine and beer from water or nothing was often no longer manifested as the act of an individual. One does not find the same sorts of references to holy women blowing on vessels or making the sign of the cross as had often been the

16   CREATING COMMUNITY WITH FOOD AND DRINK

case in Merovingian hagiography. Instead the vessel gained import, as in the cup or *poculum* of spring water that Chlotild brought to the builders of Les Andelys, and that became wine once it entered into their hands.[58] The Carolingian *vita* of Saint Sadalberga likewise contained a miracle in which a vat, or a *vas quod lingua vulgari tunnam vocant,* filled with beer prior to the arrival of Waldebert, abbot of Luxeuil, so that the monastery could provide him with refreshment.[59] Despite their differences, miracles of this sort from the Merovingian and Carolingian eras were more significant than a simple manifestation of the power of God: they also revealed clerical demonstrations of their ability to provide plentiful supplies and protection for the Christian faithful. Jo Ann McNamara has thus noted that this genre of provisionary miracles may have also been symptomatic of food shortages among clerics and, in particular, Merovingian nuns.[60]

Rather than supporting an interpretation of encounters with pagan beer sacrifices described by Jonas of Bobbio as isolated incidents, and therefore either redundant or insignificant with respect to Merovingian cultural mores,[61] these events fit into a larger context of food and drink customs in the early Middle Ages. Feasting constituted a powerful form of gift exchange and patronage, and played a highly symbolic role in the display of status and identity in sixth- and seventh-century Gaul, as elsewhere in Europe.[62] Both holy women and men were shown as actors in these bountiful displays, indicating that gender-based restrictions do not appear to have precluded the possibility of participation in such rites. This statement should not be taken as suggesting, however, that women and men had similar relationships to foodstuffs. As will be noted in chapter three, among the desert saints, as would be the case later in houses governed by *Rules* such as that of Caesarius of Arles, religious women potentially faced considerable limitations on their diet and the individuals whom they could invite to share in their meals.[63] Although the male desert saints had engaged in extreme feats of abstinence to cleanse their bodies of corruption,[64] measures governing nuns were stricter than those regulating monks, presumably stemming from the assumed link between original sin and female sexual proclivities.[65] Nuns thus faced greater obstacles to becoming patrons than their male counterparts.

Relations based upon the sharing of abundant food and drink existed not only among members of Merovingian communities, whether pagan or Christian, lay or clerical, male or female, but also between the living and the dead.[66] The links between consumption and those already in the afterlife had long existed both among pagans and Christians as a means of establishing cultural identity, social cohesion, and networks of patronage.[67] In numerous cemeteries of the Merovingian period, evidence survives of feasting at graves as well as the deposition of food and drink in individual

THE RITUAL SIGNIFICANCE OF FEASTING 17

sepulchers; both practices constituted influential expressions of competition for status and authority among the living, and they represented a means of commemorating ancestors by including them in family gatherings.[68] These uses of food and drink thus had multilayered symbolism for their contemporary participants. The relationships thereby created and maintained existed not only in a lay context, but also among monks, saints, and ascetics—groups normally associated with an ideal of renunciation rather than plenty in modern descriptions of the early Middle Ages.

Defining Christian Community through the Fear of Pollution

In order to achieve the successful longterm conversion of the population of Gaul, as we have seen, members of the clergy repeatedly legislated against the dangers of pagan sacrifice and substituted Christian feasts in their place.[69] At stake was the existence of Christian communities, the establishment and maintenance of which depended upon the ability of clerics to enforce the regulations that they codified in the canons of church councils and the chapters of monastic *Rules*. Since they could not use force beyond the level of a sound beating, the primary tool in their hands for ensuring obedience was the ability to excommunicate those who violated church prescriptions. Forbidding faithful members from mixing with those who were not yet incorporated in or already excommunicated from their ranks helped to reinforce such distinctions.

One of the most important places at which the Christian community defined itself was where its devotees gathered to break bread. Although we do not know the precise nature of these meals, they may have occurred at eucharistic, familial, or funerary celebrations. The exclusion of specific individuals or groups from the communal tables of Christians enabled clerics to identify them as outsiders in a visible and meaningful manner.[70] In the fortieth canon of the Council of Agde (506), for instance, Christians were thus commanded not to eat with Jews and heretics on pain of excommunication.[71] Clerics, too, had to be enjoined to obey these commands, and received specific instructions not to fraternize with heretics or Jews. If they did, they would suffer excommunication or beating, the latter punishment being reserved for those of junior status.[72] By means of this policy of avoidance, bishops created fear of interaction between these groups through a type of exclusionary policy that apparently had not existed previously.

One of the most illuminating accounts of the politics of the table was recounted by Gregory of Tours, who regarded mixing with Arians as one of the greatest threats to Catholic stability.[73] As a remedy, he advocated that

18   CREATING COMMUNITY WITH FOOD AND DRINK

clerics circulate descriptive models of behavior that might be emulated by the faithful.[74] In his *Glory of the Martyrs,* he thus related to his readers what was likely an apocryphal story of a Catholic woman who had invited a Catholic priest to dinner, while her husband, a heretic, also invited an Arian cleric to spite her wishes.[75] During the meal, according to Gregory, the husband goaded the Arian leader into attempting to gain a larger portion of the meal for the two of them by blessing the dishes that were intended for everyone, since he knew that the Nicene Christians would refuse to eat any food in this state. In fact, the Arian priest succeeded in doing so during four courses in a row. Thus, when the last of the dishes, a delicious concoction prepared with whipped eggs, flour, dates, and olives, was still steaming as it was brought to the table, the heretical priest apparently failed to take proper precautions. He was burnt so badly by his spoon that he expired soon afterward as punishment for his gluttony.[76] Beyond the lesson conveyed regarding the dangers of association with heretics, since in this anonymous account the abashed husband readily converted to Catholicism to avoid the fate of the Arian priest, Gregory clearly expressed his view of the basic incompatibility of those of different faiths at a communal meal. Many, however, must have treated such encounters as less fractious and more routine than he suggested to his readers in this moralizing account.

Another venue for reinforcing communal identity was through the formulation of laws regulating Christian behavior. Such practices were intended to convey the community's moral code by circumscribing what Christians did amongst their families and friends. Caesarius of Arles for this reason urged his listeners to avoid partaking in heavy drinking and feasting, or *convivia,* since drunkenness heightened the likelihood of regretful behavior and waste, as well as resembled the behavior of pagans.[77] The bishop instead advocated that Christian holidays were to be celebrated in a modest fashion.[78] Sharing in the breaking of bread more generally helped identify baptized Christians: before they ate, they made the sign of the cross, the primary ritual by which the meal was rendered orthodox. The system, however, was not without its problems. Bishops such as Caesarius of Arles, for instance, complained of Christians who thought that they might consume sacrificial foods if they first made the sign of the cross over what he referred to as demonic offerings. He thus warned his congregation that the power of the cross, if misused, might turn against them.[79] Beyond the act of Christians crossing themselves, the eighth-century Gelasian sacramentary contained more detailed references for clerics to the benedictions and prayers of thanksgiving that were to be recited before and after meals.[80]

Some measures in the Gospels related to food and drink may also be characterized as purity laws, since decrees such as Acts 15.28 promoted the

THE RITUAL SIGNIFICANCE OF FEASTING

avoidance of foods offered to idols or the meat of strangled animals as unclean.[81] In 1 Corinthians 8.4–13 and 10.1–33, Paul of Tarsus likewise identified cultic meals as incompatible with Christian life, although private meals including meat were acceptable if they did not allude to the sacred nature of the repast.[82] Clerical authors in Gaul addressed such topics at least as early as the fifth century, when Avitus of Vienne (d. circa 518) contrasted the endless quantities of fruit in Paradise with the impure eating habits of the sinning human population punished with the Flood. According to the bishop, the Garden of Eden was filled with abundance, and neither Adam nor Eve knew of hunger before the Fall.[83] By comparison, Avitus signaled the depravity and bestial nature of humanity on the eve of the Deluge with a description of its gluttonous consumption of unclean foods:

> Men grew drunk with blood, and everywhere the flesh of the slain provided torn bits of food for their unrestrained jaws. What is more, they fed on animals who had died a natural death or whom a more ferocious creature had captured and killed, seeing that neither trust nor law restrained them.[84]

The chaos of this time of evil was thereby equated by the fifth-century bishop with the violation of what were for him basic precepts governing the consumption of food and drink. A restoration of balance required reestablishing order in dietary habits following the severe punishment of the Flood.

Other accounts related to eating and drinking were frequently couched in language that communicated not only concern with the dangers of pollution but also outlined steps that might be taken to prevent contamination. Hagiographical sources pointed to the necessity of the appropriate handling of foodstuffs and beverages in a Christian context, since such activities needed to be sanctified by God, their provider. Like the Jewish traditions of Kashrut enumerated in Leviticus 11.32–37 and elsewhere, the very vessels in which such substances were conveyed became critically important. Biblical prescriptions for rituals rendering polluted containers clean had advocated the use of water, and in some cases water and ash of burnt sin offerings, before their reuse by members of the Jewish community. Tainted ceramic vessels, however, were to be broken.[85] Although Christians were warned against following the laws of Kashrut in Matthew 23.23—a lesson repeated elsewhere in the New Testament and the writings of the Church Fathers[86]—their rituals shared some similarities, whether they were entirely cognizant of these precedents or not. These measures not only reflected the need to create order within the community of the faithful, but they taught their congregations respect for God's creation, as in Leviticus 11.[87] The word of God, enacted through

20 CREATING COMMUNITY WITH FOOD AND DRINK

the signing of the cross or the recitation of prayers over containers, could bring about the destruction of impurity and hence protect the Christian community.

Historians and anthropologists have already acknowledged the manner in which traditions reinforcing the purity of food and drink were transmitted to the continent as early as the sixth century through Irish and Anglo-Saxon penitential handbooks.[88] The penitential attributed to Theodore of Canterbury in the late seventh century, for instance, existed in multiple copies on the Continent by the eighth century.[89] This document repeated biblical injunctions against the consumption of blood and semen and the meat of dead animals or those partially devoured by dogs or birds of prey; it also added prohibitions such as forbidding the drinking of liquids tainted by mice and other creatures.[90] The context of such concerns with pollution, however, extended beyond these provisions in penitential and canonical legislation. The social implications of early medieval attitudes towards the acceptability of various foodstuffs also included the purity of vessels and their contents, customs which were preserved in fifth- and sixth-century hagiographical and historical sources in Gaul.

Just as various dietary laws presented in the penitentials and in other canonical legislation prohibited Christian participation in what clerics perceived as impure and, as we have seen, demonic feasts,[91] various early medieval Christian leaders also expressed concern that the vessels themselves used to hold food and the Eucharist might spread contamination. With this objective in mind, the *Rule of St. Columbanus* directed, for instance, that monks were to motion the sign of the cross over their spoons before eating. Failure to observe the rite incurred the harsh punishment of six blows.[92] Although this policy was effectively defended against criticism, such as that of at least one sixth-century member of Luxeuil, a monk named Agrestius, who contested the practice and unsuccessfully charged Columbanus's successor Eustasius with heresy, the conflict was not fully resolved until the early seventh-century Council of Mâcon.[93] The mid-seventh-century *Rule of Donatus,* which borrowed heavily from its predecessors, moreover, included among other prescriptions very similar punishments for nuns who had begun to eat or drink without first reciting a benediction.[94] These regulations not only impressed on monastic inmates the necessity of certain sorts of decorum at the table, but they established a form of institutional control and order over the most mundane aspects of their lives.[95]

Rituals such as making the sign of the cross might also prove highly effective in sparing monastic leaders from being murdered by their detractors. Frequently attempts to eliminate holy abbots transpired with the poisoning of the contents of the vessels used in communal meals. This scenario enabled clerical authors to cast the events not only as the conse-

THE RITUAL SIGNIFICANCE OF FEASTING   21

quence of monastic corruption but as a perversion of established ceremonies. In his widely circulated *Dialogues,* Gregory I recounted that when
monks who resented Benedict of Nursia's reform efforts presented him a
drink prepared with lethal contents, the saint made the sign of the cross
over his glass. His actions caused the vessel to shatter and thereby saved his
life.[96] In a sterner warning to would-be murderers, Gregory's narrative account told of the consequences of Sabinus's near murder by an envious
archdeacon who aspired to replace the blind bishop of Canossa. Sabinus
recognized that the glass proffered to him by his subordinate contained
poison, but after making the sign of the cross, he confidently drank the
tainted contents. This act miraculously caused the poisoner to die instead
of the intended victim.[97] In this manner, clerical authors discouraged potential assailants against holy men, who were protected by divine forces
that overwhelmed their opponents' lowly tactics.

In the sacramentaries, clerics likewise made provisions to avoid contamination in sacred and profane contexts. The Bobbio Missal provided among
prayers meant to exorcise demons from water, salt, and oil, a benediction for
liturgical vessels so that they might be worthy of receiving the Eucharist.[98]
In conjunction with a blessing meant for water, the Gelasian sacramentary
also advocated that this exorcised substance be sprinkled in the homes of
Christians to rid their possessions of demonic or corrupting presences.[99] To
be certain, as early as the sixth century and increasingly thereafter, leading
clerics in Gaul deemed it necessary to guard members of monastic communities, just as the laity and even the sacraments, from the dangers of demonic pollution. This preventative action required the purification of
everyday and sacramental vessels in both public and private places.

In a number of hagiographical accounts, Jonas of Bobbio and other
contemporary early medieval authors revealed the impurity and presence
of diabolical forces infiltrating the homes of faithful Christians.[100] As will
be discussed in greater detail in the next chapter, these miracle stories focused, for example, upon the containers that held the food and drink of
unrepentant Christian nobility or those provided by individuals of unknown and hence suspect background.[101] They demonstrated consistently
that vessels could potentially cause harm if they were not properly in-
spected and used. Only a holy man or woman, moreover, had the ability
to identify and eliminate these sorts of threats because they were invisible
to most Christians prior to the point that they posed an inescapable danger to all of those present.

The *Vita Genovefae* presented one such example of the author's perception
of the potential harm that might be caused by anonymous and hence unclean
vessels. During a presumably innocent encounter between Genovefa and a
woman who had just previously bought a container, possibly of *garum* or fish

22   CREATING COMMUNITY WITH FOOD AND DRINK

sauce, from merchants, the saint demonstrated her visionary powers.[102] Upon observing the ceramic receptacle more closely, Genovefa recognized a demon that had earlier been hiding and was now sitting on the jug's lip. By blowing upon the ampule, she caused the edge to crumble and the evil spirit fell to the ground vanquished.[103] From this account, it appears that even everyday utensils purchased at markets were rendered suspect by nature of their unknown or somewhat dubious origins. Indeed, demons inhabited unsanctified worldly objects and regularly tempted the Christian faithful to renounce eternal salvation for the sake of temporary gratification.[104] Genovefa's *vita* thereby made central the necessity of the presence of an esteemed representative of the Church to identify and ward off demonic threats manifested in vessels for the consumption of food and drink.

In explaining the social significance of these rites in Merovingian traditions, especially among elites, it is also necessary to emphasize the symbolic functions of luxury vessels. Gifts of gold and silver in antiquity frequently took the form of tableware, and such ritualized presentations were similarly esteemed in the Byzantine, Merovingian, and Carolingian courts.[105] The fact that silver and bronze bowls and plates were not only used in ceremonial exchanges but were also among the most abundant of early medieval water deposits and ritually motivated hoards should indicate to us that clerical precautions with such objects were not unwarranted.[106] Such items were not limited to conveying pre-Christian ideology, but occupied a highly visible place in early medieval Christian life; if given on behalf of the poor, they represented appropriate gifts by laymen or clerics to churches.[107] Indeed, as they were potentially charged symbols of the Christian liturgy due to their association with baptism and the Eucharist, families might use them to express their membership in the community of the faithful. Such artifacts nonetheless did not lose their role as status symbols. One royal gift of silver plate bestowed upon Caesarius of Arles for his prayers allegedly weighed an impressive sixty pounds. According to the authors, because the saint was not accustomed to such luxury at his table, however, he promptly used the gift to redeem captives.[108] He thus elevated the vessel's symbolic value by making clear its association with such a worthy act.

Although tableware of silver and gold had great value and was often included in hoards, the attention paid to it as a form of aristocratic currency reflected far more than the worth of the precious metals from which eating and drinking utensils were fashioned.[109] If conveyed as a gift, for instance, eating and drinking vessels and utensils retained something of the identity of the person who had bestowed them.[110] Highlighted especially in cases when they were donated in wills and read aloud publicly,[111] presentation tableware thereby functioned as a mnemonic device commemo-

THE RITUAL SIGNIFICANCE OF FEASTING 23

rating a particular exchange or series of exchanges. In 667, for instance, Abbot Leodebodus donated property to monasteries where the monks were to be obedient to the *Rule*. Among the objects he listed in the charter were engraved silver objects that were intended for use in liturgical services and thus might serve as a reminder of his generosity.[112] A similar objective was likewise implicit in the donation of precious vessels to churches on behalf of the souls of Christians. In the will of Erminethrudis composed between the years 590 and 630/645,[113] the noble woman therefore left a number of gifts including precious jewelry, clothing, and gold and silver vessels to a number of churches in and near Paris. These donations were designated along with other sorts of property in exchange for her request to the local priests for prayers commemorating herself and her deceased son in perpetuity.[114] Even objects of lesser value, such as simple ceramic vessels typically deposited in graves of the late antique and early medieval period, appear to have held greater significance than the foods sometimes contained within them.[115]

In many Merovingian hagiographical sources describing religious communities, authors sought to outdo their lay counterparts. Because they frequently could not compete with the precious metals and stones that adorned the vessels and booty captured in war or exchanged between warriors in banquets, they instead placed emphasis on the vulnerability of the laity before demonic forces. Since secular leaders could not determine which containers were free of danger, clerics suggested through miracle stories their dependence on bishops, abbots, and holy Christians who not only had the ability to ensure the safety of Christians but could even endow ordinary vessels with special properties; in these cases, the words or gestures of the saints functioned prophylactically, protecting glass and ceramics from breakage or damage. Ampules blessed by Martin did not break, even if, as in one case, they fell from a window sill onto a marble floor.[116] Similarly, Gregory of Tours, in his *Liber in gloria confessorum*, related how he had heard from reliable witnesses that Ingenuus, a hermit from the region of Autun, regularly cooked his simple meals of vegetables in a wooden pot over an open fire. Despite the heat of the flames, the pot miraculously did not burn.[117] Just as demons might be contained in vessels used for sacrificial rituals perceived as illicit, the ascetic man's vegetable pot was not consumed by the fire since it was protected by divine forces. With the guidance of the saints, the faithful would similarly be furnished with sufficient foodstuffs and drinks for their livelihood. Christian miracle stories thereby demonstrated that the saints could compete with pagan deities and gift-bearing warlords who likewise attended to the satisfactory provisioning and good fortune of those loyal to them.

Conclusion

Various leaders of early medieval Christianity in Gaul believed that clerics could not do without the hagiographical legends that promoted their ability, whether accurate or not, to provide an abundance of food and drink; the vessels that contained these therefore became the focal point of rituals supporting such written and oft-recited traditions. Indeed, although fasting has received more prominent billing in modern accounts of the early Middle Ages, feasting and its associated vessels were central to both Christian and pagan ritual celebrations. These practices provided the opportunity for individuals to communicate publicly their status and access to limited foodstuffs.[118] The capacity to provide an abundance of food and drink was a sign of a family's wealth and power, and reflected values that continued to be emulated by Christian clerics. This is not to suggest that church leaders in early medieval Gaul never felt it necessary to restrict Christian interaction with pagan rituals. Indeed, only through baptism and associated rites of exorcism could such dangers be combated and a focal point for community integration and group identity thereby be established.[119] Merovingian bishops and abbots nonetheless gave sanction to celebrations of plenty with both pagan and Christian antecedents so that the faithful might continue to receive the benefits of social interactions strengthened through feasting. We will therefore now turn to the ways in which they dealt with these same issues within the walls of their own religious communities.

CHAPTER 2

FOOD, DRINK, AND THE EXPRESSION
OF CLERICAL IDENTITY

Defining Masculinity without Weapons:
Amicitia among Bishops

In the Merovingian kingdoms, just as in late antiquity and the later Middle Ages, sworn friendship or *amicitia* contributed in important ways to the formation of political relationships among military equals, and between lords and their followers. Fourth- and fifth-century Gallo- Roman aristocrats depended upon office-holding and networks of clients to bolster their authority;[1] similarly, early medieval elites were known to formalize and maintain agreements amongst themselves through the exchange of treasure as well as the hosting of feasts and the provision of hospitality to guests.[2] Rather than functioning as a merely symbolic expression of generosity, gift-giving and the mutual consumption of food and drink helped members of the Merovingian nobility to ritualize and thereby regulate both personal and political ties, especially in unsettled times. The initial bonds thus established and commemorated, if successful, might be honored by descendants and followers over the course of subsequent generations.[3] Although some have seen these relationships as symptomatic of the triumph of Frankish over Roman cultural traditions in Gaul,[4] such practices had Roman, Christian, and Frankish precedents and demonstrate the deep-rooted significance of such activities.

While contemporary attestations to rituals promoting *amicitia* in late antiquity and the early Middle Ages usually focused upon the lay nobility who participated in them, religious leaders were certainly not excluded from these alliances.[5] Nor did clerics distinguish ties to secular leaders as separate from their religious experience;[6] many of the distinctions that had once set apart popular and intellectual beliefs had long since been disavowed in Gaul.[7] Through letters that were directed at preserving these

26   CREATING COMMUNITY WITH FOOD AND DRINK

friendships and heightening the literary reputations of their authors, we know that such personal relationships had great emotional significance for their participants.[8] In the 640s or 650s, for instance, Desiderius of Cahors addressed a warm epistle to Bishop Audouen of Rouen. Although their days in the court of Chlothar II had taken place many years prior to his composition of this letter and the times had been filled with great uncertainty, Desiderius fondly recounted how much he valued the *amicitia* of his contemporaries, many of whom were now bishops in distant places.[9] He thus prayed that they would merit to be reunited after their deaths in the celestial palace of God.[10] Such sentiments were echoed in hagiographical literature such as the *Vita Audoini,* which drew attention to the friendship between Bishops Audouen of Rouen and Eligius of Noyon.[11]

As many, especially those who occupied episcopal positions in late antiquity, had entered religious life after having pursued secular careers, they did not cease to form alliances based on *amicitia* with lay contemporaries.[12] Not only did they retain their earlier status as members of some of the most powerful families in the kingdoms, but they gained additional prestige and authority once they occupied the office of bishop.[13] Because they often occupied previous Roman structures—many monasteries, too, were constructed from formal villas—they were often equipped to receive visitors with impressive surroundings even if they were no longer as well maintained as they had been during more prosperous times.[14] And, certainly there was long precedent for hospitality to guests in Genesis 18.1–8, when Abraham not only served three strangers who appeared at his tent, but also acted as a model of modesty and humility.[15] Naturally, some bishops were also reluctant to give up the benefits of participating in lay gatherings. Avitus of Vienne, for instance, somewhat ironically bemoaned the luxuries and delicacies of food and wine he had forsaken by taking up the office and obligations of bishop.[16]

Such sacrifices involved more, however, than missing banquets during Lent. In both late antiquity and the Merovingian period, clerics were proportionally more dependent than most noblemen upon their ability to provide gifts and hospitality in support of their roles as patrons or clients.[17] Because they could not marry, to start, they were deprived of one of the most effective means of expressing their masculinity and ensuring the loyalty of their contemporaries.[18] Neither could they adopt men as sons-in-arms.[19] In addition, they did not normally have the right to weaponry with which to defend themselves, a restriction promulgated in both the fifth canon of the First Council of Mâcon (581–583)[20] and the first canon of the Council of Bordeaux (662- 675).[21] Not all, in any case, were as skilled as Venantius Fortunatus in finding patrons who admired their prose and poetic compositions.[22] Few had holy protectors as widely acknowl-

FOOD, DRINK, AND THE EXPRESSION OF CLERICAL IDENTITY   27

edged as Martin of Tours upon whose intervention Gregory regularly depended.[23] What remained was the *auctoritas* of their office, family connections, patronage of powerful figures (and especially kings), and clerics' limited ability to participate in gift-giving rituals since they could not gain direct access to the spoils of war. Since bishops' power was based in their urban strongholds, and was certainly far from absolute,[24] their sponsorship of and attendance at feasts thus constituted one of the best opportunities to interact with and gain the support of well-armed lay contemporaries.

Early medieval authors, who were often religious leaders themselves, therefore did not hesitate to document the participation of clerics in ceremonial exchanges, feasting, and hosting of guests. Whereas early medieval ecclesiastical councils played an important role in prohibiting or at least channeling away from churches certain forms of violence,[25] banquets presented a venue at which clerics might gain insight into the volatile political scene and even come to the defense of their contemporaries. For this reason, Gregory of Tours recalled how at a royal feast he had taken the dangerous step of suggesting the innocence of a fellow bishop, Theodore of Marseilles, whom Guntramn blamed among others for the murder of his brother Chilperic.[26] In southern Gaul, where competition between cities was fierce and their futures not always certain, ecclesiastical leaders also actively vied with one another for lay backers through a variety of means, among them the sponsorship of public meals and the distribution of food.[27] For most bishops, aside from the fasting accompanying the Lenten season and other holy days, participation in feasting represented an integral part of their duties as the head of their cities' administrations.[28]

Not all church leaders, however, shared this positive outlook as to the appropriateness of involvement in secular life. Caesarius of Arles, whose training as a monk lay at the heart of his desire to promote greater asceticism in the civic community that included clerics,[29] wrote at least two sermons that specifically castigated his audience for their abuses of alcohol and eager participation in drunken banquets.[30] The bishop argued that excessive drink wounded the souls of Christians more than swords did the flesh.[31] His represented one of the few voices raised in Gaul against the temptations of a practice that had in the meantime come to be considered commonplace by most clerics. Rather than contributing to spiritual friendships, heavy drinking at *convivia,* according to Caesarius of Arles, was antithetical to their development and promoted behavior contrary to God's will.[32]

A stern warning of the dangers of drinking by clerics similarly occupied a prominent place in the seventh-century *Passio Praeiecti*. Although one brief description of Praejectus, who had recently been appointed the bishop of Issoire, demonstrated his miraculous ability to provide sufficient fish to feed his guests,[33] his biographer likewise cautioned readers to avoid

28 CREATING COMMUNITY WITH FOOD AND DRINK

the sort of behavior often brought on by gluttony and drunkenness. To illustrate this point, he recalled that Praejectus had invited the parish priests to dine with him at an Easter feast that he had prepared at his home. As all partook of the meal together, a number of the clerics began to mock those among them who had chosen to do penance. Despite Praejectus's attempt to discourage their misguided behavior, they failed to heed him and were punished by the collapse of the beams of his home, a catastrophe that left only Praejectus and the penitents alive.[34] The hagiographer showed the crisis to have been exacerbated by the lack of caution exercised by those heartily participating in the feast.

Such texts demonstrate the very conscious manner in which clerics wrote about themselves and their relationship to food and drink. Many of the scenes in hagiographical and historical texts presented here were intended to discourage behavior that cast a shadow on the upright standing of Christian leaders. In other instances, they were meant to shine the most positive light possible on their protagonists. Sometimes, the accounts also incorporated descriptions of feasting and fasting for rhetorical objectives, so as to contrast the unity of monastic communities with the extreme behavior of their eremetical competitors, or to highlight the weakness of lay adversaries before a man of God. In addition, letter collections also preserved much information about the role of food and drink in the formation of and sustenance of *amicitia* and its more spiritual cousin *caritas*—the meeting of souls—among clerics. Often written in obscure language, these epistles were meant to be read by a limited number of like-minded individuals who recognized the importance of feasting in binding their circle together.[35] Their letters thus eulogized particularly pleasurable meals, gifts of food, or occasions when they had provided hospitality. In this fashion, they flattered friends or scolded them for not maintaining more frequent contact. A complex group of factors therefore shaped the portrayal of food and drink in texts composed by clerics.

In their effort to achieve balance between fulfillment of their duties and avoidance of gluttonous revelry, clerics had to stake out a unique relationship to feasting. While meeting their responsibilities, they had to balance their actions somewhere between these two extremes. As noted by Venantius Fortunatus in one telling miracle account, the man who exhibited gluttony might literally be punished by an open mouth that would not close, a lesson of the dangers of too much meat and wine.[36] This complex set of behaviors related to the provisioning and consumption of food and drink was vital to establishing alliances, and thus represented an alternative means of expressing masculinity in early medieval Gaul. Although clerics were deprived of what have been deemed by archaeologists to have been "typical" markers of the male gender such as armament,[37] they found

FOOD, DRINK, AND THE EXPRESSION OF CLERICAL IDENTITY   29

other effective means by which they might bolster their power as men and soldiers of God in private and public arenas. Rather than encouraging extreme asceticism, bishops such as Augustine of Hippo and Faustus of Riez thus sought to promote a concept of civic masculinity that drew its strength from the interaction between society and the holy.[38] As we will see below, this approach differed significantly from that of the promoters of radical abstemiousness for virgins such as Jerome. Contemporary religious women who recognized the power of relationships formed through food, and yet deprived themselves of similar pleasures, therefore utilized a variety of strategies to overcome obstacles to their ability to provide meals to the individuals who might offer them needed protection.

Monks and the Significance of *Convivia* in Ascetic Communities

Unfortunately no early medieval equivalents to Clement of Alexandria's second-century *Paedagogus* survive with a detailed list of what constituted appropriately modest dining comportment for contemporary Christians.[39] Nonetheless, it is clear that clerical authors in Gaul recognized the influential role of eating and drinking in the socialization of its participants. Communal meals had long been utilized by monastic organizers to foster a sense of membership and comradery as well as to establish a shared identity among the inmates of male cenobitic communities in Gaul. Although in the fifth century John Cassian urged moderation in meals as necessary to the mortification of the flesh, even he identified participation in communal meals as a regular part of a monk's obligations to his brethren.[40] As made clear in the *Life* of the Jura fathers, a composition that concentrated more on monastic routine than wonder-working,[41] a balance had to be achieved between the extremes of gluttony and excessive fasting. Whereas too much food might encourage monks to disobey the *Rule* of the house of Condat,[42] Abbot Lupicinus acknowledged that too little nourishment made it impossible for inhabitants of the monastery to fulfill their duties successfully.[43] Severe asceticism weakened the body and hindered participation in monastic life. While ardent zeal for abstinence may have made the reputations of wandering holy men, it tended to breed resentment among inmates of a religious community, especially when they were also supposed to share their meals with the poor.[44]

The custom of inviting outsiders into the monastery to partake of food and drink belonging to the brethren was firmly entrenched in cenobitic culture in the West. The early sixth-century *Rule* of Saint Benedict, which was utilized in Gaul both independently and in conjunction with other *Rules* such as that of Columbanus, thus explicitly mandated that hospitality

30   CREATING COMMUNITY WITH FOOD AND DRINK

to guests and pilgrims comprise a basic pillar of the monastic way of life.[45] Even the comparatively restrictive *Rule* for monks in Visigothic Galicia formulated by Fructuosus of Braga in the seventh century made special concessions to the monks' diets of mainly vegetables and pulses with a somewhat greater quantity of fish and wine when they were hosting guests.[46] And, at least a few monks apparently knew something of food preparation, as seems clear from sophisticated emendations to recipes preserved in a cookbook by Apicius which were made by a cleric named Vinitharius at an unidentified monastery in the sixth century.[47] Monasteries were also large importers of foodstuffs, much of which traveled through the Provençal ports at Marseilles and Fos.[48] From an early eighth-century diploma recording the privilege granted by King Chilperic II to Corbie from the toll station at Fos, we know that the royal monastery annually had the right to certain quantities of oil, *garum* (fish sauce), olives, various nuts, and spices such as pepper and cinnamon.[49] Other churches such as Saint-Denis enjoyed similar advantages, indicating that at least some early medieval abbeys had sufficiently diverse provisions to entertain elite visitors in the style to which they were accustomed.[50]

In his sixth-century account of Patroclus in the *Life of the Fathers,* Gregory of Tours illustrated some of the tensions arising from different abbots' expectations of the type of behavior most appropriately exhibited by monks in their interactions with food and drink. Gregory recounted, in particular, how the holy man refused to participate in *convivia* or feasts with his brethren. Patroclus's enthusiasm for fasting, which he interpreted as too individualistic in its expression, brought rebuke from the ecclesiastical authorities and eventually resulted in his departure from the monastic community.[51] In the contemporary *Vita sancti Paterni,* Venantius Fortunatus, too, described the way in which the hermit who had limited his diet to bread, water, and raw vegetables was scolded for this highly ascetic diet. Only after abandoning it, and thus renouncing his personal ambitions, could the recluse Paternus be reintegrated into the Christian community. A less ascetic lifestyle, according to Venantius, made it possible for him to become a deacon and later a priest, and thereby serve the faithful.[52]

One might suggest from such clashes between extreme asceticism and the practical requirements of episcopal office that a bishop was understood to be qualified for clerical responsibilities only if he remained a part of this world. Sharing meals with the Christian faithful was one means by which the ecclesiastical candidate might show his aptitude for the position. Venantius Fortunatus's orderly vision of the temporal responsibilities and noble background of religious leaders such as Martin of Tours thus contrasted with Sulpicius Severus's earlier description of the saint's unkempt appearance and flight from ecclesiastical office.[53] He was nonetheless not

FOOD, DRINK, AND THE EXPRESSION OF CLERICAL IDENTITY   31

the first to present a more urbane model of the ascetic lifestyle for clerical leaders. While they did not abandon their ascetic training, some schooled at Lérins such as Caesarius of Arles acknowledged that a more moderate rhetorical approach to religious life was crucial to successful transition into ecclesiastical office and leadership of the faithful.[54]

We should not be surprised that bishops, who themselves were not often known as ascetics, regularly tempered their advice to the male devout in both late antiquity and the early Middle Ages. Even influential leaders such as Jerome, who was a strong advocate of abstinence, counseled that men, who allegedly did not suffer from the same humoral imbalances as women, take a more balanced approach to food and drink. His guidance for clerics thus differed significantly from that which he addressed to his female recipients. In his letter to Rusticus, a monk of Toulouse, for instance, he urged him to engage in moderate fasting, since that would contribute most directly to his spiritual goals and help him avoid developing an inflated pride. In addition to recommending a diet of vegetables and fruits, he counseled the young man not to live at home since there he would be subject to the temptations of the meals eaten by the rest of his family.[55] Similar to the advice offered by Augustine of Hippo, Caesarius of Arles and his contemporaries followed suit over the next two centuries by proposing a middle ground of alimentary moderation that discouraged sexual inclinations and yet did not cause bodily harm.[56] By the time of Gregory I, this brand of masculine asceticism had become so refined that clerics basically advocated what amounted to a state of mind rather than an anticipated set of physical behaviors related to food and drink.[57]

In the early Middle Ages, then, the only prompters of the type of extreme asceticism related to the eating and drinking habits of religious men were a few hermits such as Patroclus and Lupicinus who stubbornly clung to the ways of the desert. Gregory of Tours praised both men for restricting themselves to isolated cells where they inflicted a variety of privations upon themselves. In addition to abstaining from alcohol and meat, each man limited himself to a diet consisting primarily of bread and water.[58] Likewise, the hermits Aemilianus and Martius lived from the fruits of their gardens,[59] while the recluse Caluppa nourished himself with only spring water and the fish he caught.[60] Although these ascetic champions were viewed with wonder and had earned a reputation for performing healing miracles, they were not often promoted as models for early medieval clerics to imitate due to their rejection of the company of their brethren even at meals.[61] Just as such men persisted in the forests on the fringes of human society, their behavior was increasingly viewed by clerical authors such as Venantius Fortunatus as bordering on being too unrefined for clerical sensibilities. With the complete integration of Christian practice into lay society, the majority of bishops in

32   CREATING COMMUNITY WITH FOOD AND DRINK

Gaul had come to favor a brand of religious expression more familiar to those of their elite background and that of their patrons than to the sensibilities of their more ascetic predecessors.[62]

Amicitia between Clerics and Laymen

In the case of religious men, willingness to share in or provide food and drink outside of the walls of the monastery or ecclesiastical buildings was integral to the way in which they dealt with both loyal populations and intransigent lords. Rather than being viewed as indicative of worldly involvement by early medieval historians and hagiographers, gift-giving and the sponsorship of feasts or *convivia* represented a crucial part of clerical leaders' ability to enforce their will among the faithful as well as their armed competitors. Hospitality constituted a very significant part of their efforts to further their objectives with kings and noblemen, and made it possible to signal agreement upon alliances or the successful completion of negotiations. Although clerics' display of power paradoxically precluded the use of physical force (aside from the punishment with beating of some disobedient monastic brethren), their offer or refusal of hospitality might prove similarly persuasive to those much stronger in a military sense than themselves.

In the *Life* of Carilephus, for example, his anonymous biographer demonstrated that the unarmed hermit who had illegally made his home in the forest was nonetheless able to put a king in a defensive position. According to the narrator of this account, the monarch himself, Childebert, had urged the holy man to leave the plot he had cultivated in the woods. Yet, Carilephus refused to depart, and instead offered the king a drink. After rejecting the glass of wine presented by the hermit, Childebert found that his horse would not move. Consequently, the hagiographical account indicated that the dilemma could only be resolved through the monk's forgiveness and blessing; sanction of the situation and reconciliation was specifically signaled by the king's drinking of the proffered wine.[63] The actions of a man who was likely viewed by his contemporaries as marginal, and was certainly vulnerable from the perspective of the members of a warrior-society, were thus shown to have brought the king proverbially to his knees.

With reference to their elite contemporaries, the clerical nobility had to find effective means by which they might mediate between their positions as patrons or loyal clients, and the restrictions placed upon them as men of God. For this reason, accounts of clerics' participation in food and drink rites with their lay contemporaries differed in certain respects from

FOOD, DRINK, AND THE EXPRESSION OF CLERICAL IDENTITY   33

descriptions of similar bonds formed between two lay persons. An important manifestation of the unique role of the cleric in these texts, for example, lay in their reference to the supernatural, particularly with the large number of saints who functioned as guardians of the faithful. Gregory of Tours thereby promoted the veneration of Martin by recounting his own misfortunate encounter with a fishbone that became lodged in his throat and prevented him from speaking for three days. Despite the fact that he had protected himself prophylactically by making the sign of the cross before eating, Gregory emphasized that only a visit to the tomb of his patron saint gave him release from his suffering.[64] Merovingian hagiographers likewise drew attention to holy bishops' or abbots' manipulation, inversion, or rejection of traditional mores of *convivia* to demonstrate their strength in resisting brute force. In the course of a meal, by having an unforeseen impact on the vessels holding the food and drink of unrepentant members of the Christian nobility, the clerical protagonist might punish a powerful individual who disobeyed his authority.[65]

Gregory of Tours, for instance, in his *Life of the Fathers* noted that on one occasion Theuderic's right-hand man, Sigivald, tried to force the sixth-century abbot Portianus (of the monastery that is now Saint-Pourçain, dép. Allier) to bless a drinking vessel. Portianus at first declined, since he had not yet paid his respects to the king nor had he finished singing the psalms. Upon seeing that Sigivald was growing impatient and that he had no other choice, however, he lifted his right hand and made the sign of the cross. Rather than the anticipated effect of this action, the holy abbot thereby caused the cup to split in half. As the wine poured from the vessel, out slithered an immense serpent hidden within it. All present threw themselves at the feet of the saint, thereby seeking to avoid the snake's venom.[66] The lesson thereby conveyed to those who heard this account was that even a high-ranking member of the laity could not command at will the benefits of the grace of God from the hands of a cleric. God watched over the faithful and punished those who used him for worldly ends.

The saint's avoidance of inappropriate gatherings, even if it meant offending the host of the festivities, might also convey divine displeasure. Jonas of Bobbio thus recounted an instance in which Columbanus of Luxueil, following his dangerous falling out with Queen Brunhild in 607, traveled to Theuderic's villa of Époisses on the Côte-d'Or. According to the narrator of this saint's *Life,* the abbot had simply agreed to visit because he did not want to anger the royal family any further. Once he learned, however, that he was meant to participate in Theuderic's offering of a sacrificial feast and drinks, Columbanus was enraged. Not only did he denounce the king's activities, but his words caused the miraculous destruction of the

34 CREATING COMMUNITY WITH FOOD AND DRINK

king's drinking vessels and the loss of the wine.[67] Although the saint was forced soon afterwards to flee to the relative safety of Italy to avoid royal wrath, Jonas's account nonetheless gave a powerful impression of the great courage of the abbot in thwarting the will of the king.[68] This episode also allowed the hagiographer to present the abbot in a face-saving manner and to downplay the significance of the difficult circumstances that followed.

Bishops and *Civitates* in Late Antique and Early Medieval Gaul

In Gaul, indications of an urban center's prosperity and stability were often manifested in the authority and generosity of its bishop. Whereas Roman aristocrats had built edifices and sponsored public events in honor of their cities, in the Christian period these evergetistic tendencies were channeled towards church building and charity for the needy.[69] From the late Roman period, bishops in Gaul faced the consequences of the decline of their *civitates* or towns and the surrounding countryside. This trend was especially threatening to their livelihood since their power was historically tied to these bases. Besides transforming the architectural landscape by situating their churches in prominent urban locations,[70] ecclesiastical leaders typically organized festivals to bolster civic pride.[71] Likewise, they capitalized on their vast resources to distribute food and drink to gain the support of the urban population for their office. As visibility was vital to their ability to administer to Christian communities, bishops and their supporters sponsored events that drew attention to their extensive resources and the prestige of their leaders. And, certainly, there was no shortage of church holidays as occasions on which to hold them.[72] Banquets financed by bishops represented an important part of such displays and hence helped build their reputations.

Sometimes ceremonies were held at the death of a cleric and the installation of his replacement. For example, at the passing of an important leader such as Sidonius Apollinaris at Clermont in 479, the bishop's quarters (*domus*) were used to host a funerary feast for the urban population. Held in the episcopal dining room (*triclinium*), this meal was just one of a number that would be held at the site.[73] Gregory of Tours likewise recounted that with the accession of his uncle Gallus to the bishopric of Clermont (d. 551), the king held a banquet at the public's expense in the newly consecrated leader's honor. The bishop also sponsored feasts in his buildings, some of which became unruly affairs after the lay guests had imbibed vast quantities of alcohol.[74] On certain occasions, translation ceremonies also sparked celebrations involving food and drink. Such was the case of the miraculous appearance of a never-ending supply of wine

FOOD, DRINK, AND THE EXPRESSION OF CLERICAL IDENTITY   35

at the deposition of Julian of Brioude's relics at Tours; this wonder provided the monks with the resources required to entertain visitors for two full days.[75]

Given the flight from urban centers to country villas of many Gallo-Roman inhabitants of significant means, including clerics, in the course of the fifth century,[76] bishops were obliged to find alternative means to prop up their declining congregations.[77] As we have seen, Mamertus of Vienne used Rogations processions, prayers, and fasts to bring unity to a divided city following a series of earthquakes in 473. He ensured the presence of a greater number of the aristocracy by scheduling the ceremonies just after an important festival.[78] Thereafter, in 506, legislation passed at the Council of Agde forbade clerics to celebrate Mass in private chapels on important holidays, thereby encouraging Christians instead to attend services in their parish.[79] Then, in 511, those present at the Council of Orléans mandated church attendance for civic leaders on major holidays such as Christmas, Easter, and Pentecost unless they were too ill to attend.[80] By 541, however, these injunctions had been made less demanding and were reduced to including solely Easter among the services that had to be celebrated in the cities.[81] This legislation emphasized the importance of urban centers for devotional practice at the expense of rural shrines, and provided the opportunity for Christians to come together at regular intervals.[82] Although they were far from successful in extending their influence to the countryside,[83] clerics tried to make a lasting impression on the rural inhabitants who journeyed to towns to attend Masses. They therefore focused on the enlargement of their episcopal complexes, the sponsorship of lavish ecclesiastical processions on feast days, and the acquisition of powerful relics.[84]

Certain activities of early medieval bishops were more modest in proportion and pertained to ameliorating the hardships facing their congregations. Ecclesiastical responsibility for pilgrims and the poor had since the fourth century reinforced their position as the most visible and consistent patrons of urban Christians. From the sixth to tenth centuries, evidence of churches' assistance for the poor was preserved in lists at Tours, Reims, and Trier that identified the *matricularii,* namely those persons entitled to receive allocations of food and drink at regular intervals.[85] This charity was often mediated through the creation of *xenodochia* or hospices, a practice that reached its apex during the sixth and seventh centuries.[86] A number of Merovingian councils included legislation to defend these foundations, which were often located on the edges of towns or just beyond their walls, from the theft or confiscation of their sometimes enviable resources.[87] Public almsgiving, the donation of food to the poor, and hospitality, thus made bishops' presence tangible to at least urban residents.

36 CREATING COMMUNITY WITH FOOD AND DRINK

As these activities were intrinsic to bishops' activities, they were often the primary characteristics highlighted in letters and poems in their praise. Sidonius Apollinaris, for instance, celebrated the actions of Patiens of Lyons, who released grain from his own storehouses to feed the poor among the urban population.[88] For the same reasons, Venantius Fortunatus showered compliments on Vilicus of Metz in a poem he dedicated to him. Not only did the bishop of Metz defend the city and have the foresight to store grain for the population in times of need, but he was also known for offering his hospitality to guests:

> However much the wicked threatens with his vain blows, they for whom you are a wall fear no hurt, and, though the wolf should lie in ambush for the encircling sheepfold, yet with you as protector of the flock no robber will do harm there. You delight the people with your serene and cloudless countenance, and pleasing kindness nourishes the spirits of all. If a new guest asks for sustenance, you offer food; and he finds a home of his own under your roof.[89]

He could thus effectively provide for the faithful even during severe hardship. Measures promulgated at the Council of Mâcon in 585 reinforced the sense that these activities were obligatory: one canon prohibited bishops from owning dogs, since unfriendly guards might discourage those truly in need from seeking charitable assistance.[90]

Conclusion

In closing, it is helpful to reiterate the multiple functions of feasting in clerical circles in early medieval Gaul. Not only were food and drink a necessary evil for human survival, as noted by Augustine of Hippo in his *Confessions* in the fifth century,[91] but the provisioning of and participation in shared meals provided opportunities for religious men and women to demonstrate their role as leaders in Christian communities. As documented by sixth-century authors in Gaul, clerics increasingly recognized that feasts represented venues at which they could distinguish themselves not only as generous patrons of the poor but also as loyal clients of more powerful and armed members of the nobility. In the context of hagiographical works, moreover, interactions involving food and drink might be manipulated by abbots and bishops who found themselves in the dangerous position of facing an angry king or lord. Their resistance to compliance with demands that they found unacceptable, for instance, might take the form of miraculously shattering the bonds normally created in the course of a shared meal. At the heart of this rhetoric was their recognition of the ritual symbolism and practical applications of eating and drinking in the creation and maintenance of Christian communities. The attempt to forbid religious women from participating in such important activities—an effort that was ultimately unsuccessful because it proved so deleterious to gaining necessary support and protection for their monastic foundations—should therefore now receive our attention.

CHAPTER 3

GENDER AND AUTHORITY: FEASTING AND FASTING IN EARLY MEDIEVAL MONASTERIES FOR WOMEN

Feasting and the Power of Hospitality

Food and drink occupied an important, albeit incongruous, position in the lives of religious women in early medieval Gaul. In late antiquity and the early Middle Ages, nuns were frequently lauded for their ability to provide hospitality in the manner of Martha's devotion to Jesus and the apostles.[1] Yet while supplying memorable repasts to their guests, they themselves only ate sparingly. This sort of generosity, practiced in conjunction with extreme personal abstinence, was far from being uniquely female in its manifestation;[2] as we saw in the last chapter, hagiographical sources reveal that moderation in food and drink, charity, and the taking in of guests all constituted general obligations of monastic life among both religious men and women.[3] Although such behavior was encouraged in monastic regulations for male houses, some early medieval *Rules* for nuns nonetheless prohibited or limited women's ability to sponsor banquets. As noted by Avitus of Vienne in a poem on virginity addressed to his sister Fuscina, scriptural precedents such as Luke 10.38–42 meant that laboring to provide food was not the Lord's highest priority. Jesus had revealed that Mary and not Martha had chosen the best portion, since the latter was caught up in the ways of the world.[4] Making meals clearly distracted women from a higher calling as virgins of Christ.

Our study of the context in which and reasons for which generosity with food and drink took place in early medieval Gaul has revealed that the provisioning of feasts connoted power and authority. For many, as we saw above, the activity had great symbolic value, since it was one of the few opportunities for clerics to express masculine identity since they were

40   CREATING COMMUNITY WITH FOOD AND DRINK

deprived of the ability to carry weapons or marry. In the case of female houses, which were often founded by elites on behalf of their daughters, families considered them both sacred spaces and worldly property. Unlike ecclesiastical institutions, monasteries were identified closely with these kin groups, which meant, for one, that they often suffered attack when enemies of relatives took retribution.[5] The responsibilities and repercussions of these familial connections probably also led to the expectation that the house might be used regularly by kin for a variety of secular purposes, including providing hospitality for them and their associates. Clerics such as Caesarius of Arles, seeking to shelter the nuns from unnecessary external obligations, hence discouraged the sponsorship of feasts as an inappropriate activity for female members of monastic houses. The restriction of nuns' movement through the imposition of permanent claustration, while intended to guard them from external threats, nonetheless resulted in their exclusion from networks of political, religious, and military patronage. Caesarius's ban on the hosting of meals for visitors to the monasteries was a particularly severe addition to restrictions on nuns' movements, since it meant that they could no longer easily court the support of powerful protectors. Because they recognized that the friendships of influential leaders were vital to the well-being of their monastic houses and their own authority, sixth-century abbesses and monastic founders sought a variety of means to circumvent such limitations on their access to this form of exchange.

The push and pull between nuns' sparing ingestion of food and drink and their need to provide nourishment in quantity to others elucidates some of the vagaries of the path between two contrasting models of holy behavior. Despite the striking compartmentalization of women's activities in early medieval monasteries, the role of female religious houses in the provision of feasting has generally received scant attention. Modern scholars more frequently associate Merovingian convents with images of the radically abstinent behavior of monks and consecrated virgins inherited from the traditions of the desert fathers and the Irish.[6] In his general survey of medieval food customs, for instance, Massimo Montanari has posited that:

> [T]he monastic regulations of northern Europe (for example, those of the Irish Columban[us]) were the strictest and most severe in establishing fasts, penitence and excluded foods; these were clearly conceived as reactions or "negative" references to the prevailing dietary models. They represented the repudiation of a society which placed eating first among worldly values; so among spiritual values it was the refusal of food which held pride of place.[7]

GENDER AND AUTHORITY

Measures for nuns, in particular, were based on the type of lifestyle lauded in late antique letters to virgins and saints' *Lives* describing holy women; these emphasized a need for asceticism stemming from medical descriptions of the physiological shortcomings of the female body and scriptural examples of women who had succumbed to temptation with disastrous consequences. In his *Paedagogus,* Clement of Alexandria noted that women's immodest behavior at meals was sufficient to provoke illicit sex with their male counterparts.[8] Those of the female sex were therefore advised by Jerome not to eat excessively and to avoid wine altogether, since both increased the heat of the body and thereby inflamed the genitals.[9]

Although *Rules* for women in Gaul such as that written in the early sixth century by Caesarius of Arles officially discouraged extreme asceticism,[10] the *vitae* of Radegund of Poitiers (d. 587) and Rusticula of Arles (d. 632), both of whom lived in houses regulated by these prescriptions, celebrated virtually the opposite sort of behavior.[11] Similarly, Monegund, a mother of two who left her husband after her daughters died, shut herself in a cell where she lived on little more than water and the barley bread she made for herself.[12] In each of their cases, this radical behavior appears to have been self-imposed; Ceasarius of Arles and others viewed severe forms of fasting as a platform for expressing resistance to the highly restrictive codes typically applied to religious houses for women. Since women had fewer opportunities to isolate themselves than did male hermits, however, they had little choice other than to achieve such privations within the confines of their convents. While such feats marked the individual strength of the nuns who chose to undertake them, radical abstention from food and drink by one or a few contributed to a sense of disunity in female monastic houses. Extreme behavior presumably created a wide gap between ascetic athletes and the other members of their cloistered communities.

Thus, descriptions of extreme fasting such as by the former prostitute Pelagia of Antioch,[13] or the widow Blaesilla and the virgin Furia in the letters of Jerome,[14] while indeed relevant to the development of monastic life in Gaul, were not the only sources from which early medieval clerics drew inspiration. At least in the case of monastic *Rules* composed by fifth-century Christian authors such as Augustine and John Cassian, rituals relating to the presentation and consumption of food and drink in early medieval religious communities often took a more moderate form.[15] The need to chasten the body through abstinence from sufficient foodstuffs, for instance, did not outweigh all else. On Sundays, even relatively strict monastic *Rules* such as that of Caesarius of Arles forbade fasting.[16] As remarked by Venantius Fortunatus, relatively generous meals on feast days acted as a physical reminder of the glory which would be enjoyed in the afterlife.[17] This emphasis on

42 CREATING COMMUNITY WITH FOOD AND DRINK

moderation differed from the castigation of gluttony symbolized by Adam's encounter with forbidden fruit in the Garden of Eden, an event referred to in Ferreolus of Uzès's late sixth-century *Rule* for monks.[18] Women nonetheless faced enormous obstacles to achieving a similar balance as men in their relationship to food, since contemporary clerics repeatedly reminded them of Eve's culpability in disobeying God's command and eating from the tree of knowledge. Avitus of Vienne, for instance, blamed Eve's pride for her successful effort on behalf of the serpent to persuade her mate to partake of the apple after she had done so herself.[19]

As we have seen, religious life provided many opportunities for gift exchange involving food and drink in early medieval Gaul.[20] However, rather than constituting evidence of the laxity of the regulations governing the inhabitants of monastic houses,[21] early medieval feasts or *convivia* celebrated God's generosity and were integral to nunneries' survival. Prior to the sixth-century composition of *Rules* restricting nuns' contact with the world, their foundation of *xenodochia* or *hospites* for the housing of pilgrims and the needy had allowed monastic communities to reinforce their bonds with the population beyond the convent walls.[22] Sulpicius Severus specifically praised nuns for the hosting of *convivia* for the faithful.[23] Despite prescriptions limiting women's ability to provide hospitality that appeared in monastic *Rules* starting in the early 500s, miracle stories continued to draw attention to the beneficial actions of female saints who interacted positively with food and drink. Virgins thereby humbly imitated or expanded upon precedents established by Jesus during his lifetime. In the *Life* of Rusticula (d. 632), for instance, the future abbess of Saint-Jean, Arles, when still a young girl caught a fish of incredible size with a cloth she had been wearing. As Jesus had done, she provided sustenance to the faithful who accompanied her.[24] Nuns thus reaped both holy reputations and the practical rewards of relationships fostered through food.

The Claustration of Nuns in Sixth-Century Gaul

A thorough assessment of rites and regulations involving the exchange and consumption of food and drink will allow us to achieve a better understanding of the workings of early medieval monastic communities. In the context of monasteries, however, just as in many other settings used to highlight differences in the lives of women from those of men, the oft-used categories of domestic and public spaces are less than optimal for interpretive purposes. Monastic institutions clearly incorporated important aspects of both spheres. Regarding female houses, historians may nonetheless learn much from nuns' private and public interactions with food and drink. Although religious women were largely excluded from power struc-

GENDER AND AUTHORITY

tures that relied on military prowess, they nonetheless participated in patron-client relations just as they had done in secular society. To be certain, however, among the aristocratic women who lived in religious houses, gender differences were highlighted to a greater extent than in the outside world where such practices were simply a matter of accepted oral tradition. By codifying nuns' behavior in a more permanent fashion, monastic *Rules* contained written provisions that concretely reinforced gender-based distinctions between male and female religious. The requirements for nuns' behavior in the sixth century thus differed in significant ways from those composed on behalf of their male contemporaries.

For nuns in Gaul, customs regarding food and drink were formalized in monastic *Rules* from the early sixth century, when Caesarius of Arles composed his *Rule for Virgins*.[25] In this document, the bishop established a means by which to regulate the lives of religious women far more than had been the case in either the late fourth or fifth century. Although consecrated virgins had come under episcopal authority since at least the fourth century,[26] Caesarius advocated a degree of control over their movements far greater than evidenced by the active lifestyles led by earlier religious women in Gaul and Italy such as Genovefa or Scholastica, the latter being the sister of Benedict of Nursia.[27] In writing a *Rule* for the nuns in his sister Caesaria's house of Saint-Jean, Arles, Caesarius specified in the prologue that he had specially adapted its contents for the needs of women.[28] Most significantly, for the first time documented in a communal setting in Gaul, he advocated cloistering the nuns on a permanent basis.[29] Once they took monastic vows, the nuns were never to leave again during their lifetimes.[30] This measure was reinforced in 549 at the Council of Orléans, which indicated that once nuns took their vows and accepted monastic dress, they could not subsequently change their minds and leave their religious communities.[31]

To the best of our knowledge, Caesarius' *Rule* diverged significantly not only from others in Gaul but those that preceded it in various parts of the Mediterranean, where bishops often composed instructions by which their sisters might guide the nuns under their charges. In Augustine of Hippo's more general letter of advice to his sister's congregation, for instance, he encouraged relatively moderate ascetic practices; if nuns could not adhere to the dietary regime, he indicated that they were entitled to additional food so long as they did not consume it outside of meal times.[32] There is also no evidence that the now lost *Rule* of Honoratus, written for the monks at Lérins and influential in shaping Caesarius's composition, advocated any measures as restrictive as those proposed by Caesarius for the nuns of Arles. Similarly, Ambrose of Milan's prescriptions for his sister Marcellina emphasized a balanced approach to monastic life. This set of measures encouraged sensible attitudes toward food and drink

44   CREATING COMMUNITY WITH FOOD AND DRINK

as the best way to maintain both the health and the full participation of the sisters of the religious house.[33] John Cassian's *De institutis coenobiorum* likewise urged moderation in all activities, including fasting and vigils.[34] Caesarius's decision to institute perpetual claustration at his own foundations represented a break from the practices advocated by Cassian, since Caesaria herself received her training at Cassian's nunnery in Marseilles before leaving to direct the monastic house at Saint-Jean, Arles.[35]

With so many options available to them, it thus seems astonishing that any religious women agreed to take on Caesarius's stringent measures. Around 567, however, Radegund of Poitiers (d. 587) chose Caesarius's *Rule* to regulate the lives of the nuns at her monastic foundation at Poitiers. Despite its rigid requirements regarding the cloistering of inmates, it favored the relative independence of the nuns and protected their urban houses from the direct interference of the local bishop. Radegund, who found herself in repeated conflict with the bishop of Poitiers, likely saw the *Rule* as a means of thwarting any malicious efforts by him or his successors to intervene in decisions affecting her foundation and its possessions.[36] Although the monastery of Saint-Jean apparently enjoyed full exemption from episcopal interference bestowed by the pope, and Radegund's house at Poitiers likely also benefited from similar protections, it remains improbable that this privilege was extended automatically to all houses that adopted Caesarius's *Rule*.[37]

Why did the desire to cloister nuns first arise? Claustration was not advocated by the *Rule* in response to the biological or physical needs of women,[38] nor was it a response to so-called abuses perpetuated by religious women prior to this time.[39] Caesarius's flesh and blood, his sister Caesaria, after all, was affected directly by these measures. The bishop justified restricting nuns' freedoms, however, by intimating that a good number of activities might cause greater temptation to religious women than to men. Since their behavior affected not only their holy status but also his own reputation and prestige as their sponsor, Caesarius wanted to reaffirm the validity of the nuns' prayers by closely regulating their lifestyles.[40] While it is unknown whether Caesarius consciously sought to alter their roles from lay women, whose obligations had traditionally included the provision of food and drink,[41] the impact of the *Rule* on their lives should not be underestimated. While its quantitative influence cannot reliably be measured in the random surviving textual sources,[42] Caesarius's monastic regulations specific to nuns reinforced and legitimated unequal access to modes of production and social wealth.[43] Although certainly not thought of in terms of a formal gender ideology in the early Middle Ages, his *Rules* sanctioned clear distinctions between the expected behavior of monks and nuns living in Caesarius's foundations and the other houses that adhered to their prescriptions.

Caesarius' *Rule* for Nuns
and the Prohibition of *Convivia*

A comparison of the *Rule* for nuns written by Caesarius of Arles for his sister Caesaria's congregation of Saint-Jean first in 512, and later revised by him in 534, with the *Rule* that he wrote for monks in the first decade of the sixth century just after leaving Lérins,[44] demonstrates some of the important distinctions between the two. Both of Caesarius's compositions derived their inspiration largely from Augustine's writings on monastic life, Honoratus's *Rule* for Lérins, and John Cassian's *De institutis coenobiorum.* Adaptations to these earlier compositions revealed Caesarius's desire to establish greater constraints on the distribution of food among women than among men. Whereas both religious men and women were prohibited from partaking in meals of meat or poultry unless sick,[45] in Caesarius's *Rule* for nuns, he specifically gave authority to the cellaress to regulate the sisters' access to wine and gifts of food and drink.[46] Monks, conversely, only received brief instructions indicating that they should limit their eating and drinking to mealtimes and remain silent when partaking of food in order to listen to religious readings. Such measures would help them achieve the spiritual nourishment contained in the word of God.[47]

Caesarius's concern with controlling the nuns' access to food did not mean, however, that he instituted measures encouraging them to abstain in a more extreme fashion than their male cohorts. Both monks and nuns were obligated to fast in the appropriate seasons, especially in the weeks before Christmas and during Lent.[48] Monks, however, more frequently had to fast daily whereas the nuns were instructed to do so every other day.[49] Caesarius incorporated additional clauses in the *Rule* for nuns giving the abbess flexibility to temper fasts to the abilities of the virgins under her charge.[50] The reasons for this surprisingly accommodating attitude might perhaps be attributed to Caesarius's perception of religious women as requiring greater leniency due to their alleged physical deficiencies. Yet, as indicated in a letter from Caesarius to his sister, these measures were more plausibly related to his emphasis in the *Rule* on moderation in the nuns' activities.[51] The bishop apparently wanted to discourage the nuns under the abbess's charge from engaging in the type of heroic feats that would gain them the sort of followings achieved by fifth-century ascetics such as Jerome' pupil Blaesilla or Melania the Younger.

Of great importance regarding foodways in Caesarius's *Rule* for nuns was a section entirely absent from the one that he composed for monks. Caesarius forbade the virgins from preparing *convivia* or feasts inside or outside the monastery for bishops, monks, clerics, laymen, women in secular clothing, and relations of the abbess or nuns.[52] The only exceptions to

46   CREATING COMMUNITY WITH FOOD AND DRINK

these prescriptions were in the case of visits by other religious women, on whose behalf the nuns were permitted to prepare feasts.[53] This legislation appeared in the main body of the *Rule* and was repeated a second time in its *Recapitulatio.*[54] A similar passage was also included in the monastic *Rule* of Donatus, bishop of Besançon, written in the mid-seventh century for the abbess Gauthstrude and the nuns of Jussamoutiers, among them his mother Flavia.[55] This document borrowed heavily from the monastic regulations of Benedict of Nursia, Caesarius of Arles, and Columbanus.[56] The detailed nature of these prohibitions make it easy to dismiss the suggestion that the measures were strictly a reflection of the preservation of cloistered life or that they stemmed solely from the desire to protect the nunneries from the imposition of burdensome obligations.

The absence of similar provisions in the *Rule* for monks, moreover, cannot be attributed to the fact that the brethren never provided meals to outsiders. In the *Rule* of Saint Benedict, a nearly contemporary piece, a central tenet of the monastic way of life was the insistence that abbots provide guests and pilgrims with a place at their table.[57] In fact, the only monastic *Rule* for a male house containing similar provisions was the mid-sixth-century composition of Aurelian, Caesarius's successor in the see of Arles. This set of regulations unusually forbade monks from hosting *convivia* in a passage directly borrowed from chapter 39 of Caesarius's *Rule* for nuns.[58] There is, however, much that is unique about Aurelian's composition as it applied a very strict standard of behavior for the brethren, mainly by mandating claustration in the male community! Not thought to have been in use outside of Aurelian's one foundation, these reform measures applied an equal emphasis on the need for the male religious to remove themselves from contact with the world. This experiment was likely resisted by monks as too limiting a regimen, and was abandoned much sooner than was the case in female houses.

Although Caesarius desired to bring an end to the powerful form of gift exchange embodied in the provision of feasts by virgins, his efforts were not successful in either the short or long term. After his lifetime, as far as is known, only two clerics in Gaul in the next century and a half attempted to establish such a severe regime for Christians who took vows as monks or nuns. Aurelian, who as mentioned above tried to prohibit monks from sponsoring banquets, nonetheless did not incorporate a similar prohibition of *convivia* in his *Rule* for nuns, written for a female congregation in Arles in 548.[59] It is unclear whether this lacuna was an error or a sign of recognition that the effort had been unsuccessful among Caesaria's nuns a generation earlier. Donatus of Besançon, who did include in his monastic *Rule* for nuns Caesarius's prohibition of hosting of meals for persons outside the monastery, modified this measure significantly. He indicated that relations of the nuns could supply provisions to them, so long as these gifts passed through the hands of the porter.[60] In Visigothic Spain, Leander of Seville's *De institutione virginum et contemptu mundi,* written for his sister Florentina in the late sixth century, advocated moderation of food and wine consumption, but made no reference to the sponsorship of banquets by the nuns.[61] Widespread resentment towards measures prohibiting *convivia* arose because these restrictions hindered the type of alliances viewed as necessary to maintaining the well-being of monastic foundations.

Radegund of Poitiers's Relationship to Food and Drink

It is now useful to assess in greater detail an example of the application of Caesarius of Arles's prescriptions for nuns to a monastic house. As we noted above, Radegund, former queen and founder of an important monastery at Poitiers in the mid-sixth century, chose Caesarius's *Rule* for her community; the wealth of surviving eaccounts of her activities makes her house a particularly apt case study. Although she should not be viewed as representative of the women who provided direction for communities subject to this *Rule,* the abundance of evidence for her ascetic lifestyle makes her an important candidate by which to evaluate the daily implications of these tight restrictions on nuns' activities. Not only does the analysis of her behavior and accomplishments benefit from the existence of two contemporary *vitae* by close friends of both sexes, but brief parts of Gregory of Tours's historical and hagiographical corpus also give important details about the former queen and the rebellion of the nuns at her foundation two years subsequent to her death.[62] In the poetry of Venantius Fortunatus, multiple examples of short poems or *carmina* refer to his interactions with both Radegund and Agnes, the abbess of her monastic house. These poetic works provide significant contrast with the contents of his hagiographical oeuvre.[63]

Due to her political and social connections as former queen, Radegund appears to have gained rather than lost authority upon her retreat from her royal husband and subsequent entry into her monastic foundation at Poitiers.[64] Most notable was her facility at flouting contemporary canonical measures that made bishops responsible for monastic houses located *intra muros,* that is, within the walls of their cities. In 511, this legislation was promulgated at the Council of Orléans,[65] and repeated at a council in the same city in 533.[66] Referring to bishops' responsibility for enforcing the monastic *Rule* in religious houses was also the second canon of the Council of Arles in the year 554.[67] Georg Scheibelreiter has thus characterized Radegund's attitude and those of the royal nuns who rebelled in

48   CREATING COMMUNITY WITH FOOD AND DRINK

589 as symptomatic of the tensions that existed between lay traditions of accruing privileges through status and clerical interpretations of the religious authority of the episcopal hierarchy.[68] In addition to the connections she maintained with traditional institutional bodies and her access to considerable economic resources, Radegund utilized more "informal" networks to secure the future status of the nuns at her foundation of Sainte-Croix at Poitiers. Her flexibility in achieving religious ends was reflective of the active brand of sanctity more characteristic of that which was exhibited in Gaul during the fourth and fifth centuries by such figures as Martin, Genovefa, and Chlotild.[69]

Yet, the sources of power that Radegund manipulated clashed with Caesarius's conservative formulation of the type of behavior that he considered appropriate among Merovingian nuns. Her maintenance of contact with her lay contemporaries and her insistence on providing hospitality for both the needy and those in elite circles afforded her important opportunities to act as a patroness and spiritual leader of her monastic house. The visibility of these activities highlighted certain distinctions from the undertakings of her male contemporaries, who were not forbidden the same privileges. Just as the choice of burial in specifically female relics, such as the worn veil of a holy woman, forcefully projected a gender-specific brand of sanctity,[70] Radegund's conscious violation of the prescriptions regarding feasting and fasting in Caesarius's *Rule* for nuns protected the use of this prerogative for other nuns. Radegund's relationship to food and drink, which was often very different from that which was envisioned by Caesarius, had a measurable impact not only during her lifetime but also following her death.

The interpretation of Radegund's activities has long been recognized as being somewhat clouded by the existence of very different rhetorical frameworks informing the compositions of her biographers. Yet, complementary hagiographical representations of her sanctity by the future bishop Venantius Fortunatus and the Poitevan nun Baudonivia, while often at odds with one another, both used the saint's interaction with food to demonstrate her power.[71] Although Gregory of Tours observed that Radegund was famous for her prayers, fasts, and charity,[72] her ascetic lifestyle within the monastic house that deprived her of nourishment nonetheless contrasted starkly with her lavish generosity when providing others such as Venantius Fortunatus with food.[73] The latter, a direct violation of Caesarius's *Rule* chapters 39–40, reveals contradictions among the sources and thereby provides a window into some of the informal power structures at Radegund's disposal.[74]

As has been demonstrated by Caroline Bynum for the high Middle Ages, fasting and ingestion of the Eucharist provided great contrast to one

GENDER AND AUTHORITY   49

another but were closely related activities. They had special although not exclusive significance for religious women.[75] In late antiquity and the early Middle Ages, too, women were considered the "weaker vessel." Yet, self-deprivation was an important source of strength because it made the soft female body hard: the more withered their appearance, the more man-like their bodies became.[76] Fasting provided the means by which female fragility and vulnerability were transformed and eliminated.[77] Abstention from most types of food and wine was thus one form of behavior besides prayer and chastity through which nuns achieved higher spiritual status than otherwise open to them.

At Radegund's foundation of Poitiers regulated by Caesarius's *Rule* for nuns, contemporaries acknowledged Radegund's indelible imprint on the cloister's reputation. In her *vita,* which might be characterized as the more conservative of his writings about the saint, Venantius Fortunatus portrayed Radegund as a true virago, a woman who had gained the bearing of a man through her actions.[78] Her dietary habits also received extensive attention from one of her biographers. Not only was the saint very sparing in her intake of bread, but Venantius Fortunatus lauded the fact that she abstained from pure wine, mead, and beer. Even when faced with illness, Radegund ate nothing but legumes and green vegetables, refusing all animal products, meat, fish, and fruit. During Lent, she deprived herself further, and abstained from bread, oil, and salt, and drank little water.[79] She acted in this manner against the advice of Caesaria II (d .559), her contemporary and the abbess of Saint-Jean in Arles, who counseled moderation since extreme asceticism would only make her sick and thus set her back in her program of abstinence.[80] Citing 1 Timothy 4.3, Fortunatus and Agnes likewise urged Radegund deferentially to take a little wine for the sake of her health.[81]

Baudonivia, a nun who had grown up at Radegund's house, later supplemented Venantius Fortunatus's hagiographical account of the former queen. She noted in passing the saint's ascetic observances, and emphasized how they brought her significant bodily, though not spiritual, weakness.[82] Her briefer allusions to Radegund's highly ascetic behavior owed much to the complementary nature of her *vita* to that of Fortunatus. Yet, her version of Radegund's life also responded to other more pressing concerns in the period when she wrote following the tumultuous events of the rebellion in 589. Whereas Fortunatus urged the nuns to retain a rigorously ascetic lifestyle as promoted by Radegund, Baudonivia used Sulpicius Severus's prototype of Martin's aggressive Christian leadership to highlight Radegund's activism in a time when the house was under great pressure by local authorities.[83] The differences between the two biographies of Radegund were also linked to Baudonivia's desire to show Radegund as a powerful patroness, using, among other things, food to retain the loyalty of

50   CREATING COMMUNITY WITH FOOD AND DRINK

her protectors. Rather than the secret expression of extreme asceticism of the virago promoted by Venantius Fortunatus, Radegund's self-denial as described by Baudonivia, was matched by her ability to secure influential supporters.

This diversity of opinion as to Radegund's achievements matched more general characteristics distinguishing the two authors from one another. Whereas Fortunatus focused on Radegund's excessive zeal within the monastic house, he neglected the more public and thus worldly aspects of her life. Although he praised these same activities in his poetry,[84] he omitted from her *vita* any discussion of her acquisition of a piece of the Holy Cross by embassy, her regular correspondence with bishops and kings, and even the controversy surrounding her funeral when Bishop Maroveus refused to officiate.[85] Baudonivia, like Gregory of Tours, directly referred to the abbess as a contemporary Helena in their hagiographical works; she eagerly engaged in worldly as well as spiritual interchange to promote the prestige and well-being of her monastic foundation.[86] These efforts incorporated hospitality, food, and drink to ensure the patronage of powerful supporters.

Not many nuns who lived in or visited the monastic house at Poitiers could have followed as meager a diet as did Radegund. In doing so, Radegund showed disregard for obeying the *Rule* to the letter. While all authors insisted that Radegund alone engaged in these feats of restraint, the precedents set by the former queen were somewhat uneven in nature. Just two years after Radegund's death, in the course of a rebellion at her foundation in 589, charges brought against Abbess Leubovera by resentful nuns included accusations that she had provided feasts for pilgrims, the poor, and other guests. During the inquiry that followed, the abbess responded that because she had not herself participated in the feasts, she had not violated the example established by Radegund. As a result, the authorities deemed permissible her transgressions of the *Rule*.[87] Even within the boundaries of activities sanctioned by Caesarius's *Rule,* there was clearly room for maneuvering. One measure, for example, specified that those who cooked would receive a mixture of wine according to their labors. The cellaress was likewise instructed to apportion wine to the sick and those of "delicate upbringing." As noted above, feast days were an occasion for wine, whereas fowl and other meat were reserved for the ill.[88]

Although it violated the *Rule,* Radegund's regular charitable activities included her serving of bread and meat to the infirm and impoverished laity who visited the nuns; she also cooked for the sisters and cleaned the kitchen afterwards.[89] In his poetry, Fortunatus often celebrated as pleasurable and filling the meals to which he had been invited by Radegund and Agnes.[90] Whereas Fortunatus did acknowledge in his hagiographical *oeuvre* the miraculous ways in which Radegund protected those who supplied

GENDER AND AUTHORITY 51

the monastery with food, Baudonivia was more apt to describe Radegund's activities in terms reminiscent of the acts of Jesus in the Gospels. For instance, she attested to the cask in the cellar that never ceased to fill miraculously with wine much to the joy of the nuns residing at Sainte-Croix.[91] Both types of wonders appeared regularly in fifth- and sixth-century hagiographical works that praised the accomplishments of holy monks and nuns in Gaul.[92] While Jo Ann McNamara has characterized these sorts of food miracles as symptomatic of concern for sufficient food-stuffs for the nuns,[93] the symbolic implications of these wondrous activities were also of great significance for readers of the *vitae*. By sponsoring charitable meals, Radegund brought marginalized individuals back from the point of death and reintegrated them with the Christian community through the food and drink they required. By extending the hospitality of *convivia* to visiting clergy members, she became their patroness.

While her biographers were exceedingly careful to specify that Radegund herself did not participate in the consumption of the various delicacies that she offered to those who visited the monastery, her actions, however generous, constituted a direct violation of Caesarius's prohibition to nuns against providing meals to either male clerics or lay persons of any status. The sisters were only allowed to provide food to fellow religious women, and it was forbidden for even the abbess to eat outside of the monastic house.[94] Both the extreme asceticism cautioned against by Caesarius in and outside of the *Rule,* and the regular practice of *convivia* at Poitiers testified to Radegund's flagrant resistance of monastic custom.[95] She likely recognized that her provision of feasts and remarkable feats of fasting heightened her authority among the nuns as well as outside the walls of her foundation.

Measuring the impact of this type of expression of power remains particularly difficult. While the two primary hagiographical descriptions of Radegund were written at cross-purposes, their very different descriptions of her relationship to food complemented one another. Venantius Fortunatus desired to portray the former queen as a figure of great sanctity who underwent privation by choice, whereas Baudonivia recalled Radegund as a generous patroness as would have befitted her role as queen. Despite Radegund's perilous balancing act between royal and episcopal leaders, she successfully exercised a number of unwarlike activities that furthered her influence.[96] Both Venantius Fortunatus's and Baudonivia's description of the monastic founder showed the potential power accessible to religious women who successfully manipulated, among other things, their ingestion and provisioning of food and drink.

Although the significance of hosting *convivia* is now evident, one final example demonstrates the close association between Radegund's fasting and power. Indeed, abstinence from food and drink represented a means of

52   CREATING COMMUNITY WITH FOOD AND DRINK

resisting a variety of obstacles as well as a means of preparing for a religious experience.[97] The most revealing incident of Radegund's manipulation of food followed her successful negotiations with the Byzantine emperor Justin II and his consort Sophia to obtain a relic of the Holy Cross. After a successful embassy to Constantinople, achieved with the help of a petition by King Sigibert and poems by Venantius Fortunatus written on her behalf, Radegund received a piece of the holy relic. Yet, she was unable to install it in her monastery because the bishop of Poitiers, Maroveus, refused to perform the appropriate liturgy on the occasion of the translation.[98] Presumably he was angry that the relic was not destined for his own church. As described by Baudonivia, Radegund conducted vigils and fasted as a means of garnering Sigibert's support for an effort to sidestep the bishop of Poitiers. She thereby pressured Eufronius, the bishop of Tours, to install the relic instead, despite his lack of jurisdiction in the see of Poitiers.[99] Interestingly, in his account of the events, Gregory of Tours, who was Eufronius' successor, omitted any reference to the saint's fasts on this occasion from his description of the incident. He must have seen Radegund's use of ascetic behavior to overcome ecclesiastical resistance as inappropriate: it made her appear more powerful than the bishops involved in the incident since they bowed to her will. Gregory of Tours instead attributed Radegund's success to a letter that she sent to the king to urge him to act on her behalf.[100]

In the end, Radegund's efforts were fruitful. Remaining conflict at the arrival of the fragment of the Holy Cross at Poitiers, however, meant that the *adventus* ceremony did not have all the usual trappings of community consensus and solidarity.[101] This controversial translation, which occupied a central role in Baudonivia's account, was nonetheless absent altogether from Venantius Fortunatus's biography of Radegund. Despite his participation in the negotiations and extensive praise of the Holy Cross in his poetry, Venantius Fortunatus was also a cleric with political ambitions. He was evidently not in a position comfortable enough to denigrate Bishop Maroveus directly.[102] Nor would it make sense to weaken the office he eventually hoped to occupy. Only in the words of Baudonivia did fasting and other ascetic activities become Radegund's weapons to overcome her adversaries. Not only did she thereby ensure the future legacy of her monastic foundation through the installation of a relic of the Holy Cross, but she demonstrated the potential power of tools at the disposal of every aspiring nun.

Conclusion

Extreme food deprivation and the provisioning of meals, both activities contrary to the prescriptions laid out by Caesarius of Arles, enabled Rade-

GENDER AND AUTHORITY 53

gund to gain access to avenues of power that the bishop specifically prohibited to the inhabitants of monastic houses regulated by his *Rule*. Indeed, she was not the only religious woman to engage in a mixture of these two complementary practices. Twelve years prior to Radegund's death in 587, Rusticula, the eighteen-year old abbess of Saint-Jean at Arles, began her practice of severe fasts, eating only every third day while she prayed and kept vigils on behalf of the nuns in her charge.[103] Yet, the abbess also showed herself to be a capable patroness during her lifetime as well as after her passing some time in her seventies. Written shortly after her burial in 632, Florentius of Tricastrina's *vita* of the saint prominently confirmed Rusticula's role in providing food and drink even in death; his recitation of miracles included those provoked by the consumption of minuscule fragments of her relics. On one occasion, for instance, a man possessed by a demon in the city of Sens tried to consume her hand (*manus beatissimae devorare conabatur*), since presumably she used it to make the sign of the cross. Her hair, clothing, and bed also became conduits of healing miracles. When mixed with water and drunk by infirm individuals, the saint's remains effected wondrous cures and exorcism.[104]

The anonymous seventh- or eighth-century *Rule* for nuns that is often referred to as the *Regula cuiusdam patris ad virgines*,[105] furthermore demonstrates that Caesarius's effort to prohibit the nuns' provision of *convivia* was not considered a priority by other bishops and abbots. For the nuns who may have employed this *Rule* or ones like it, including the inhabitants of Burgundofara's double monastery of Faremoutiers,[106] the author made hospitality to guests and the poor a central obligation. The presence of both male and female religious inhabitants would have no doubt made Caesarius's restrictions infeasible. The legislation nonetheless specified that inmates of the house were not permitted to eat together with those who benefited from their patronage.[107] Judging from an account of allegedly gluttonous nuns in Jonas of Bobbio's description of Faremoutiers appended to his *vita* of Columbanus, some religious women in Burgundofara's house apparently still rebelled in reaction to the harshness of measures regulating their consumption of food. Despite transgressing the monastic prescriptions for food and drink, however, both of the nuns successfully repented and thereby avoided the suffering of eternal damnation.[108] Included among descriptions of holy women who were received in heaven directly after their deaths, this story served as a warning for future nuns who desired more than their share of food. The work circulated not only in this monastery but in all houses in possession of a copy of the *vita* of Columbanus.

Radegund thus for a time triumphed in her resistance to restrictive legislation regulating women's interaction with food and drink: her successful manipulation of these mores may have inspired at least in part the abandonment of some of Caesarius's central objectives in monastic *Rules* for women in Merovingian Gaul written during the next century. Through a model of what might be called non-institutional forms of influence, early medieval noble women in monastic houses gained access to greater authority both as a result of their patronage of feasts and abstinence from food and drink. Due to the conditions in which their actions transpired, nuns' complex relationships to food and drink had symbolism unique to their sex. Timely manipulation of customs of feasting and fasting allowed religious women to create and reinforce existing bonds of allegiance with those within as well as outside the walls of their monastic houses. At the same time, their own ascetic behavior was worthy of emulation and veneration in the centuries following their deaths.

CHAPTER 4

FOOD AS A SOURCE OF HEALING AND POWER

Healing Alternatives in Late Antiquity and the Early Middle Ages

When Christians in Gaul became ill, a variety of options were available to them in the sixth and seventh centuries. Some families, mainly those residing in cities south of the Loire or those presumably of means in more isolated locations, sought the assistance of physicians.[1] Severe maladies required visits by doctors who diagnosed diseases by means of patients' urine and pulse, and then chose the appropriate course of action from among a variety of techniques, including bleeding, cauterization, pharmaceutical remedies, dietetic regimens, the application of prosthetic devices, and surgery. While there is plentiful evidence of practicing physicians throughout late antiquity and the early Middle Ages, the number of theoreticians in western Europe with extensive knowledge of classical medicine had declined dramatically.[2] The last major compilation written in Gaul based on the work of ancient and contemporary Greek authors before the high Middle Ages was the Gallo-Roman Marcellus of Bordeaux's *De medicamentis,* written for the sons of the Emperor Theodosius II circa 408.[3] This treatise gave extensive attention to the role of herbs in healing as had been done most famously in the first century by Pliny the Elder in his *Natural History* and Dioscorides in his *De materia medica.* The latter was a Greek pharmaceutical text translated to Latin some time before the sixth century.[4] As in their works, Marcellus, who was not himself a physician, emphasized the role of mineral, vegetable, and animal substances in curing disease. By providing patients with some important translations of the teachings of classical Greek medicine, Marcellus gave them, at least theoretically, the means to cure themselves without a doctor.[5] Many of these remedies made an explicit connection between food, drink, and health.

56 CREATING COMMUNITY WITH FOOD AND DRINK

Although the reasons for a decreasing call for the services of physicians are complex and poorly documented in contemporary sources, they represent in part a consequence of a more general decline in the quality of urban life in the late Roman empire. Increasingly few scholars in the West could read Greek; the number of Latin translations of medical works available to them, moreover, remained limited and the vocabulary of these was somewhat specialized.[6] While some have suggested the existence of formal schools of medicine in late antiquity and the early Middle Ages,[7] the training of physicians in the Roman period had likely always been an informal affair. Practitioners passed knowledge of medical techniques from father to son, mother to daughter, or master to apprentice or slave.[8] By late antiquity, these traditions had become more tenuous. The practice of medicine had by now essentially become a trade: treatment of the human body had lost most of its theoretical basis and focused almost exclusively on the proper administration of remedies to the ill.[9]

Although they occupied prestigious positions, the livelihoods of physicians in early medieval Gaul were not always assured. On the one hand, doctors moved with ease between influential households: the deacon and physician Helipidius of Lyons found employment in the Ostrogothic court under Theoderic;[10] Reovalis, one of the few in the West to have studied medicine in Constantinople, served the bishop of Poitiers as an *archiater* (medical officer) at the end of the sixth century.[11] Those who had written works in their name, even if compilations, could also spread their reputations further afield.[12] Their professions seem to have afforded specialists more mobility and a higher status than the positions into which they had been born. Success nonetheless required developing and maintaining a close relationship with their patrons. While Marileif, the court physician of Chilperic, achieved great wealth in the course of his career, he lost it in the aftermath of the siege of Poitiers in 576 and the death of his royal sponsor in 584.[13]

On the other hand, in a time when there was not uniform confidence in the abilities of medical practitioners, becoming a physician must have represented a fairly dangerous choice of profession. For this reason, in seventh-century Spain, while doctors had to pay a deposit before surgery, they were protected from retribution in Visigothic legislation; if the patient died, this sum was forfeited but the practitioner could not be sued for malpractice.[14] In Merovingian regions, however, the wrong procedure or the failure to cure the member of a powerful family occasionally resulted in exile or even murder of the unlucky physician. When Queen Austrechild, having fallen victim to an epidemic, lay on her deathbed in September, 580, for example, she allegedly took revenge on the two doctors who had not been able to cure her of dysentery. According to Gregory of Tours, who rarely came to

FOOD AS A SOURCE OF HEALING AND POWER 57

the defense of the medical profession but condemned this particular act as evil, she ordered that her physicians be executed. Her unjust command was carried out after her death by her husband Guntramn.[15] Considering the level of medical learning available in Gaul in the sixth and seventh centuries, doctors must have thus felt anxious about taking on royal patients who had a reputation for a quick temper or a thirst for vengeance.

Underlying these difficulties were even more basic changes in attitudes towards physicians, illness, and the causes of sickness. While clerics in Gaul such as Caesarius of Arles (d. 542) were not opposed to using doctors in certain circumstances, others expressed less confidence in the efficacy of medical treatments.[16] For instance, the failure of physicians to respond effectively to epidemics such as the episodic plagues that severely affected Mediterranean port cities and the Rhône valley nearly every decade from the 540s to 600, must have eroded many inhabitants' faith in medicine.[17] Great numbers of Christians instead opted for divination, amulets, herbal potions, and other forms of traditional healing,[18] about which Caesarius was far less enthusiastic.[19] Unfortunately we know very little about these practices, since our primary evidence largely consists of clerical denunciations of the alleged supernatural dealings or demonic dabbling of lay and religious practitioners. At ecclesiastical councils such as Agde in 506, magicians and enchanters, among them some clerics, were defined as those who used amulets. The penalties for such mild forms of sorcery nonetheless included condemnation and excommunication.[20] Bishops such as Gregory of Tours accused popular healers, including one named Desiderius of Bordeaux, of a combination of necromancy and quackery. According to Gregory, Desiderius deceived and harmed numerous local residents of Tours before being run out of the city by authorities.[21]

From a modern perspective, many of these alleged cures appear to have been virtually indistinguishable from the work of physicians in all but name. Many medical recipes, like amulets, relied upon occult powers for their effectiveness.[22] And, the work of such healers also resembled the cures of the saints in everything but the alleged source of their power. Consequently, when reading the primary evidence, readers today may find that religious authorities seemed inconsistent in their policies. For instance, they did not necessarily condemn natural magic as demonic, especially when it served the objective of healing the sick and occurred in an appropriate setting.[23] The most apparent cause of the opposition of medieval clerics to traditional healers, depending upon their techniques and popularity, was that they lured Christians away from churches with fabulous reports of cures.[24] Their alleged ability to heal must have outpaced similar claims by both lay practitioners of medicine and clerical leaders promoting the miraculous cures of the saints.[25]

58   CREATING COMMUNITY WITH FOOD AND DRINK

Conversely, the language of medicine had long permeated religious literature despite the fact that actual knowledge of medical practice did not always extend as far. This familiarity likely made clerical authorities more amenable than they would have otherwise been to cures effected by physicians. Such an observation should not be altogether surprising in light of the emphasis in the Benedictine *Rule* on the necessity of having an infirmary in every monastic house for the care of sick brethren.[26] Monastic libraries also played a role in preserving classical manuscripts on a wide variety of topics, including medicine.[27] Some clerics such as Eumerus, bishop of Nantes, were also trained as physicians.[28] In the Ostrogothic kingdom, Cassiodorus, who seems to have been relatively well-informed in classical medicine, urged the monks of his foundation of Vivarium to study the works of Dioscorides, Hippocrates, Caelius Aurelianus, and Galen in Latin, copies of which were kept in the monastery library.[29] In his *Rule,* which was not as well informed as Cassiodorus's regarding medical practice, Benedict of Nursia nonetheless made an analogy between the responsibilities of an abbot in tending for his flock and those of a wise physician caring for his patients. At both of their disposal were a broad selection of remedies ranging from soothing unguents to the knife of amputation, which each leader might metaphorically or literally apply to combat spiritual and physical ailments.[30]

Christian Cures: Blessed Oil and Holy Relics

In many circumstances, clerics such as Caesarius of Arles prescribed not doctors but rather advised Christians to request that priests anoint the sick with blessed oil and administer communion to them.[31] Holy oil, once exorcised of demonic forces, could bring healing from illness, pardon from sin, and celestial health.[32] For Caesarius, purification of the soul and preparation for eternal life through the communion wine and wafer were far more important than physical healing.[33] Indeed, unction of the sick and ministration of the Eucharist helped ensure the salvation of Christians; as noted by the biographer of Eligius, bishop of Noyon, even in the instance that they died, the faithful gained through the Mass a greater chance of receiving the incomparable reward of eternal life.[34] Although some clerics recognized the benefits of using capable physicians who were able to cure even ascetics,[35] religious leaders impressed upon Christians the far more enviable gift of heavenly repose that resulted from spiritual and not physical healing.

The reception of these ideas among the Christian faithful must have been somewhat mixed. Although contemporary accounts, all written from the perspective of clerics, do not directly point to widespread resistance to

FOOD AS A SOURCE OF HEALING AND POWER   59

their teachings, some reveal a persistent campaign by individual religious leaders to discredit physicians, who represented their direct competitors.[36] Jerome's *Adversus Jovinianum* 2.6 ridiculed the foolishness of a variety of medical techniques. Why would anyone turn to food to heal a variety of illnesses, when faith in God was within reach of every Christian?[37] In the sixth century, Gregory of Tours, moreover, characterized reliance on physicians as a sign of spiritual weakness.[38] He warned Christians that those who went to doctors, especially after receiving healing from a saint or cleric, demonstrated a basic lack of faith. This transgression sometimes merited divine punishment since such ignorance represented an affront to God, the source of the miraculous cures. The archdeacon Leunast, whose eyes were initially cured by a visit to the church of Saint-Martin, thus lost his sight again, this time permanently, after consulting a Jewish practitioner.[39] Even in tales that lacked cautionary warnings of the errors of those who consulted physicians, the alleged efficacy of cures and exorcism of even the poor under the care of benevolent saints such as Junianus made their services highly desirable.[40]

Some hagiographers contrasted the faithlessness of those Christians who sought out lay practitioners with the more praiseworthy behavior of the saints who chose to view their illnesses as an opportunity for spiritual preparation. Rather than seeking a physical cure from a lay physician, they eagerly embraced their imminent deaths. The anonymous author of Balthild of Neustria's (d. 680–681) *vita* therefore emphasized the variety of expressions of the former queen's sanctity once she entered her foundation of Chelles.[41] After she joined the monastery against her will, many of her contemporaries, including some of the nuns of Chelles, doubted the sincerity of her religious vocation.[42] Yet, when she was confronted with her death, her biographer praised her preference for salvation over a cure for her poor health.[43] In choosing this *topos,* or hagiographical motif, to describe Balthild, the author was responding to a trend increasingly common among contemporary hagiographers. A similar example is contained in the description of the Frankish monk Barontus's late seventh-century vision of the afterlife at a monastery now known as Saint-Cyran-en-Brenne (Indre). Following the horrifying revelation of how he would suffer in the afterlife, Barontus wisely decided to seek a course of spiritual reconciliation rather than focusing on his physical health.[44] One prayer in the Burgundian liturgical manuscript known as the *Missale Gothicum* (circa 690–710) likewise petitioned the Lord for the gift of celestial medicine rather than a bodily cure on behalf of ailing Christians.[45] Even if God chose not to cure the sick, far greater rewards lay within His power.

Although liturgical remedies leading to eternal salvation were fitting for saints and Christians facing imminent death, they must not have offered

60   CREATING COMMUNITY WITH FOOD AND DRINK

great solace to the population in times of catastrophe such as plague epidemics. Those suffering from chronic ailments that were not life-threatening but which were nonetheless debilitating must have similarly craved more concrete alternatives. Some illnesses such as leprosy resulted in the alienation of the sufferer from community life and intimate contact with contemporaries;[46] lameness and blindness might make it impossible for that Christian to earn a living by anything but begging. Sickness, moreover, if we may rely on contemporary clerical descriptions, was in many cases portrayed as a manifestation of divine punishment for sins perpetrated by individuals or communities.[47] Those who worked on Sunday, according to Gregory of Tours, risked paralysis in their hands or loss of their eyesight until they relinquished the offending activities.[48] While Gregory was quickest to attribute illness to sin when describing his enemies or in order to use such diagnoses to teach a moral lesson, his selective application of this notion revealed his understanding of God's role in Christian society.[49] Not only did such sufferers require a cure, but they needed to undergo some sort of public ritual that would enable them to be reintegrated into the community of the faithful. The arena in which this process most often transpired was at the tomb of a powerful intercessor. Reverence for the saint, as expressed through fasting, prostration, and prayer before the holy relics, was often answered with healing. This experience thereafter also elevated the status of the petitioner through his or her unique relationship to the saint.[50]

This last form of healing, in the course of which the saint became the patron by curing the faithful of their serious or chronic ailments, was logically the one promoted most vociferously by clerical authorities. Their enthusiasm for this type of treatment stemmed from the fact that the majority of the miraculous cures were effected by relics rather than by living holy men and women, the latter of which had a long tradition of exhibiting unpredictable behavior.[51] Control over the shrines in which sacred remains were housed and the saints' *Lives* that commemorated their achievements, were guarded jealously by clerics, since they recognized the power that such sites gave them over the faithful.[52] They thereby theoretically had the ability to dictate who might enter these holy places and under what conditions. Similarly, they might shape the accounts that heralded the types of cures most frequently performed by Christ through the relics in the possession of their churches.

The selection of potential patients might occur in a variety of ways. Some of the sick received holy visions with instructions as to which shrines they should visit or which saint they should petition for a successful cure; such revelations, if recognized as legitimate by clerical guardians of the saints, sanctioned their presence before particular relics.[53] During a

FOOD AS A SOURCE OF HEALING AND POWER   61

plague epidemic, by contrast, one set of relics might be sufficient to redeem an entire community, as was the case of the holy shroud of Remigius that saved the population of Reims in 543.[54] Certain saints, however, only healed a few types of ailments exhibited by petitioners: the Burgundian king and martyr Sigismund (d. 523), for instance, was best known by the time of Gregory of Tours for reducing fevers;[55] his cures were nonetheless unusual in that they did not occur exclusively at his shrine at Agaune, likely the site of a former pagan sanctuary.[56] From at least the late sixth century, miraculous cures in Sigismund's name also spread to wherever the Mass written in his honor was performed.[57] While this practice allowed a greater number of the ill to be healed, at the same time, it meant a reduced income from pilgrims for the monks who guarded Sigismund's relics.

Yet, because a cure at a saint's shrine usually required travel, the need to make pilgrimage excluded all of those who lacked the means or were already too sick to make the journey.[58] Some diseases, especially those suffered by women, likewise tended to be neglected at many relic shrines or at least in the accounts of cures preserved in some churches and appended to the saints' *vitae* as evidence of the efficacy of their healing ability. The dwindling number of alternatives such as sacred springs meant that women who were ill had few options to effect their recoveries, and only a small number of those solutions were deemed acceptable in the eyes of clerics.[59] A minority of holy women such as Monegund of Tours (d. 570) successfully integrated folkloric healing into their ascetic routines by combining herbal remedies with Christian practices such as making the sign of the cross to effect cures.[60] Nonetheless, few female healers in the surviving hagiographical evidence seem to have received official approval as health practitioners. Not only did bishops and abbots zealously guard against competitors in healing, but on at least a few instances they discredited women active in caring for the sick: many of those accused of wrongdoing and exiled or executed as sorceresses by lay contemporaries must have been midwives or other sorts of traditional healers.[61]

Anthimus's Guide to a Proper Diet
for a Merovingian King

But how does this discussion of sixth- and seventh-century healing practices in Gaul relate to our understanding of food and drink in the early Middle Ages? The most basic answer is the way in which all of the above-mentioned methods of dealing with illness relied at least tangentially upon the ingestion of substances deemed suitable for countering different ailments. Whether the recommendation was for a particular pharmaceutical substance, the Eucharist, or even the dust from a saint's tomb mixed with water,[62] many types of healers shared in common the belief that an effective way to vanquish the symptoms caused by disease was to treat the patient with an ingested remedy. As will be discussed below, at the root of such approaches was the general notion that oral therapies were often efficacious in reestablishing a balance of the humours. For similar reasons, medical and religious treatises also emphasized the beneficial effects for the ill of dietary regimens or periodic abstention from most liquids and solid foods. Fasting could realign the bodily fluids, just as it was seen as an expression of self-control, and it thus represented an appropriately humble preparation for pilgrimage to a holy shrine. Abstinence constituted an important part of the process of purification required of the petitioner who sought the saint's assistance. Rigorous fasting also made possible miraculous visions, such as the vivid dream of the afterlife that left Salvius, bishop of Albi (d. 584), cured of the fever that had nearly killed him.[63]

Clerics also promoted abstinence as a means of discouraging inappropriate behavior, particularly among women. Jerome argued that a limited regimen calmed the sexual appetite and allowed those such as youths and women perceived to be of weaker constitution to avoid temptation and to focus more clearly on their devotions.[64] In particular, he saw fasting as a means of cooling the body. It thus had the opposite effect of wine and meat on human physiology. Those who wished to achieve religious perfection were hence to avoid these dangerous substances.[65] Yet, this harsh outlook on the ingestion of food and drink by women was nonetheless not shared by all of the Church Fathers, since Augustine of Hippo noted that severe self-mortification had negative repercussions on those who sought a closer relationship with God.[66] Rather than recommending that they fast more, he argued that monks and nuns had to find a middle ground—a tempered approach to fasting—so that they could continue to function fully in community life.[67] As Venantius Fortunatus also concluded, partaking in meals and hence participating in communal activities, represented obligations necessary to the good health of nuns so long as they ate and drank in moderation.[68]

As has been noted by John Riddle, the practice of medicine in the early Middle Ages had not so much declined from Roman imperial standards as it had shifted its course.[69] As we have seen, the attention of doctors came to rest primarily on the regulation of diet and the ministration of pharmaceutical remedies to the ill.[70] Extant works related to the writings of physicians in Gaul between the fifth and eighth century thus largely consisted of recipes and regimens rather than addressing other approaches to patients' health, particularly those suffering from severe conditions. By contrast, more theoretical medical approaches, like those of Hippocrates, Aristotle, and Galen, which had heretofore circulated widely but had largely not been translated, no longer found much of an audience in the West. Those works that did address larger themes, like the anonymous early medieval treatise known as the *Sapientia artis medicinae,* mainly focused on the very broad schematization of bodily functions. In this case, the author drew attention to the four humours, four parts of the human body, four phases of the life cycle, and how these were affected by the four seasons.[71] The practical application of such information to the care of patients is nonetheless more difficult to assess, since the author proposed few actual treatments of specific ailments.

Although it does not often deal directly with sickness but rather concentrates on preventative health care, one source that allows us to focus more narrowly on practical approaches to human health is the early sixth-century medical treatise composed by the Byzantine physician Anthimus on behalf of the Frankish king Theuderic (d. 534). Exiled from Constantinople after being charged by Emperor Zeno with treasonous conspiracy, Anthimus fled to relative safety in Ravenna, where he served the Ostrogothic king Theoderic (d. 526) in a variety of capacities, including his participation in at least one embassy to the Frankish king. His letter, known as *De observatione ciborum (On the Observance of Food),* written some time after 511 and perhaps in northern Gaul, outlined for the monarch the beneficial effects of a balanced regimen.[72] Not only does this work provide a fascinating glimpse of the role that food and drink were believed to play in the maintenance of good health, but it highlights the significant attention that nourishment might merit in diplomatic relations and royal life in general. An assessment of the Byzantine physician's suggestions in their historical context also allows us to propose the possible reaction they were likely to have engendered among members of the Frankish aristocracy.[73]

That such a work, adapted to the needs of its Frankish readers, should have emerged from the Ostrogothic court is not altogether surprising. Cassiodorus, who served Theoderic as *quaestor* (legal expert) during roughly the same period at which Anthimus worked for the same, wrote a brief instructional treatise for the chief *archiater* or medical officer of the king. Although the text cannot be dated precisely to a particular year of Theoderic's reign, Cassiodorus preserved it by including it in his collection known as the *Variae* (compiled circa 537–538).[74] Among the duties of the *archiater,* Cassiodorus noted that it was the responsibility of the royal doctor to impose a dietary regimen on his patients. These recommendations might even include fasting, if this approach was seen as the necessary course for good health.[75] It is very likely that Anthimus served as the Ostrogothic court physician, since he had presumably quickly gained an influential position in Ravenna as one of the few practitioners with the type of medical training then available in Constantinople. In monitoring the

64   CREATING COMMUNITY WITH FOOD AND DRINK

health and diet of Theoderic, and possibly also spending time in the Frankish king Theuderic's circle, he must have gained considerable experience in Germanic dietary mores prior to his composition of a manual outlining a healthy regimen for the Frankish monarch.[76]

Borrowing heavily from the Roman authors Apicius and Galen, Anthimus formulated his dietary recommendations on the basis of the classical belief that the body was composed of four humours: blood, phlegm, black bile, and yellow bile. A rounded diet was hence one that promoted good health by fostering a balance of these fluids.[77] The wrong combination of foods, by contrast, contributed not just to indigestion but generated more serious ailments such as bloody fluids, pungent carbuncles, and belching.[78] Comparing the functioning of the human stomach to the mixing of mortar, Anthimus organized his recipes so as to ensure proper blending or digestion of the building materials. These constitued the basis for a strong edifice.[79] He nonetheless adapted his advice to appeal to the tastes and resources of elite Franks who were great lovers of meat and beer. His reference to the use of lard as a condiment instead of olive oil, the latter of which was a Mediterranean standard, must have been intended to increase the interest of Theuderic and his followers; they were likely unaccustomed to traditional Roman culinary mores.[80] Butter, too, was not simply a salve as suggested by Galen, but in Anthimus's composition, it was promoted as an important medicament for those with lung ailments.[81] Of necessity, Anthimus also made concessions to other Frankish dietary staples such as beer and mead,[82] and must have struggled not to be openly critical of their surprising predilection for raw bacon as both nutriment and medication.[83] Clearly the text's objective was to flatter rather than to offend the Frankish king; in order to achieve this end, a few adjustments to the contents were necessary to make more palatable the classical approach to diet as the basis for good health.

During the past century and a half, Anthimus's *De observatione ciborum* has largely been overlooked by late antique and early medieval historians.[84] Nonetheless, the work has intrinsic value for any assessment of how early medieval descriptions of dietary mores varied from their classical predecessors. Sixth-century authors such as Anthimus and Vinitharius, for instance, surprisingly employed a more varied array of spices than did the second-century Roman author Apicius.[85] As such works made their way into monastic centers in the seventh and eighth centuries, they may have in turn influenced the types of spices imported by houses such as Corbie and Echternach for the health of the members of these communities.[86] Moreover, as Anthimus was a non-native speaker who learned to speak Latin in Italy, his writing has significant value for linguistic scholars, who have found much of interest in his creative uses of Vulgar Latin and words borrowed from Greek.[87]

Yet, Anthimus's work should also be recognized as having value as a historical record of the unique nature of Ostrogothic-Frankish relations in the early 500s. Despite the presence of the Burgundians between them as a buffer, the Ostrogoths appear to have viewed the political aspirations of the sons of the Frankish king Clovis (d. 511) as potentially dangerous and used a number of tactics such as marriage alliances and their relationship with the Byzantine empire to press their advantage. Although Theoderic was powerful and did not suffer directly from the expansionist ambitions of the Franks in his own time, his successors would soon face the devastating effects of the Frankish armies of Theuderic's son Theudebert in 533.[88] Theoderic and Theuderic were divided, however, not only by political but also religious differences, with the Ostrogoths practicing the Arian faith and the Franks by now having converted to the tenets of the Nicene Creed. Although Theoderic maintained a mostly constructive relationship with Catholics within his own kingdom,[89] the two monarchs had to find a neutral language by which to communicate diplomatically. The mutual appreciation of food and drink may well have represented such a medium.

Well-provisioned feasts, such as those prepared by Leo, the cook of Gregory, bishop of Langres, were commonly acknowledged as capable of winning trust and lulling even the most stubborn opponents into complacency. Gregory of Tours, for one, recalled the instance in which an unnamed Frankish nobleman held Gregory of Langres's nephew Attalus in slavery, and would not cede to the bishop's request to redeem him through purchase. The bishop's cook therefore received permission from his lord to infiltrate the nobleman's household by having himself sold to the latter; after winning the Frank's confidence by cooking a number of extraordinary meals for him and his guests, Leo assisted Attalus in escaping to safety.[90] From the perspective of this account, we may see Anthimus's letter to the Frankish court as a more theoretical rendition of a well-prepared banquet. Presenting this dietary manual on Theoderic's behalf allowed Anthimus to use once again the medical education that he had already applied to good effect to win himself not only asylum among the Ostrogoths but also a prominent place in the court at Ravenna. Although he may not have been the one who conceived of Anthimus's plan to write such a composition, Theoderic must have also agreed that such a treatise on medicine constituted an appropriate gift for the Franks. Rather than sending precious objects, Theoderic chose to impress his Frankish contemporary with the wealth of medical knowledge present in the Ostrogothic court but not otherwise available to the Merovingian king. Couched as concern for the well-being of the monarch, the work was nonetheless also intended to highlight the Ostrogoths' mastery of Roman *civilitas*.[91] This expression of the sophistication of the royal court

66   CREATING COMMUNITY WITH FOOD AND DRINK

in Ravenna was but one means of subtly demonstrating the shortcomings of the cultural achievements of the Franks.[92]

Like any gift, however, the currency of Theoderic's offering was only as valuable as its intended recipient's understanding of its significance. Disappointingly, surviving sources do not include any account of Theuderic's reaction upon receiving Anthimus's treatise, nor is there any way to divine the spirit in which the work was accepted by the Frankish monarch. No extant sixth-, seventh-, or eighth-century manuscripts of Anthimus's *De observatione ciborum* have been identified, and ninth-century copies reveal only the barest information about the preservation and circulation of this dietary manual in monastic libraries.[93] Hence, we are left wondering what the place of such advice was in the lay context of the Frankish court, and whether the king would have preferred a bountiful feast to a dietary manual. It is uncertain what impact, if any, Anthimus had in modifying royal foodways. However, although it may be impossible to reconstruct with any certainty Theuderic's perception of this unique gift, we should note that this composition was the last of its kind written in Gaul for several centuries. Judging from the increasingly broad appeal and growing authority of the cult of saints in healing in the early medieval West,[94] moreover, its timing was likely poor. Anthimus's work was clearly not memorable or influential enough to encourage others in the Frankish court to embark on similar projects. Ironically, but perhaps fittingly, the work's main audience in subsequent centuries were not high-ranking members of the laity but rather those clerics appointed to oversee the ill who were housed in monastic infirmaries.

Conclusion

Anthimus's desire to regulate the intake of food and drink for the sake of good health likely met with significant resistance among the lay nobility on whose behalf he wrote. In large part, the effort may have failed because the concept of a successful dietary regimen demanded that individuals master their own habits.[95] Unlike the nuns and monks who were accustomed to curbing their will through the practices of abstinence and chastity, since the perfection of the body mirrored that of their souls, lay elites were unaccustomed to this type of self-imposed restraint on their personal freedom. As we have seen in chapter two, feasting represented an integral component of their interactions; any challenge to that structure posed a threat to the mechanisms of power upon which they depended to negotiate their place in the social hierarchy in Gaul. Although physical health constituted a matter of considerable importance for many, the ability to provide abundant meat and beer to their guests had more immediate results: it conveyed the standing of individuals who hosted feasts in their communities. Similarly, one of the most important opportunities to communicate status and identity occurred at the funerals of relations and the celebrations of subsequent anniversaries of their deaths. Food and drink played a role in sending off those who did not find a cure among physicians, healers, or the saints. In the next chapter, we will thus explore the different manifestations of funerary feasting in early medieval Gaul from both historical and archaeological perspectives. The written and material evidence will allow us to propose the reasons why rituals involving food and drink in this last phase of the life cycle persisted for centuries after Christian clerics had begun encouraging the faithful to abandon these ancient customs due to their alleged associations with pagan tradition.

CHAPTER 5

FUNERARY FEASTING
IN EARLY MEDIEVAL GAUL
AND NEIGHBORING REGIONS

Ancient Sources and Early Medieval Practices

One last, but certainly not the least important, aspect of rituals related to food and drink to be discussed here, pertains to ceremonies conducted in conjunction with burial and anniversaries of the deaths of ancestors. Of all of the topics covered thus far, this set of practices was the most ubiquitous in early medieval communities until at least the seventh century. Yet, it was also the most poorly documented by clerics in Gaul. The most vivid images of funerary feasting date not from the early Middle Ages but Roman antiquity when such customs were widespread and received extensive attention in the writings of contemporary pagan authors. Some of the most impressive remains of cemeterial meals also derive from Gallo-Roman sites (Figure 5.1). In excavations in 1851 and 1893 at Martres-de-Veyre (Puy-de-Dôme), for instance, a number of extremely well-preserved second-century graves with remains of food deposition rites were uncovered. Along with an assortment of ceramic and glass vessels and woven baskets, the sepulchers contained fragments of nuts and seeds from grapes and apples or pears; the glass vessels exhibited residues of liquid that may have been a grape- or a honey-based beverage. Although none of the organic materials were retained by the excavators, and many of these items crumbled soon after being exposed to air, Auguste Audollent noted with astonishment the unique state of their survival.[1] He nonetheless did not feel the need to offer additional commentary on the significance of these remarkable discoveries, since the burial of food and drink with the dead was well known to scholars of Roman antiquity.

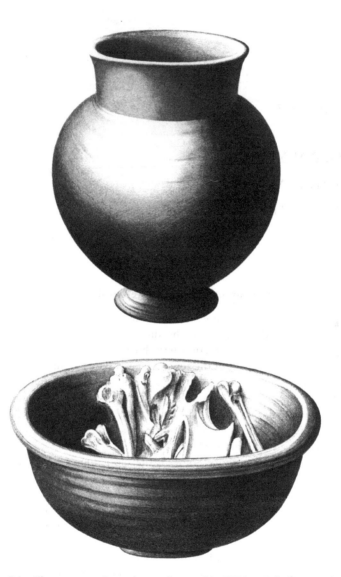

Figure 5.1. These two ceramic vessels were discovered in 1885 in a Gallo-Roman inhumation grave at the cemetery of Nampteuil-sous-Muret (Aisne). The bones contained in the bowl, which like the vase above it was produced from gray clay on a wheel, were identified by Frédéric Moreau as being those of a chicken or cock. He noted that this burial custom was typical of this cemeterial site, but he provided little documentation of similar finds in his journal. Image reproduced from Frédéric Moreau, "Les fouilles de Nampteuil-sous-Muret (Aisne) et fin de celles d'Aiguisy," in *Album Caranda: Sépultures gauloises, gallo-romaines et mérovingiennes* (Saint-Quentin: Imprimerie typographique et lithographique Charles Poette, 1886), pl. 51, nouvelle série, with permission of the Musée des antiquités nationales de Saint-Germain-en-Laye.

FUNERARY FEASTING IN EARLY MEDIEVAL GAUL 71

Due to the paucity of early medieval sources describing funerary meals, scholars have traditionally looked back to prolific classical Roman historical and archaeological sources to explain in greater detail surviving features of this custom commemorating the dead in the early Middle Ages. One of the most frequently cited passages derives not from a historical account but is a part of Gaius Petronius's (d. 65) *Satyricon*. In this work, Petronius depicted the life of Trimalchio, a fictional freedman from Asia Minor. After Trimalchio settled in southern Italy, his ill-breeding and rapidly acquired wealth caused him to engage in vulgar displays of his fortune. In addition to specifying the enormous size of his future tomb housing his ashes, which was to be thirty meters long and twice as deep and guarded by one of his former slaves, Trimalchio insisted that his tomb contain a dining room replete with large jars of wine and a fresco of many people enjoying themselves at his expense. Besides mocking the folly of the *nouveaux riches,* Petronius's satirical composition suggests that Trimalchio viewed his sepulcher as the home in which he would spend eternity. Hence he prepared for his stay as one might plan for the construction of a lavish villa. He thus required what he viewed as suitable refreshments for entertaining, something Petronius evidently viewed as being in poor taste.[2]

While such a literary description of excess might be fairly useful as a caricature of the festivities celebrated in conjunction with Roman funerals of the newly moneyed, it is questionable to what degree this fictional image may be applied to research on cemeterial feasting in a later period. Surviving written and archaeological evidence of Christian funerary meals in imperial and early medieval Gaul seem to indicate the existence of rites with substantial differences from their antecedents both with regard to their scale and content.[3] An exclusive focus on late antique and early medieval sources helps avoid conflation of first-century Roman materials with those of later periods (Figure 5.2). The resulting data, while often contradictory, creates an independent basis for a discussion of the social dynamics that came into play at the loss of members of early medieval Christian communities in Gaul. Funerary feasting, as embodied in the celebration of *convivia* in cemeteries at the time of burial as well as on anniversaries of the death of loved one, demonstrated the central role of food and drink throughout the Christian life cycle. Beyond marking the successful passage of Christians into the afterlife, such public events helped to restore the fabric of families and communities rent by death. By including the dead in activities associated with daily life, however, feasting also reminded Christians of their continued obligations to the deceased.[4] Integrated in this fashion into the consciousness of surviving kin and contemporaries, *convivia* at cemeteries represented an important vehicle for the sustenance of the memory of the dead in successive generations.

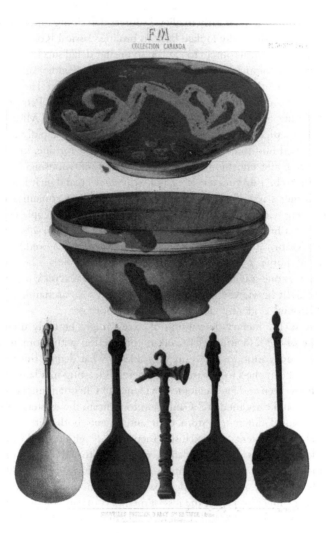

Figure 5.2. One of the difficulties in excavating early medieval cemeteries such as Arcy-Sainte-Restitue (Aisne) was that the occupation of the burial grounds continued for many centuries. In this image, Frédéric Moreau documented the fairly common discovery of fifteenth- and sixteenth-century ceramic vessels together with artifacts of a much earlier period: the bronze spoons probably dated from the Gallo-Roman era. Both sorts of objects were likely deposited with the deceased in their respective eras, but crowding at the cemeterial space caused the contents of the graves to become intermingled. Image reproduced from Frédéric Moreau, "Sépultures mérovingiennes: Nouvelles fouilles d'Arcy-Sainte-Restitue (Aisne)," in *Album Caranda: Sépultures gauloises, gallo-romaines et mérovingiennes* (Saint-Quentin: Imprimerie typographie et lithographique Charles Poette, 1885) with permission of the Musée des antiquités nationales de Saint-Germain-en-Laye.

FUNERARY FEASTING IN EARLY MEDIEVAL GAUL   73

Another of the obstacles to studying funerary meals in the Merovingian period stems from the paucity of written as opposed to material sources for this era: it is very difficult to establish the precise relationship that existed between the historical and archaeological evidence because they frequently contradict one another.[5] Since the consumption of food and drink took place in cemeteries still little regulated by clerics, our knowledge of these rites from written sources is sharply limited aside from descriptions of the funerals and celebrations at the sepulchers of saints. A picture of the normative traditions of Christians buried in rural row grave cemeteries, by contrast, is far more difficult to reconstruct except from the archaeological evidence. The majority of negative characterizations of funerary feasting, for instance, were expressed not in the Merovingian period but rather by ninth- and tenth-century clerics; hence they are not accurate indications of prevailing attitudes three centuries earlier. Whereas Regino, abbot of Prüm, categorized eating and drinking in the presence of the deceased together with *carmina diabolica* or demonic songs,[6] sixth- and seventh-century clerics did not characterize such practices in such a derogatory fashion. Even in the few extant Merovingian-period sources addressing funerary feasting, the sentiments expressed only an ideal of what clerics viewed as appropriate behavior by mourners at a grave site. To what extent these prescriptions and prohibitions circulated and whether they were heeded cannot be easily assessed. Yet, changing attitudes towards funerary feasting, a rite pagan in its origin but not necessarily in its continued practice, help us envision some of the tensions arising from clerical expectations of behavior in Christian communities that were not likely met.

Just as with many other manifestations of feasting in early medieval society, *convivia* in association with funerals or anniversaries of the death of Christians represented an opportunity for families to strengthen or renew their connections to their contemporaries. In a gift-giving society, funerary feasting provided a means of participating in existing networks of patronage.[7] In particularly lavish examples, by presenting more food than could be physically eaten by participants and offering a symbolic portion to the deceased, families may have consciously created a situation in which their expenditure caused them loss. But this loss allowed them to outdo their rivals.[8] Although we cannot measure the quantity of food consumed, we may suggest that by means of these rites families fulfilled obligations to their ancestors. When spouses, children, and more distant descendants celebrated funerary meals in commemoration of their deceased relations, they perpetuated a century-old tradition intended to honor the dead. The practice also served to comfort those still remaining with the reassurance that similar efforts to care for their spiritual and physical needs would be made after their own passing.[9] The ties created through funerary meals thus

74   CREATING COMMUNITY WITH FOOD AND DRINK

functioned simultaneously on two levels: that of the surviving community and that of the more difficult to define relationship between this world and the next.

Christian Attitudes toward Funerary Meals in Early Medieval Gaul

In the late Roman period, written and archaeological sources underline the importance of the widespread custom of funerary feasts as part of the obligations owed by kin in commemorating their blood and artificial relations. Central, then, to the practice of *convivia* were their legal and social manifestations. The choice of exquisite tableware, sometimes including fine earthenware such as *terra sigillata* and intricate glass cage cups to accompany the cremated remains of the dead, underlines the implications of the rite for the status of the deceased.[10] Meals associated with cemeteries also had religious associations, deriving from the custom of pagan ceremonies paying respect to the dead and the *Manes,* or general community of spirits of the dead. Not only did Roman families end their period of mourning with a sacrifice and banquet known as the *novemdial sacrificium,*[11] but they also partook of food and drink at the graves of relatives on anniversaries of their deaths as well as during the more general holiday of the *Parentalia* lasting from 13 to 21 February.[12] Early Christians integrated such funerary customs very quickly into their own practices with the addition of the *agape* or love feast, central to which was the offering of the Eucharist. Although it is disputed how widespread this custom became, the familial rite clearly gained new vitality with its inclusion of the sacrifice of Christ.[13] The survival of funerary feasting among Christians thus owed much to the communal and social functions of the tradition.

While it is not known how frequently priests performed Masses in commemoration of the dead in the actual presence of corpses or at sepulchers during funerals (*depositio*), the ceremony was more commonly celebrated at specified intervals following Christians' deaths, either in churches or less often at actual sepulchers.[14] By the early fifth century in North Africa, Augustine of Hippo noted that a priest could perform the Mass at the grave site on the third day following the interment of the deceased.[15] Most funerary ceremonies and those marking subsequent anniversaries of relatives' deaths, however, were undoubtedly more simple than described in ecclesiastical or hagiographical texts that focused on the deposition of saints. At their most basic level, the rites honoring the dead involved a gathering of mourners around a stone table (*mensa*) over or near the grave for food and drink.[16] Holes carved in the lids or upper walls of some late antique sarcophagi reveal that they served the purpose of allowing participants to pour libations into the sepulchers. This rite enabled them to include the commemorated in such celebrations.[17]

Although little opposition was voiced against funerary feasting in the eastern Mediterranean in late antiquity, bishops in the West desirous of making stronger distinctions between Christians and pagans discouraged funerary meals as sacrilegious.[18] They condemned votive offerings of food and drink even in conjunction with the resting places of the saints.[19] Clerics were clearly wary of non-Christians criticizing these rites as derivative: mere imitations of their own more venerable funerary customs. As recalled by Augustine in his *Confessions,* Ambrose of Milan therefore famously advised Augustine's mother Monica that she should not take wine, cakes, and bread to the tombs of the martyrs; he specifically stated that he perceived such activities as too close to their pagan counterpart, the *Parentalia*. Rather than her making such offerings at the graves of the dead, he encouraged Monica to donate the food to the poor who would benefit more from her charity.[20] Apparently such precautions were not widely heeded: a pseudo-Augustinian sermon composed soon afterward castigated libations and other offerings made not just at *martyria* but also at the sepulchers of other Christians. The anonymous author argued: "I see that pernicious error increases today among certain unfaithful, so that they confer drinks and wine over the tombs of the dead, as if the carnal souls, having exited from the bodies, required drinks."[21] In his view, such private banquets commemorating deceased family members fulfilled no constructive purpose. Rather, among Christians, he feared that these rites perpetuated ancient and unorthodox beliefs in the physicality of souls of the deceased.

In early medieval Gaul, the alleged association between the *Parentalia* and funerary feasting was repeatedly insinuated by clerics and thus had negative repercussions on the rite's reception. In the first half of the sixth century, the stricter bishops who referred in derogatory tones to the custom of funerary feasting were not surprisingly the same who denounced those Christians who made superficial conversions and reverted to their former lifestyles after baptism. The need to forbid such customs was thus not indicative of the survival of paganism as an alternative faith,[22] but of contemporary challenges faced by Christian leaders who demanded a high level of obedience and commitment from their followers. Clerics apparently had significant difficulty in convincing their congregations of the importance of embracing Christianity in more profound ways than evinced by the ability to recite the Nicene Creed properly. Many members of the faithful resisted abandoning the customs such as funerary meals that had long served to honor their families and instilled a sense of communal stability after grievous loss. Yet, since these foodstuffs were not identified by contemporaries as intended for transport to the afterlife, funerary feasting

76 CREATING COMMUNITY WITH FOOD AND DRINK

and drinking were discouraged practices but not identified by most early medieval clerics as contrary to Christian belief.[23]

As noted by Gregory of Tours with disapproval in his account of the events that transpired after the death of bishop Sidonius Apollinaris (d. 479), even priests on occasion encouraged Christians to join in funerary meals.[24] Because the celebrations were held at the expense of the church, Gregory attributed this particular incident to the greed of a misguided cleric who had a reputation as a rapacious climber. Although his misuse of ecclesiastical resources and shameless ambition made him an inappropriate candidate for an episcopal title, the account revealed the political incentives for holding such feasts in the course of building the type of consensus necessary for a successful bid for religious office.[25] Moreover, it is clear that there was a very thin line between funerary feasting and more overt attempts to gain authority in a community. While such celebrations were often portrayed in hagiographical accounts as charity for the sake of the deceased's soul in the form of foodstuffs for the poor, their distribution in honor of an elite Christian's death might serve a variety of less altruistic purposes.[26] Sponsorship of alms and funerary feasting highlighted not just the generosity but also the status, resources, and power of the deceased and his or her surviving family or religious community.

Known for his conservative stances on Christian behavior, Bishop Caesarius of Arles was one of the few in sixth-century Gaul to condemn outright food offerings for the dead. Rather than weighing the merits of the situation in which they occurred, as did many of his contemporaries, he viewed them as entirely sinful. In his sermons, Caesarius suggested that the rite implied that souls required sustenance.[27] In particular, what he found highly insidious was the way in which Christians celebrated feast days honoring the saints with the sorts of ceremonies that composed the *Parentalia*. He cited drunkenness, dancing, and singing as the most blatant manifestations of demonic behavior, and argued that such activities did not contribute to an increase in religious devotion.[28] And he was not alone. In 567, the Council of Tours specifically castigated those who defiled the anniversaries of martyrs with the celebration of ancient errors, especially on the feast day of St. Peter.[29] Commemorated as late as on the fifth-century calendar of Polemius Silvius, this holiday was particularly vulnerable to abuses as it fell on 22 February. This date was traditionally the one on which Romans celebrated the *Caristia* or *Cara cognatio,* the repast honoring the cult of parents just after Roman families had traditionally observed the *Parentalia* and the *Feralia* from 13–21 February.[30] Nor were problems regarding the survival and transformation of ancient holidays confined to Gaul. Further south, the twenty-second canon of the Council of Toledo held in 589, likewise prohibited inappropriate revelry and the singing of the *carmen funebris* at graves of the saints; participants at the Visigothic synod suggested that the recitation of psalms should replace such popular practices.[31]

More general outcry against allegedly sacrilegious inebriation and dancing was related but certainly not limited to complaints about feasting honoring the dead. Sixth-century legislation of Childebert I sought to enforce what the bishops had not succeeded in doing: the Merovingian king outlawed drunken vigils and threatened the unfree with a beating if they ignored these regulations.[32] Because he left the terms of the actual enforcement of these measures vague, however, it is difficult to determine whether violations were dealt with at the royal or local level. Presumably such words dampened at least some of the raucous behavior among the faithful at funerary celebrations and other gatherings. But, as will be discussed below, they did not directly affect the deposition of vessels, food, and drink in the graves of many Christians. While the interment of foodstuffs with the dead appears to have declined widely over time, ceramics and glass vessels appeared regularly in burials for at least another few generations.

The first half of the sixth century marked a high point in legislation against funerary celebrations involving feasting, and in clerical rhetoric against the activities allegedly characteristic of pagans. Few religious leaders after Caesarius, however, tackled the subject directly. In Visigothic territories, Martin of Braga (d. 580) banned Christians from participating in the custom of bringing food to the dead; he suggested that the Eucharist would be a more acceptable sacrifice.[33] A later exception in Gaul was the writing of the seventh-century bishop and goldsmith Eligius of Noyon, who borrowed extensively from the works of Caesarius.[34] By contrast, most clerics focused instead on the obligations of Christian families or their servants with regard to the resting places of their dead. The Council of Paris, held some time between 445 and 573, had taken up the subject of perpetual care for the sepulchers of ancestors.[35] Venantius Fortunatus, in his sixth-century *Life* of Marcellus, bishop of Paris, also gave attention to the spiritual needs of the dead. He warned that Christian sinners should fear the consequences of their actions on the status of their souls; no amount of expenditure for a lavish funeral would compensate for their sins. In this piece, he cautioned readers further with the vivid example of a frightful serpent that devoured the remains of an unrepentant Christian woman after her burial.[36]

This horrifying image of the damned provides a sharp contrast to Gregory of Tours's laudatory description of the celebration of the Eucharist on the outdoor sepulchers of holy abbots on the thirtieth day following their deaths.[37] The saints enjoyed the reward of a feast at their graves, a rite incorporating the transubstantiation of the flesh and blood of Christ. In the

78   CREATING COMMUNITY WITH FOOD AND DRINK

writings of Gregory, the celebration of the Mass thus outweighed the significance and power of anything that might be criticized as pagan ritual. For devout members of the laity, Gregory also pointed out that those who made gifts of food and drink in honor of the Mass would be recognized by God. To support this view, he related a story of a widow of Lyons who brought wine imported from Gaza to honor her deceased husband at Mass. Deceived by the sub-deacon who replaced it with vinegar in the chalice, she received a vision from her late spouse complaining about the poor taste of the offering. When the fraud of the cleric was exposed, she merited a miracle as a consequence of her unwavering faith and good intentions in commemorating the dead in this fashion.[38] Clearly Gregory's lesson to his readers was that offerings of food and drink on behalf of the dead were acceptable in controlled circumstances under the watchful eye of church leaders.

Although positive reinforcement of the benefits of being a devout Christian successfully prevented some from further aggravating clerics, Gregory of Tours and others were not shy about castigating those who fell into error. Gregory mocked, for instance, the ignorance of the *rustici* who left *ex-voto* offerings at the sarcophagus of Saint Benignus in Dijon. Interestingly enough, however, he did not specifically refer to either excessive feasting or food and drink donations among their activities, although they are certain to have occurred.[39] Likewise, a surviving letter from Pope Gregory I to Queen Brunhild in September 597, condemned the poor devotion of her subjects. In violation of the sacrament of baptism, they continued to make sacrifices and offerings to idols.[40] This papal document nonetheless failed to mention directly the celebration of the *Parentalia*. It is thus difficult to determine to what extent these prohibitions even pertained to celebrations in honor of the dead, and whether funerary feasting still represented a significant concern in Gaul during the second half of the sixth century.

In the late seventh and especially the eighth century, Merovingian clerics granted an increased amount of attention to eucharistic celebrations on behalf of the dead and correspondingly less to funerary feasting. With the growing importance of liturgical commemoration in ensuring the well-being of the dead in the afterlife, burial places, too, came under closer scrutiny of church officials.[41] If no one attended the grave site of a deceased Christian, it was feared that the identity of the interred, especially in an unmarked sepulcher, might be forgotten before he or she attained relief from purgatorial suffering. In the late seventh-century *Visio Baronti,* for instance, the monk Barontus was given the task of caring for the sepulcher of one of his late brethren, Framoaldus, whose remains were buried at the entrance of the church. His specific responsibilities involved

FUNERARY FEASTING IN EARLY MEDIEVAL GAUL

sweeping the tomb of the young boy regularly and reciting the prayer *Misere mei Deus* on his behalf.[42] The eighth-century Gelasian sacramentary likewise assuaged concerns for the souls of the dead with the performance of outdoor Masses in cemeteries on the seventh and thirtieth days following death.[43]

Funerary feasts outside of the Mass, to whatever extent they were still celebrated in the eighth century, did not usually fall into the purvey of clerics if one may judge from the dearth of written sources limiting or even describing such activities. Those ceremonies of this nature that did survive, however, became increasingly questionable in their legitimacy as priests expanded their authority at grave sites. In 742, the *Concilium germanicum* therefore forbade sacrifices to the dead,[44] just as the *Indiculus superstitionum et paganiarum* (744–745) definitively banned funerary meals and libations.[45] This latter piece was the strictest extant legislation formulated up to this time, but it seems to have been promulgated after the deposition of food and drink in Christian graves had largely ceased as a funerary practice. In both cases, it is extremely difficult to confirm the laws' successful application due to the widespread lack of archaeological evidence for burial traditions at this date. Presumably, clerical condemnations of the raucous singing and dancing associated with cemeterial feasting sought to limit the type of rituals used by Christians to commemorate the dead. Although they recognized the opportunities provided by funerary rites for renewing natural and artificial bonds between members of Christian communities following the loss of one or more of the faithful, clerics perceived these particular means as beyond their control and hence viewed them as entirely unacceptable.[46]

Interpreting Early Medieval Archaeological Evidence for Feasting

In turning to the prolific archaeological remains of the Merovingian period, however, we are immediately confronted by the great contrast between the material evidence and the few written references to clerics' disapproval of funerary feasting. Evidence for such rites is most abundant in pagan graves of the fourth and fifth centuries and extends far beyond the borders of Gaul; I have included some examples of these for the sake of comparison. Not only rural graves but also elite sepulchers in Christian structures have produced material remains attesting to this custom. In some cases, burials in churches included wide selections of food and drink offerings. In two fifth-century graves resting under the church of St. Severinus in Cologne, for instance, there were deposits of eggs, chicken, and other fowl prepared with honey, meat cooked with fat, mustard, and sage,

80   CREATING COMMUNITY WITH FOOD AND DRINK

and beer and wine. Under the cathedral of Cologne, the lavish sepulchers of a woman and young boy likewise contained the remains of fruit, nuts, and water.[47] In the sixth and seventh centuries, however, evidence of such deposits in graves drops precipitously. Yet, the rite did not cease altogether. At Réville (Manche), the cemetery was utilized from the early sixth to the late seventh century, and its sepulchers included depositions of a variety of foodstuffs and vessels; approximately 62 of the necropolis's 152 graves contained animal bones, and a slightly higher number revealed remains of shells of marine creatures.[48] In the recently excavated and still unpublished cemetery of Erstein in the Rhine basin, at least seven of a representative sample of nineteen graves included the remains of egg shells and animal bones. Interpreted by the archaeologists as evidence for the custom of food offerings, the burials date from the second half of the sixth century onward. Although the interred whose graves included foodstuffs were identified as predominantly female, the small sample included a man and a child laid to rest with similar items.[49]

Before engaging in a discussion of archaeological remains, we must be careful to note the distinctions between deposition rites involving food and feasting by contemporaries. Food and drink placed in graves are more easily documented archaeologically because meals consumed in cemeteries left comparatively few traces beyond scattered ash and bone in grave fill; such remains could have also resulted from a variety of other activities that required fire or from previous occupation of the site. Excavated data thus tends to favor or overplay the significance of vessel depositions as opposed to other features of funerary feasting (Figure 5.3). Yet, the written sources conversely fail to mention rites involving the deposition of vessels, food, and drink in individual sepulchers. Rather than specifically addressing such practices, late antique and early medieval authors focused on regulating meals at the anniversaries of the death of relatives and at ceremonies on the same day as the funeral. As we have seen, clerics were most concerned with condemning the uncontrolled behavior with which feasting usually ended. We thus need to be aware of the ways in which surviving sources influence our understanding of early medieval funerary rites. Although one would never know it from early medieval evidence due to the historical and archaeological sources' exclusive concentration on one or the other practice, funerary feasting and the placement of vessels or food in graves were presumably part of the same or closely related traditions.

Another methodological problem affecting our understanding of funerary feasting relates to the current state of our knowledge of ceramic production, distribution, and consumption in the Merovingian period.[50] In many cases, due to the simplicity of the vessels found in early medieval graves, it is difficult to ascertain their date or provenance with any degree

Figure 5.3. A. Ponchon recorded the appearance of a skeleton at the time of its excavation at Marchélepot. C. Boulanger identified the deceased as an alleged *chef franque* on the basis of his weaponry. Dated by Boulanger to the sixth century, the grave contained among other items one large gray-black ceramic vessel deposited between the shins of the deceased. Image reproduced from C. Boulanger, *Le cimetière franco-mérovingien et carolingien de Marchélepot (Somme): Étude sur l'origine de l'art barbare* (Paris: Imprimerie nationale, 1909), pp. 123–1224, pl. 18, with permission of the Musée des antiquités nationales de Saint-Germain-en-Laye.

82   CREATING COMMUNITY WITH FOOD AND DRINK

of accuracy or reliability.[51] A lack of comprehensive or comparative studies of ceramics of the Merovingian era, in contrast to numerous studies of contemporary brooches and weaponry from the same graves, is largely a consequence of the historic lack of interest in the uninspiring workmanship of these artifacts. The manner of their production and the ubiquitous nature of such finds also render their study more difficult to pursue. Scholars should therefore be aware that most vessels, particularly ceramics, but also glass containers, the age of which is notoriously difficult to estimate, have been dated in conjunction with other objects from the same graves or settlement sites. Their chronology has largely not been established on the basis of a typological survey of their style or production, and hence their dating is likely inaccurate and currently ill-suited for quantitative analyses.

In the current understanding of the history of funerary feasting in Gaul from an archaeological perspective, Bailey Young and others have noted that fourth-century rites involved the placement of primarily ceramic but also more rarely glass or bronze vessels in graves. Relatives at least sometimes filled these containers with various types of food or drink, including water, and deposited them at the feet or less frequently at the head of the deceased. In Saint-Seurin, Bordeaux, for instance, one sarcophagus contained a glass vessel marked by wine residues.[52] These same graves often also included a coin, thought to be Charon's *obol,* or the fee for the ferryman to cross the Cocytus river, if placed in the mouth or hand. Over the next two centuries, these funerary customs became more sparing in their expression but continued in conjunction with the deposition of a wide range of objects related to clothing and weaponry (Figure 5.4). By the sixth century, the deposit of ceramics often comprised only a single vessel, if any, at the foot of the corpse; food offerings had normally ceased to constitute a recognizable part of the rite (Figure 5.5).[53] There were important exceptions, however, such as the well-known sixth-century grave no. 1782 at the cemetery of Krefeld-Gellep, which included a large roasting spit, a drinking vessel, and bowls filled with food including beef ribs.[54] Nonetheless, on the whole, the deposition rite became less complex.

In discussing these developments, the archaeologist Bailey Young has sought to document this decline quantitatively. He proposes that approximately 75 percent of late imperial sepulchers in Gaul included ceramic vessels, versus his rough estimate of 16 percent of Merovingian-period graves in Gaul having similar deposits.[55] While these statistics are helpful in comprehending the general enormity of the changes in this ritual, they are also somewhat misleading. Aside from the dangers of creating statistics based upon an arbitrary collection of excavated graves, since many early archaeological surveys did not document ceramic finds,[56] it is important to note that

Figure 5.4. Philippe Delamain noted that virtually all of the Merovingian-period sepulchers at Herpes (Charente) contained a ceramic vessel to the left or right of the head of the deceased. Although the shape and size of the containers varied significantly, they were rarely found in other positions at this site. They had been deposited in poorly-equipped graves as well as in those that were richly appointed. Nearly all the turned ceramics were black in color and some may have originally contained liquid despite the fact that no traces were discernable on their porous interior surfaces. Image reproduced from Philippe Delamain, "Les sépultures barbares d'Herpes," in his *Le cimetière d'Herpes (Fouilles et collection Ph. Delamain)* (Angoulême: Chez L. Coquemard, 1892), pp. 15–17; pl. 18, with permission of the Musée des antiquités nationales de Saint-Germain-en-Laye.

Figure 5.5. This water-color by Anatole Lablotier of a glass vessel depicts one of only two found relatively intact among the Merovingian-period graves of Bourogne excavated between 1907 and 1909. In this cemetery, glass and more frequently ceramic vessels were normally placed at the feet, between the legs, or in the corner of the sepulcher near the left foot of the deceased. Image reproduced from Ferdinand Scheurer and Anatole Lablotier, *Fouilles du cimetière barbare de Bourogne* (Paris: Berger-Levrault, Éditeurs, 1914), pp. 6; 56–57, pl. 18, with permission of the Musée des antiquités nationales de Saint-Germain-en-Laye.

FUNERARY FEASTING IN EARLY MEDIEVAL GAUL 85

burial customs varied considerably from cemetery to cemetery, and region to region. These averages do not give sufficient attention to the necropoleis that did not fit into these patterns. In the cemeteries excavated in the French Alps, for instance, the only Merovingian-period sites to have revealed use of ceramics were in Haute-Savoie. To date, the other provincial *départements* in this region have not yet produced any remains.[57] There were often much higher or lower numbers of graves furnished with eating and drinking containers at specific sites than Young's estimates suggest to readers.

Measuring such archaeological manifestations of the declining popularity of the placement of food in vessels deposited in graves in the course of the sixth century also remains difficult. Young has suggested, for instance, that, even early in the Merovingian period, the principal element of the offering was the dish itself rather than the food presented in it.[58] Yet, scholars have seldom studied these vessels more than visually for organic residues, and have rarely noted anything beyond wine stains, bones, and pits (Figure 5.6). Since excavated vessels are frequently washed before being catalogued and stored, there is no way to rectify this situation or to ascertain the accuracy of Young's assertions in the majority of early medieval cemeterial sites.[59] What is clear is that many Christians continued to include vessel and less often food depositions in their funerary ceremonies long after the period of the conversions.[60] Although the rite may have originated in Gallo-Roman communities, it was not characteristic exclusively of that population. Just as other features of burial custom were transmitted between ethnic groups, food and drink offerings were not limited to only those of Gallo-Roman heritage. Nor has the rite been observed to have regularly favored one sex over the other with regard to the quality or quantity of vessels or perishables deposited.[61]

Archaeological evidence in many Merovingian-period cemeteries in Gaul reveals that the deposition of vessels in graves ceased for the most part by the seventh century. There are, however, a few exceptions: knives, with many potential symbolic functions besides eating, continued for as much as another hundred years.[62] Why the inclusion of vessels in sepulchers became less appealing as much as a century prior to the final decline in the deposition of grave goods is less clear. We cannot explain a cessation in their use as the result of some process of "Christianization" or "spiritualization" of Christian life. As we have seen, food and drink deposits resulted neither from the survival of actual pagan cults nor from belief in the consumption of these offerings by the dead. If they had, more sharply condemnatory legislation by clerics would have undoubtedly been preserved. Contemporary hagiographical works, by contrast, indicate that many saints, in imitation of the life of Jesus as recounted in the Gospels, provided Christians with abundant food and drink as a display of their power. Early

Figure 5.6. This hand-colored plate illustrates some of the fine glass serving vessels discovered at the cemetery of Herpes (Charente) in the late nineteenth century. Colored pale green or clear yellow, the pieces were highly fragile and some broke in the course of excavation. Philippe Delamain, the excavator and subsequent owner of this material, noted that some of the vessels contained a dried red residue, perhaps that of wine, but he did not pursue further this line of inquiry. Image reproduced from Delamain, "Les sépultures barbares d'Herpes," pp. 17–20, pl. 25, with permission of the Musée des antiquités nationales de Saint-Germain-en-Laye.

medieval feasting, whether in conjunction with graves or not, thus potentially celebrated the miraculous bounty of God. Once paganism no longer represented an active threat to Christian bishops, a harsh stance on the subject of food and drink offerings was no longer required so long as these rites did not lead to excessive or inappropriate revelry. Only when clerics decided to expand their graveside authority more generally, a process most clear in the early Carolingian era, did funerary feasting merit the type of attention required to eradicate it completely.[63]

Drinking vessels, knives, and other eating implements found in Merovingian interments also conveyed other types of symbolism related to the identity of the deceased. Guy Halsall has suggested that alimentary and vessel donations at graves constituted an important form of gift-giving in antiquity just as in the early Middle Ages. In a similar manner to other types of grave goods, the deposition of food and drink vessels, in at least some cases replete with food and drink, heightened the status or defined the identity of a family in a community.[64] The decision to bury specific types of food or a particular vessel, however, may have had personal connotations as well, such as the desire to offer the deceased a gift a favorite food or drinking glass. Our interpretations must thus be frustratingly tentative, since these meanings can no longer be discerned with our great distance from the event. Despite the small number of contemporary written documents that address the theme of feasting, we must avoid the temptation to define the symbolism of these rites based upon later vernacular texts. The application of Scandinavian sources to early medieval mortuary feasting, common in the scholarly literature as late as the 1970s, is problematic at best. It is highly unlikely that absolute continuity of belief existed over the course of a millennium in northwestern Europe.[65]

Although this discussion has concentrated mainly on the deposition remains of food and vessels, early medieval archaeological evidence also reveals the practice of including in sepulchers whole or partial animal remains that had not been prepared for consumption. These customs may have, at least at first, been related to funerary feasting, since the *Parentalia* included sacrificial rites. By the early Middle Ages, however, animal deposits were no longer necessarily related to food rites, and did not retain uniquely pagan connotations.[66] No Christian legislation seems to have addressed or forbidden the practice until the mid-eighth century, long after the evidence for the rite disappears from the archaeological record in Gaul. More specifically, the practice of interring animals in conjunction with high status graves ended fairly early in Merovingian regions: in northern parts of Gaul the rite continued only until the mid-sixth century. In southwest Germany and Alemannic regions, by contrast, the rite continued as late as 700.[67] Two early medieval cemeteries recently excavated by the Bayerische Landesamt für Denkmalpflege at Wenigumstadt (Lkr. Aschaffenburg) and Zeuzleben (Lkr. Schweinfurt), for instance, have produced fairly late evidence of partial skeletons of horses, pigs, goats, sheep, dogs, and chickens, as well as eggs and fish. At the former cemetery, about 26 percent of sepulchers contained animal remains, whereas at the latter it was as many as 80 percent. These statistics reveal the diversity and unique combinations of funerary rites employed in individual cemeteries despite more general trends in burial practices.[68]

The purpose and symbolism of these customs, needless to say, is obscure. Consequently, we should avoid reading too much into the evidence. Caution, first, is required to distinguish between scattered bone and shell remains from previous occupations of the burial site and contemporary funerary use. We should also recognize the complexity of the different applications of animal depositions. Édouard Salin, for instance, argued that animals interred in their entirety in human graves comprised part of a rite distinct from food rituals in which animals deposited in sepulchers were prepared for consumption. Because of the significant expenses incurred in earmarking domestic animals for an early death, Salin interpreted their deposition in entirety as functioning little differently than costly weapons, jewelry, or amulets placed in early medieval graves.[69] Today, however, we instead tend to envision both of his categories of animal deposits as contributing to the expression of the status and identity of the deceased.

Judith Oexle has most recently characterized as grave goods, rather than as sacrificial offerings, animals such as horses, dogs, sheep, deer, oxen, and falcon, that were interred at or near human cemeteries dating from the Merovingian period.[70] Her conclusions mirror observations made at the Merovingian-period cemetery of Vouciennes (Marne) in the 1940s. As noted by Amaury Thiérot and Raymond Lantier, the animals buried in or near well-furnished graves, but rarely in direct contact with human skeletons, reflected an important aspect of the ideal representation of the warrior elite.[71] Of these animals, not only were horses precious commodities, but they were most frequently beheaded in the course of funerary celebrations or possibly some time afterward. In the absence of a horse, relatives of deceased elites might substitute objects associated with riding horses, such as bits, halters, and rings. Nonetheless, from a modern perspective, it is impossible to distinguish between which animal remains constituted offerings and which status-related artifacts. It is likely that the categories were also blurred for their medieval contemporaries.

A more tenuous type of archaeological material associated possibly with feasting includes evidence of the presence of fires in early medieval cemeteries. These customs associated with fires are less than satisfactorily understood, but seem to have survived well into the seventh century. While small-scale conflagrations may have been related to funerary feasts or sacrificial practices, they may have also formed a component of purificatory rites preceding burial or ceremonies involving partial incineration of the body subsequent to interment. In cases in which charred matter is discovered in grave fill mixed with ceramic shards and animal bones, this organic material provides stronger but not solid evidence of the celebration of funerary feasts or the provision of alimentary offerings.[72] Remains of meals might have been dispersed into the sepulchers when earth was shoveled back into trenches dug to house the bodies.[73] In some examples, however, such as at Ennery (Moselle), scattered bones may have been the consequence of contamination of the site by previous occupants during the Gallo-Roman period.[74] More convincing evidence of contemporary feasting includes pits filled with the remains of bones, grains, and ceramics such as found at the Merovingian cemetery of Noiron-sous-Gevry (Côte-d'Or) in the early part of the twentieth century. One may easily imagine these facilities containing the leftovers of feasting or food offerings as was similarly the case at Samson in Belgium, Hermes (Oise), and Morley (Meuse).[75]

Bailey Young has made a number of observations with respect to the distribution of incineration rites in cemeteries in the northeast of Gaul during the Merovingian period. At the cemetery of Mazerny (Ardennes), for example, he has pointed to at least fifty-eight examples of charcoal remains or ritual fire dating from the seventh century, that form the equivalent of 26 percent of the observable graves. The majority of these inhumations contained evidence that fires had been lit in or near the sepulchers since charcoal traces were scattered throughout the fill of the graves.[76] Young has also importantly noted that at Mazerny, the frequency of rites leaving behind small traces of fire in the form of charcoal or burnt stone tended to increase with the wealth and quality of the objects found in a particular grave. The sorts of nonextreme remains of fire rituals associated with funerary meals appeared most often in conjunction with sepulchers containing armament.[77] Contemporaries thus apparently performed such ceremonies at least in part to display their elite identity in the same way in which they utilized grave goods as a form of symbolic expression.[78] More extensive uses of fire resulting in the creation of a layer of ash at the bottom of graves, by contrast, probably first came into use in the later Merovingian period. The sepulchers in which these rites have been observed contained reduced numbers of burial objects or none at all, a consequence not of the social status of the deceased but more likely the late date of these inhumations.[79] Such changes in these rites, the meaning of which remains unclear, signaled the rise of new traditions in the seventh century. Most were probably unrelated to funerary feasting.

Future Directions for Research

In assessing the material evidence, then, more consistent collection of data and new paradigms for interpreting the symbolic uses of mortuary feasting are much needed. In the past, the deposition of vessels, food, and drink in graves was considered a Gallo-Roman rite as opposed to the alleged Germanic mortuary custom of burying weaponry and jewelry with the dead. Yet, scholars can no longer accurately use evidence of funerary meals to posit the presence of persons of a specific religious affiliation or ethnic identity. Because a common tendency has been to focus on particularly lavish graves without looking at less impressive contemporary examples, it is difficult to give an accurate picture of "representative" burial practices. It is clear, however, that by taking these deposits out of context, their larger significance is lost. Although such artifacts played an important role in individual graves, their distribution pattern in a particular cemetery may reveal many features of community dynamics and diachronic changes.

A number of important questions might therefore be posed in the future about archaeological remains of food, drink, and vessels in and near graves. Along with other aspects of the burial rites, an assessment of whether all or certain vessels appeared more frequently in men's or women's burials, or in adolescents' or adults' sepulchers, would prove very useful. These distinctions would suggest some of the possible connotations of feasting rites and whether they were directly linked to particular gender- or age-identities. This sort of survey would also allow us to determine distinctive behavior in individual cemeteries. Examination of which sets of grave objects included food vessels, and with what sort of containers food most often appeared, would also be very helpful, as would a comparison of evidence of the discovery of certain sorts of vessels in settlements as opposed to cemeteries and vice versa.[80] Regular chemical analysis of ceramic and glass containers might also reveal whether vessels were new or used, and if small quantities of food residue were still on the containers, whether all food and drink deposits declined between the fourth and seventh centuries. The use of ceramics of different styles at a particular necropolis or fewer vessels per grave might also serve to explain, if any, the effects of the condemnation of feasting. This information, if it could be satisfactorily dated, would be especially interesting in regions such as in or near Arles or Tours, since these towns were the source of much of the negative ecclesiastical legislation against this ancient practice. Finally, comparison of regional differences would help determine to what extent the rite radiated from the south of Gaul as has traditionally been posited.

Identifying some of the subtleties of the evidence for funerary feasting would allow scholars to posit far more about the dynamics of the communities in which they were practiced. These rites, about which we still know relatively little, might help us discern which members of the early medieval population were most frequently commemorated in this fashion by their contemporaries, and to what extent the rites were influenced typically by the age, sex, and status of the deceased. Although these goods could no longer nourish the dead in a physical sense, they played an effective symbolic role in building bonds between disparate generations of kin groups and contemporary inhabitants of neighboring settlements. The utility of remembering the dead by means of a rite that brought together the living represented grounds for funerary feasting's continued popularity among Christians in Merovingian Gaul at least until the beginning of the seventh century. Long after the original significance of the *Parentalia* celebrations had been forgotten, partaking of food and drink with the dead remained an important means of honoring and commemorating kin and community members. And, when it was at last condemned, funerary feasting might effectively be replaced with the more acceptable celebration of the Eucharist, thereby allowing the faithful to commemorate their ancestors under the watchful eye of the Catholic clergy.

EPILOGUE

Some time in the second half of the sixth century, a married woman named Monegund living in Chartres gave birth to two daughters. After she lost both to untimely illnesses, she found no consolation for her grief and thus decided to devote the rest of her days to God. She courageously left her husband and built a cell in Chartres in order to model her life after that of the female desert saints. Allowing herself contact with the world solely through a small window, Monegund humbled herself by becoming entirely dependent on the good will of a local servant girl. The latter brought her flour and water so that she could bake the small loaves that formed the mainstay of her diet. Despite such meager resources, Monegund always managed to leave some of her bread for the poor. Yet, Monegund was tested more than once in her resolve to lead such an ascetic existence; on one occasion, her servant decided not to come for ten days in a row. Halfway through this predicament, the recluse ran out of food and water. Her prayers were answered by God, who supplied snow through the window of her cell so that she might make bread from her remaining flour and nourish herself for some additional time.[1]

Monegund's struggle was not confined to combating her hunger: she also faced the obstacle of her husband's resistance to her religious calling. After her independent pilgrimage to Tours to visit the shrine of Martin, Monegund's husband brought her back home to her cell in Chartres. Only after she secretly fled to Tours and established a small community of nuns was she no longer bothered by her former spouse.[2] Her unwavering faith in the face of grave hardship showed the depth of her sanctity and rendered her worthy of enacting miraculous cures. According to Gregory of Tours, from the time of her flight to Tours, Monegund gained a reputation for the ability to heal the sick suffering from a variety of illnesses. In one case, she expelled worms from a youth with a parasitic infection. After having not been able to eat or drink anything for days, he immediately regained his appetite.[3] In contrast to her rigorous and self-imposed withdrawal from nearly all food and beverages, Monegund, like Radegund, recognized its necessity for others and hence made it possible for them to partake in meals and thus community life.[4]

The relationship of this holy woman to food thus defined her last significant connection to the needs that characterized the lives of the rest of humanity. Having exchanged her home for the stark comfort of a cell, and later gaining the company of a few female followers, Monegund allowed herself only the most minimal requirements for continued survival. Her determination to overcome the weakness of her body manifested itself in the power of her spirit.[5] As a healer whose cures were effected by Jesus through the medium of her transformed body, Monegund was able to reach beyond herself and help others overcome their illnesses.[6] Her ascetic behavior not only defined her identity as a saint, but like the miracles of Rusticula, it confirmed that a holy woman's body might become the blessed conduit of efficacious acts on behalf of the most needy and marginalized members of Christian communities.[7] The struggle to overcome the fragility of the female sex through self-imposed abstinence resulted in the elevation of the moral status and authority of the most exceptional nuns, even when they lived in the shadow of powerful bishops such as those of Arles and Tours.[8]

As we have seen in the course of this discussion, power and authority in early medieval communities derived from a variety of sources, not all of them formal or institutionalized. One of the most important of the routes to self-empowerment was the ritual use of or abstention from food and drink; how religious contemporaries chose to contextualize such behavior in written accounts determined how such acts would be remembered. From both a lay and clerical perspective, feasting and fasting were central to social interaction. Not only were they a concern of lay elites eager to fill their halls with loyal supporters, but they also represented basic tools at the disposal of bishops, priests, nuns, and monks in their contact with the laity and in their private devotions. The consumption of nourishment was not negative in and of itself, since after all, the Gospels memorialized how Jesus had recognized the need for plenty in times of celebration such as at Cana. He had also used the breaking of bread during the Last Supper as an opportunity to impart wisdom to His disciples. Because eating and drinking occupied such an integral place in Christian tradition, religious authors thus did not condemn these acts as long as they occurred in appropriate settings and in moderation. Instead, they focused on discerning how the behavior of clerics in conjunction with foodstuffs differed in distinctive ways from their lay counterparts.

Foodways played a substantial role in the organization of Christian communities. The prescription of specific mores for the consumption of food and drink helped define what it meant to be Christian beyond the rites of baptism. Just as excommunication served to exclude individuals who had violated Christian law from continued interaction with the faithful, the identification of certain types of edible substances as unclean meant that those who consumed them might be considered impure. Even in the case of acceptable foods, refusal by clerics to participate in bountiful meals provided by sinners marked out a hierarchy that was not based upon rank but rather spiritual status. The sponsorship of feasts among the faithful on religious occasions conversely strengthened relationships between clerics and lay persons. In the case of hospitality to the wealthy, the provision of food and drink helped monks and nuns to retain powerful protectors; although their generosity to the poor often had more altruistic objectives, these charitable activities likewise established the reputation of clerics as benefactors. All the while, clerics' conscious abstention from such festivities marked them as different in the eyes of their contemporaries and at least theoretically underlined their spiritual superiority. Dining habits clearly represented an integral component of their religious identity.

Among the laity, food and drink, or fasting, represented ritual activities with significant social consequences even from a clerical perspective. Dietary regimens were important to maintaining health, and in the case of those who were ill, ingested substances played a significant role in the process of healing, whether the remedy was taken at the advice of a physician, healer, cleric, or saint. Not only did Christians' choices of what to eat affect the state of their spirits, but they also modified the general balance of the humours in the human body. Finally, at funerals, shared meals helped the living to express their solidarity both with surviving kin and deceased ancestors. As long as it occurred under the watchful eye of the clergy, the consumption of food and drink in cemeteries underscored the need for families to fulfill their obligations to the dead by visiting their resting places. Throughout the Christian life cycle in early medieval Gaul, rituals involving food and drink or abstention from them defined Christian community. Feasting and fasting played a transformative role in clerical descriptions of and prescriptions for the activities and spiritual concerns of the faithful.

NOTES

Note to the Acknowledgments

1. Although early medieval Gaul itself has not been the exclusive subject of such a work due to the incomplete nature of the primary sources, some helpful resources include: Don Brothwell and Patricia Brothwell, *Food in Antiquity: A Survey of the Diet of Early Peoples,* expanded ed. (Baltimore: The Johns Hopkins University Press, 1969); Jean-Louis Flandrin and Massimo Montanari, eds., *Food: A Culinary History from Antiquity to the Present* (New York: Columbia University Press, 1999); Kathy L. Pearson, "Nutrition and the Early-Medieval Diet," *Speculum* 72 (1997), pp. 1–32; Ann Hagen, *A Handbook of Anglo-Saxon Food and Drink,* 2 vols. (Hockwold cum Wilton: Anglo-Saxon Books, 1992–1995).

Notes to the Introduction

1. Among the recent introductory works on the political organization of Merovingian Gaul, see: J. M. Wallace-Hadrill, *The Long-Haired Kings,* Medieval Academy of America Reprints for Teaching (Toronto: University of Toronto Press, 1982); Eugen Ewig, *Die Merowinger und das Frankenreich,* Urban-Taschenbücher 392 (Stuttgart: Kohlhammer, 1988); Patrick J. Geary, *Before France and Germany: The Creation and Transformation of the Merovingian World* (New York: Oxford University Press, 1988); Edward James, *The Franks* (Oxford: Basil Blackwell, 1988); Reinhold Kaiser, *Das römische Erbe und das Merowingerreich,* revised edition, Enzyklopädie deutscher Geschichte 26 (Munich: R. Oldenbourg Verlag, 1997); Roger Collins, *Early Medieval Europe 300–1000,* second edition (New York: St. Martin's Press, 1999), pp. 161–172.

2. Gender and women were not categories, for instance, officially addressed in the five-year project entitled "Transformation of the Roman World" sponsored by the European Science Foundation (1993–1997). Thomas F. X. Noble, "The Transformation of the Roman World: Reflections on Five Years of Work," in *East and West: Modes of Communication. Proceedings of the First Plenary Conference at Merida,* edited by Evangelos Chrysos and Ian Wood, TRW 5 (Leiden: E. J. Brill, 1999), p. 269; Julia M. H. Smith, "Did Women Have a Transformation of the Roman World?" *Gender & History* 12 (2000), pp. 552–553.

98 CREATING COMMUNITY WITH FOOD AND DRINK

3. Ian Wood, *The Merovingian Kingdoms 450–751* (London: Longmans, 1994), pp. 120–139.

4. For the recent state of the field, see: Hans-Werner Goetz, *Frauen im frühen Mittelalter. Frauenbild und Frauenleben im Frankenreich* (Weimar: Böhlau Verlag, 1995), pp. 395–397.

5. Janet Nelson, "Queens as Jezebels: Brunhild and Balthild in Merovingian History," in her *Politics and Ritual in Early Medieval Europe* (London: Hambledon Press, 1986), pp. 1–48.

6. Elizabeth A. Clark, "The Lady Vanishes: Dilemmas of a Feminist Historian after the 'Linguistic Turn,'" *Church History* 67 (1998), p. 31.

7. Suzanne Fonay Wemple, *Women in Frankish Society: Marriage and the Cloister 500 to 900* (Philadelphia: University of Pennsylvania Press, 1985), pp. 28–31.

8. Isabel Moreira, *Dreams, Visions and Spiritual Authority in Merovingian Gaul* (Ithaca: Cornell University Press, 2000); Lynda Coon, *Sacred Fictions: Holy Women and Hagiography in Late Antiquity* (Philadelphia: University of Pennsylvania Press, 1997); Guy Halsall, *Settlement and Social Organization: The Merovingian Region of Metz* (Cambridge: Cambridge University Press, 1995); Giselle de Nie, *Views from a Many-Windowed Tower: Studies of Imagination in the Works of Gregory of Tours,* Studies in Classical Antiquity 7 (Amsterdam: Rodopi, 1987).

9. Michael Mann, *The Sources of Social Power,* 1: *A History from the Beginning to A. D. 1760* (Cambridge: Cambridge University Press, 1986), pp. 1–27.

10. Fredrik Barth, "Towards Greater Naturalism in Conceptualizing Societies," in *Conceptualizing Society,* edited by Adam Kuper (London: Routledge, 1982), pp. 17–33.

11. For an exploration of the difficulties of retrieving accurate evidence about women in early medieval Irish society since all extant records were written from the perspective of men, see: Lisa M. Bitel, *Land of Women: Tales of Sex and Gender from Early Ireland* (Ithaca: Cornell University Press, 1996).

12. Averil Cameron, "Social Language and its Private Deployment," in *East and West: Modes of Communication. Proceedings of the First Plenary Conference at Merida,* edited by Evangelos Chrysos and Ian Wood, pp. 122–125.

13. Dick Harrison, *The Age of Abbesses and Queens: Gender and Political Culture in Early Medieval Europe* (Lund: Nordic Academic Press, 1998), pp. 18–19, 75–76.

14. Jürgen Hannig, "*Ars donandi:* Zur Ökonomie des Schenkens im früheren Mittelalter," in *Armut, Liebe, Ehre: Studien zur historische Kulturforschung,* edited by Richard van Dülmen (Frankfurt: Fischer Taschenbuch Verlag GmbH, 1988), pp. 11–37.

15. Although he recognizes the challenges faced by women who wished to assert authority, Hans-Werner Goetz denies the existence of gender-specific qualities that characterized women's methods or contributions. Hans-Werner Goetz, "Frauenbild und weibliche Lebensgestaltung im fränkischen Reich," in his *Weibliche Lebensgestaltung im frühen Mittelalter* (Cologne: Böhlau Verlag, 1991), pp. 21–29.

NOTES 99

16. Catherine Peyroux, "Gertrude's *furor:* Reading Anger in an Early Medieval Saint's *Life*," in *Anger's Past: The Social Uses of an Emotion in the Middle Ages,* edited by Barbara H. Rosenwein (Ithaca: Cornell University Press, 1998), pp. 36–55.

17. Even biased inquisitorial records can help historians gain important insights into popular belief. See Carlo Ginzburg, "The Inquisitor as Anthropologist," in his *Clues, Myths and the Historical Method,* translated by John and Anne Tedeschi (Baltimore: The Johns Hopkins University Press, 1986), pp. 156–164.

18. James Fentress and Chris Wickham, *Social Memory* (Oxford: Basil Blackwell, 1992), pp. 146–154.

19. For a convincing assessment of the potential contributions to be made by hagiography to research on early medieval Gaul, see: Paul Fouracre, "Merovingian History and Merovingian Hagiography," *Past and Present* 127 (1990), pp. 3–38; Ian Wood, "The Use and Abuse of Latin Hagiography in the Early Medieval West," in *East and West: Modes of Communication. Proceedings of the First Plenary Conference at Merida,* edited by Evangelos Chrysos and Ian Wood, pp. 93–109.

20. Mann, *The Sources of Social Power* 1, pp. 22–23.

21. Andrew McGowan, *Ascetic Eucharists: Food and Drink in Early Christian Ritual Meals* (Oxford: Clarendon Press, 1999), pp. 3–7.

22. Massimo Montanari, *The Culture of Food,* translated by Carl Ipsen (Oxford: Blackwell, 1994), pp. 15–16.

23. Paul Connerton, *How Societies Remember* (Cambridge: Cambridge University Press, 1989), pp. 45–47; Maurice Halbwachs, *On Collective Memory,* edited and translated by Lewis A. Coser (Chicago: University of Chicago Press, 1992), pp. 87–88.

24. Marcel Mauss, *The Gift: Forms and Functions of Exchange in Archaic Societies,* translated by Ian Cunnison (New York: W. W. Norton & Company, Inc., 1967), pp. 10–12.

25. Georges Bataille, "The Notion of Expenditure," in *Visions of Excess: Selected Writings, 1927–1939,* edited and translated by Allan Stoekl, Theory and History of Literature 14 (Minneapolis: University of Minnesota Press, 1985), pp. 120–123.

26. Mary Douglas, "Deciphering a Meal," in *Food and Culture: A Reader,* edited by Carole Counihan and Penny van Esterik (New York: Routledge, 1997), pp. 41–45.

27. Carl Deroux, "Des traces inconnues de la *Diététique* d'Anthime dans un manuscrit du Vatican (Reg. Lat. 1004)," *Latomus* 33 (1974), p. 685; Mireille Corbier, "The Broad Bean and the Moray: Social Hierarchies and Food in Rome," in *Food: A Culinary History from Antiquity to the Present,* edited by Jean-Louis Flandrin and Massimo Montanari (New York: Columbia University Press, 1999), pp. 128–140.

28. John Moreland, "Concepts of the Early Medieval Economy," in *The Long Eighth Century,* edited by Inge Lyse Hansen and Chris Wickham, TRW 11 (Leiden: E. J. Brill, 2000), pp. 18–34.

100 CREATING COMMUNITY WITH FOOD AND DRINK

29. Christine A. Hastorf, "Gender, Space and Prehistory," in *Engendering Archaeology: Women and Prehistory,* edited by Joan M. Gero and Margaret W. Conkey (Oxford: Basil Blackwell, 1991), pp. 132–136.

30. Stéphane Lebecq, "The Role of Monasteries in the Systems of Production and Exchange of the Frankish World between the Seventh and the Beginning of the Ninth Centuries," in *The Long Eighth Century,* pp. 129–133.

31. Caroline Walker Bynum, "Fast, Feast and Flesh: The Religious Significance of Food to Medieval Women," in *Food and Culture: A Reader,* pp. 138–141.

32. Rudolph Arbesmann, "Fasting and Prophecy in Pagan and Christian Antiquity," *Traditio* 7 (1949), p. 8.

33. Igor Kopytoff, "The Cultural Biography of Things: Commoditization as Process," in *The Social Life of Things: Commodities in Cultural Perspective,* edited by Arjun Appadurai (Cambridge: Cambridge University Press, 1986), pp. 64–70.

34. Walter Pohl, "Telling the Difference: Signs of Ethnic Identity," in *Strategies of Distinction: The Construction of Ethnic Communities, 300–700,* edited by Walter Pohl and Helmut Reimitz, TRW 2 (Leiden: E. J. Brill, 1998), pp. 17–69; Bonnie Effros, "Appearance and Ideology: Creating Distinctions between Merovingian Clerics and Lay Persons," in *Encountering Medieval Textiles and Dress: Objects, Texts, Images,* edited by Janet Snyder and Désirée Koslin (New York: Palgrave Macmillan, forthcoming).

35. Paul Fouracre, "The Work of Audoenus of Rouen and Eligius of Noyon in Extending Episcopal Influence from the Town to the Country in Seventh-Century Neustria," in *The Church in Town and Countryside. Papers Read at the Seventeenth Summer Meeting and Eighteenth Winter Meeting of the Ecclesiastical History Society,* edited by Derek Baker, Studies in Church History 16 (Oxford: Basil Blackwell, 1979), pp. 82–83.

36. Mary Douglas, *Purity and Danger: An Analysis of the Concepts of Pollution and Taboo* (New York: Praeger, 1966), pp. 50–52.

37. Peter Brown, "The Decline of the Empire of God: Amnesty, Penance and the Afterlife from Late Antiquity to the Middle Ages," in *Last Things: Death and the Apocalypse in the Middle Ages,* edited by Caroline Walker Bynum and Paul Freedman (Philadelphia: University of Pennsylvania Press, 2000), pp. 51–59, 280–283.

38. Arbesmann, "Fasting and Prophecy," pp. 32–37.

39. Hans-Werner Goetz, "Social and Military Institutions," in *The Cambridge Medieval History,* edited by Rosamond McKitterick (Cambridge: Cambridge University Press, 1995), pp. 478–479.

40. Gerd Althoff, "Der frieden-, bündnis- und gemeinschaftstiftende Charakter des Mahles im früheren Mittelalter," in *Essen und Trinken im Mittelalter und Neuzeit: Vorträge eines interdisziplinären Symposions vom 10.–13. Juni 1987 an der Justus-Liebig-Universität Gießen,* edited by Irmgard Bitsch, Trude Ehlert, and Xenja von Ertzdorff (Sigmaringen: Jan Thorbecke Verlag, 1987), pp. 14–15.

NOTES 101

41. Matthias Hardt, "Silbergeschirr als Gabe im Frühmittelalter," *Ethnographisch-Archäologisches Zeitschrift* 38 (1997), pp. 431–444.
42. Annette B. Weiner, *Inalienable Possessions: The Paradox of Keeping-While-Giving* (Berkeley: University of California Press, 1992), pp. 4–7.
43. Caesarius of Arles, *Ad regularum virginum* 39, edited by Germain Morin, in *Sanctus Caesarius episcopus Arelatensis, Opera omnia* 2 (Brugges: Jos. van der Meersch, 1942), p. 112.
44. Frederick S. Paxton, "Sickness, Death and Dying: The Legacy of Barbarian Europe in Ritual and Practice," in *Minorities and Barbarians in Medieval Life and Thought,* edited by Susan J. Ridyard and Robert G. Benson (Sewanee: University of the South Press, 1996), pp. 223–224.
45. This miracle account was likely recorded in the Carolingian period. Wilhelm Levison, ed., *Vita Anstrudis abbatissae Laudunensis* 32, in MGH: SRM 6 (Hanover: Impensis bibliopolii Hahniani, 1913), p. 76; Moreira, *Dreams, Visions and Spiritual Authority,* pp. 128–129.
46. Valerie I. J. Flint, *The Rise of Magic in Early Medieval Europe* (Princeton: Princeton University Press, 1991), pp. 252–253
47. Valerie I. J. Flint, "The Early Medieval 'Medicius,' the Saint—and the Enchanter," *Social History of Medicine* 2(1989), pp. 131–143.
48. Mark Grant, trans. and ed., *Anthimus, De observatione ciborum* (Blackawton: Prospect Books, 1996), pp. 9–44.
49. Peter Brown, *The Cult of Saints: Its Rise and Function in Latin Christianity* (Chicago: University of Chicago Press, 1981), pp. 113–120; Raymond Van Dam, *Saints and their Miracles in Late Antique Gaul* (Princeton: Princeton University Press, 1993), pp. 82–115.
50. Frederick J. Paxton, *Christianizing Death: The Creation of a Ritual Process in Early Medieval Europe* (Ithaca: Cornell University Press, 1990), pp. 50–51.
51. Edward James, "A Sense of Wonder: Gregory of Tours, Medicine and Science," in *The Culture of Christendom: Essays in Medieval History in Commemoration of Denis L. T. Bethell,* edited by Mark Anthony Meyer (London: The Hambledon Press, 1993), pp. 52–59.
52. Veronika E. Grimm, *From Feasting to Fasting, the Evolution of a Sin: Attitudes to Food in Late Antiquity* (London: Routledge, 1996), pp. 162–196.
53. On written sources for burial in early medieval Gaul, see: Bonnie Effros, *Caring for Body and Soul: Burial and the Afterlife in the Merovingian World* (University Park: Pennsylvania State University Press, 2002).
54. Walter Janssen, "Essen und Trinken im frühen und höhen Mittelalter aus archäologischer Sicht," in *Liber castellorum: 40 Variaties op het Thema Kasteel,* edited by T. J. Hoekstra, H. L. Janssen, and I. W. L. Moerman (Zutphen: De Walburg Pers, 1981), pp. 327–328.
55. Paul-Albert Février, "La tombe chrétienne et l'Au-delà," in *Le temps chrétien de la fin de l'antiquité au moyen âge IIIᵉ-XIIIᵉ siècles, Paris, 9–12 mars 1981,* Colloques internationaux du CNRS 604 (Paris: Éditions du CNRS, 1984), pp. 171–176; Bailey K. Young, "Pratiques funéraires et mentalités

102 CREATING COMMUNITY WITH FOOD AND DRINK

païennes," in *Clovis: Histoire et mémoire. Le baptême de Clovis, l'événement,* edited by Michel Rouche (Paris: Presses de l'Université de Paris-Sorbonne, 1997), pp. 19–23.

Notes to Chapter 1

1. The cask was described as a:"vasque magnum, quem vulgo cupam vocant." Jonas of Bobbio, *Vitae Columbani abbatis discipulorumque eius, libri II* 1.27, edited by Bruno Krusch, in MGH: SRG 37 (Hanover: Impensis bibliopolii Hahniani, 1905), pp. 211–214; Karl Hauck, "Rituelle Speisegemeinschaft im 10. und 11. Jahrhundert," *Studium generale* 3 (1950), pp. 612.

2. Here the drinking ceremony utilized: "gentile ritu vasa plena cervisae." Jonas of Bobbio, *Vita Vedastis episcopi Atrebatensis* 7, edited by Bruno Krusch, in MGH: SRG 37, pp. 314–316.

3. Marc van Uytfanghe notes the desire of authors of such accounts from the seventh century onward to show the monastery as a place of plenty. Marc van Uytfanghe, *Stylisation biblique et condition humaine dans l'hagiographie mérovingienne (650–750),* Verhandelingen van de Koninklijke Academie voor Wetenschnappen, Letteren en Schone Kunsten van België, Klasse der Letteren 49, vol.120 (Brussels: Paleis der Academiën, 1987), pp. 161–169; Michael J. Enright, *Lady with a Mead Cup: Ritual, Prophesy and Lordship in the European Warband from La Tène to the Viking Age* (Dublin: Four Courts Press, 1996), pp. 16–17.

4. Yitzhak Hen, *Culture and Religion in Merovingian Gaul, A. D. 481–751* (Leiden: E. J. Brill, 1995), pp. 189–194. Ian Wood, by contrast, does not challenge the veracity of these passages or the concerns of holy men such as Columbanus with the continued existence of pagan practice in border regions of the Merovingian kingdoms. Ian Wood, *The Missionary Life: Saints and the Evangelisation of Europe 400–1050* (Harlow: Longman, 2001), pp. 32–35.

5. Caesarius of Arles was a leader in this respect. Robert A. Markus, "From Caesarius to Boniface: Christianity and Paganism in Gaul," in *Le septième siècle: Changements et continuités. Actes du colloque bilatéral franco-britannique tenu au Warburg Institute les 8–9 juillet 1988,* edited by Jacques Fontaine and J. N. Hillgarth (London: The Warburg Institute, University of London, 1992), pp. 156–161.

6. L. Carless Hulin, "The Diffusion of Religious Symbols with Complex Societies," in *The Meaning of Things: Material Culture and Symbolic Expression,* edited by Ian Hodder, One World Archaeology 6 (London: Unwin Hyman, 1989), pp. 90–94.

7. C. E. Stancliffe, "From Town to Country: The Christianisation of the Touraine 370–600," in *The Church in Town and Countryside. Papers Read at the Seventeenth Summer Meeting and Eighteenth Winter Meeting of the Ecclesiastical History Society,* edited by Derek Baker, Studies in Church History 16 (Oxford: Basil Blackwell, 1979), pp. 43–59.

NOTES 103

8. Donald Bullough, *Friendship, Neighbours and Fellow Drinkers: Aspects of Community Conflict in the Early Medieval West,* Chadwick Lecture 1990 (Cambridge: Department of Anglo-Saxon, Norse and Celtic, 1991), p. 8. I thank Julia Smith for bringing this piece to my attention.

9. Ramsay MacMullen, *Christianity and Paganism in the Fourth to Eighth Centuries* (New Haven: Yale University Press, 1997), pp. 43–48.

10. "Siquis autem laicus manducaverit aut biberit iuxta fana, si per ignorantiam fecerit, promittat deinceps quod numquam reiteret, et XL diebus in pane et aqua paeniteat. Si vero per contemptum hoc fecerit, id est postquam sacerdos illi praedicavit quod sacrilegium hoc erat, et postea mensae daemoniorum communicaverit, si gulae tantum vitio hoc fecerit aut repetierit, III quadragesimis in pane et aqua paeniteat; si vero pro cultu daemonum aut honore simulacrorum hoc fecerit, III annis paeniteat."

G. S. M. Walker, ed. and trans., *Paenitentiale Columbani* 24, *Sanctus Columbanus, Opera,* Scriptores latini Hiberniae 2 (Dublin: The Dublin Institute for Advanced Studies, 1957), pp. 178–179. The English translation is taken from this edition.

11. Mireille Corbier, "The Ambiguous Status of Meat in Ancient Rome," *Food and Foodways* 3 (1989), p. 234.

12. Charles de Clercq, ed., *Conc. Aurelianense a.533* c.20, in *Concilia Galliae a.511-a.695,* CCSL 148a (Turnhout: Typographi Brepols editores pontificii, 1963), p. 102.

13. De Clercq, ed., *Conc Clippiacense a.626–627* c.16, in *Concilia Galliae,* CCSL 148a, p. 294.

14. Paul Fouracre, "The Work of Audoenus of Rouen and Eligius of Noyon in Extending Episcopal Influence from the Town to the County in Seventh-Century Neustria," in *The Church in Town and Countryside,* pp. 82–83.

15. Rob Meens, "Pollution in the Early Middle Ages: The Case of the Food Regulations in the Penitentials," *EME* 4 (1995), pp. 16–19.

16. Richard Kieckhefer, *Magic in the Middle Ages* (Cambridge: Cambridge University Press, 1989), pp. 44–47.

17. De Clercq, ed., *Conc Aurelianense a.533* c.12, in *Concilia Galliae,* CCSL 148a, p. 100.

18. "Isti enim infelices et miseri, qui ballationes et saltationes ante ipsas basilicas sanctorum exercere nec metuunt nec erubesunt, et si christiani ad ecclesiam veniunt, pagani de ecclesia revertuntur; quia ista consuetudo ballandi de paganorum observatione remansit." Caesarius of Arles, *Sermones* 13.4, edited by Germain Morin, revised edition, CCSL 103 (Turnhout: Typographi Brepols editores pontificii, 1953), p. 67.

19. Childebert I's capitulary recorded inappropriate drunken dancing among Christians in his kingdom. Alfred Boretius, ed., *Capitularia regum Francorum* 2, in MGH: Leges 2, Capitularia 1 (Hanover: Impensis bibliopolii Hahniani, 1883), pp. 2–3.

20. Gregory the Great, *Registrum epistolarum libri VIII-XIV* 8.4, edited by Dag Norberg, CCSL 140a (Turnhout: Typographi Brepols editores pontificii, 1982), p. 521; Robert A. Markus, *Gregory the Great and his World* (Cambridge: Cambridge University Press, 1997), pp. 173–175.

21. "Si quis maialem sacriuum furauerit et hoc [cum] testibus, quod sacriuus fuit, potuerit adprobare, mallobergo barcho anomeo chamitheotho hoc est, DCC denarius qui faciunt solidos XVII semis culpabilis iudicetur excepto capitale et dilatura." Karl August Eckhardt, *Pactus legis salicae* 2.16, MGH: Leges 4.1 (Hanover: Impensis bibliopolii Hahniani, 1962), p. 26; Ruth Schmidt-Wiegand, "Spuren paganer religiosität in den frühmittelalterlichen Leges," in *Iconologia sacra: Mythos, Bildkunst und Dichtung in der Religions- und Sozialgeschichte Alteuropas. Festschrift für Karl Hauck zum 75. Geburtstag,* edited by Hagen Keller and Nikolaus Staubach (Berlin: Walter de Gruyter, 1994), pp. 256–257.

22. Avitus of Vienne, *Epistolarum ad diversos libri III* 76, edited by Rudolf Peiper, in MGH:AA 6.2 (Berlin: Apud Weidmannos, 1883), p. 92; Danuta Shanzer, "Two Clocks and a Wedding: Theodoric's Diplomatic Relations with the Burgundians," *Romanobarbarica* 14 (1996–1997), p. 244.

23. Annette B. Weiner, *Inalienable Possessions: The Paradox of Keeping-While-Giving* (Berkeley: University of California Press, 1992), pp. 4–7.

24. Dieter Harmening, *Superstitio: Überlieferungs- und theoriegeschichtliche Untersuchungen zur kirchlich-theologischen Aberglaubensliteratur des Mittelalters* (Berlin: Erich Schmidt Verlag, 1979), pp. 231–235.

25. These activities do not differ significantly from the practice of "potlatch" among the native peoples of the American Northwest, although the volume of expenditure involved in the latter was likely significantly greater. Igor L. de Garine, "Food, Tradition and Prestige," in *Food, Man and Society,* edited by Dwain N. Walcher, Norman Kretchmer, and Henry L. Barnett (New York: Plenum Press, 1976), pp. 150–159.

26. Aron J. Gurevich, *Categories of Medieval Culture,* translated by G. L. Campbell (London: Routledge & Kegan Paul, 1985), pp. 221–248.

27. Gregory of Tours, *Liber vitae patrum* 1.3, edited by Bruno Krusch, in MGH: SRM 1.2, revised edition (Hanover: Impensis bibliopolii Hahniani, 1969), pp. 215–216; Alain Schnapp, *The Discovery of the Past: The Origins of Archaeology* (London: British Museum Press, 1996), p. 87; Bonnie Effros, "Monuments and Memory: Repossessing Ancient Remains in Early Medieval Gaul," in *Topographies of Power in the Early Middle Ages,* edited by Mayke de Jong and Frans Theuws, TRW 6 (Leiden: E. J. Brill, 2001), pp. 109–110.

28. Karl Hauck, "Rituelle Speisegemeinschaft im 10. und 11. Jahrhundert," *Studium Generale* 3 (1950), pp. 611–621.

29. Andrew McGowan, *Ascetic Eucharists: Food and Drink in Early Christian Ritual Meals* (Oxford: Clarendon Press, 1999), pp. 73–79.

30. Rudoph Arbesmann, "Fasting and Prophecy in Pagan and Christian Antiquity," *Traditio* 7 (1949), pp. 32–36.

31. MacGowan, *Ascetic Eucharists,* pp. 169–170.

NOTES 105

32. Venantius Fortunatus, *De uita sanctae Radegundis libri II* 1.15, edited by Bruno Krusch, in MGH: SRM 2, new edition (Hanover: Impensis bibliopolii Hahniani, 1956), p. 369. For a discussion of the significance of vegetarianism as a facet of Merovingian asceticism, see: Pierre Bonnassie, "Consommation d'aliments immondes et cannibalisme de survie dans l'Occident du haut moyen âge," *Annales ESC* 44 (1989), pp. 1036–1037.

33. Judith W. George, *Venantius Fortunatus: A Latin Poet in Merovingian Gaul* (Oxford: Clarendon Press, 1992), pp. 169–173.

34. G. Sartory, "In der Arena der Askese. Fasten im frühen Christentum," in *Speisen, Schlemmen, Fasten: Eine Kulturgeschichte des Essens,* edited by Uwe Schultz (Frankfurt: Insel, 1993), pp. 71–82.

35. Sidonius Apollinaris, *Epistulae* 5.14, edited by Christian Luetjohann, MGH: AA 8 (Berlin: Apud Weidmannos, 1887), pp. 87–88.

36. De Clercq, ed., *Conc. Aurelianense a.511* c.27, in *Concilia Galliae,* CCSL 148a, pp. 11–12; De Clercq, ed., *Conc. Lugdunense a.567–570* c.6, in *Concilia Galliae,* CCSL 148a, p. 202; Arbesmann, "Fasting and Prophecy," pp. 47–50.

37. H. J. Schmitz, ed., *Die Bussbücher und die Bussdisciplin der Kirche* 1 (Mainz: Verlag von Franz Kirchheim, 1883); Paul Willem Finsterwalder, ed., *Die Canones Theodori Cantuariensis und ihre Überlieferungsformen* (Weimar: Hermann Böhlaus Nachfolger, Hof-Buchdruckerei GmbH, 1929); Ludwig Bieler, ed., *The Irish Penitentials,* Scriptores latini Hiberniae 5 (Dublin: The Dublin Institute for Advanced Studies, 1963).

38. Peter Brown, "Vers la naissance du purgatoire: Amnistie et pénitence dans le christianisme occidental de l'Antiquité tardive au Haut Moyen Age," *Annales: Histoire, Sciences Sociales* 6 (1997), pp. 1247–1261.

39. Jörg Jarnut, "Konsumvorschriften im Früh- und Hochmittelalter," in *Haushalt und Familie in Mittelalter und früher Neutzeit: Vorträge eines interdisziplinären Symposions vom 6.–9. Juni 1990 an der Rheinischen Friedrich Wilhelms-Universität Bonn,* edited by Trude Ehlert (Sigmaringen: Jan Thorbecke Verlag, 1991), pp.121–122.

40. Arbesmann, "Fasting and Prophecy," pp. 36–37.

41. McGowan, *Ascetic Eucharists,* pp. 270–271.

42. Peter Brown, "*Gloriosus obitus:* The End of the Ancient Other World," in *The Limits of Ancient Christianity: Essays on Late Antique Thought and Culture in Honor of R. A. Markus,* edited by William E. Klingshirn and Mark Vessey (Ann Arbor: University of Michigan, 1999), pp. 302–310.

43. Harmening, *Superstitio,* pp. 231–235.

44. Hermann Wasserschleben, ed., *Die irische Kanonensammlung* 56.1–4, second edition (Leipzig: Verlag von Bernhard Tauchnitz, 1885), pp. 221–222.

45. Peter Brown, *Power and Persuasion in Late Antiquity: Towards a Christian Empire* (Madison: University of Wisconsin Press, 1992), pp. 92–93.

46. Jean-Claude Schmitt, "'Religion populaire' et culture folklorique," *Annales ESC* 31 (1976), pp. 941–948; M. Lauwers, "'Religion populaire,' culture folklorique, mentalités: Notes pour une anthropologie culturelle du moyen âge," *Revue d'histoire ecclésiastique* 82 (1987), pp. 243–249.

106   CREATING COMMUNITY WITH FOOD AND DRINK

47. Bridget Ann Henisch describes the medieval Church as "flawed and tarnished" due to its alleged relinquishment of early standards of austerity. Bridget A. Henisch, *Fast and Feast: Food in Medieval Society* (University Park: Pennsylvania State University Press, 1976), pp. 2–10.

48. It should be noted, however, that meat was absent from these meals. McGowan, *Ascetic Eucharists*, pp. 95–135, 140–142.

49. On later tensions between abstinence and participation in the eucharistic sacrifice, see: Caroline Walker Bynum, *Holy Feast and Holy Fast: The Religious Significance of Food to Medieval Women* (Berkeley: University of California Press, 1987). This is still a paradoxical relationship among modern nuns. A. M. Iossifides, "Wine: Life's Blood and Spiritual Essence in a Greek Orthodox Convent," in *Alcohol, Gender and Culture*, edited by Dimitra Gefou-Madianou (London: Routledge, 1992), pp. 80–86.

50. "Si vero pro infirmitate aut quia longo tempore se abstinuerit et in consuetudine non ei erit multum bibere vel manducare aut pro gaudio in natale domini aut in pascha aut pro alicuius sanctorum commemoratione faciebat et tunc plus non accipit quam decretum est a senioribus nihil nocet." Finsterwalder, ed., *Die canones Theodori Cantuariensis* U1.1, c.4, p. 289; Bullough, *Friends, Neighbours*, p. 10, n. 18.

51. Augustine of Hippo, *Confessionum libri XIII* 6.2.2, edited by Lucas Verheijen, CCSL 27 (Turnhout: Typographi Brepols editores pontificii, 1981), pp. 74–75; Otto Gerhard Oexle, "Mahl und Spende im mittelalterlichen Totenkult," *FS* 18 (1984), pp. 404–405.

52. Jonathan Z. Smith, *To Take Place: Toward Theory in Ritual* (Chicago: University of Chicago Press, 1987), pp. 92–95.

53. The author carefully described the vessel as a: "vas, in quo potum dilatum fuerat, quod cupam noncupamus." Bruno Krusch, ed., *Vita Genovefae virginis Parisiensis* 21, in MGH: SRM 3 (Hanover: Impensis bibliopolii Hahniani, 1896), p. 224.

54. Ralph W. Mathisen, "Crossing the Supernatural Frontier in Western Late Antiquity," in *Shifting Frontiers in Late Antiquity*, edited by Ralph W. Mathisen and Hagith S. Sivan (Aldershot: Ashgate Publishing Limited, 1996), pp. 317–320.

55. Giselle de Nie, *Views from a Many-Windowed Tower: Studies of Imagination in the Works of Gregory of Tours* (Amsterdam: Rodopi, 1987), pp. 112–113; Gregory of Tours, *Liber de virtutibus sancti Juliani* 36, edited by Bruno Krusch, in MGH: SRM 1.2 (Hanover: Impensis bibliopolii Hahniani, 1885), p. 129; Venantius Fortunatus, *Vita sancti Marcelli* 20, edited by Bruno Krusch, in MGH: AA 4.2 (Berlin: Apud Weidmannos, 1885), p. 51; Gregory the Great, *Dialogi* 1.9.1–5, edited and translated by Adalbert de Vogüé, SC 260 (Paris: Les Éditions du CERF, 1979), pp. 76–81.

56. The object of this miracle, an "ampulla vitrea," was blessed for the wife of Avitianus. Sulpicius Severus, *Dialogi* 3, edited by Karl Halm, in CSEL 1 (Vienna: Apud C. Geroldi Filium, 1866), pp. 200–201.

57. Krusch, ed., *Vita Genovefae virginis Parisiensis* 52, in MGH: SRM 3, p. 236.

NOTES   107

58. Bruno Krusch, ed., *Vita sanctae Chrothildis* 12, in MGH: SRM 2 (Hanover: Impensis bibliopolii Hahniani, 1888), pp. 346–347.

59. Bruno Krusch, ed. *Vita Sadalbergae abbatissae Laudunensis* 20, in MGH: SRM 5 (Hanover: Impensis bibliopolii Hahniani, 1910), p. 61.

60. Jo Ann McNamara, "A Legacy of Miracles: Hagiography and Nunneries in Merovingian Gaul," in *Women of the Medieval World: Essays in Honor of John Mundy,* edited by Julius Kirshner and Suzanne Wemple (Oxford: Basil Blackwell, 1985), pp. 45–46. This hypothesis has recently been substantiated quantitatively in a demographic survey based on textual and archaeological evidence. Kathy L. Pearson, "Nutrition and the Early-Medieval Diet," *Speculum* 72 (1997), esp. pp. 20–28.

61. Hen, *Culture and Religion,* pp. 189–194. On the continuing significant role of pagan religion and sacrifice in Gaul and Byzantium, see: Aline Rousselle, *Croire et guérir: La foi en Gaule dans l'antiquité tardive* (Paris: Fayard, 1990); K. W. Harl, "Sacrifice and Pagan Belief in Fifth- and Sixth-Century Byzantium," *Past and Present* 128 (1990), pp. 7–27.

62. Enright notes the importance of the lord's table, at which "seating order was a public visual statement of the hierarchy of the warband community while also expressing and renewing the bond which joined all who ate or drank from it." Enright, *Lady with a Mead Cup,* p. 49.

63. Pearson, "Nutrition," p. 27.

64. Peter Brown, *The Body and Society: Men, Women and Sexual Renunciation in Early Christianity* (New York: Columbia University Press, 1988), pp. 219–224.

65. Jerome, *Adversus Jovinianum* 2.6, edited by Jacques-Paul Migne, in PL 23, reprint edition (Turnhout: Brepols, 1983), pp. 306–307; Veronika E. Grimm, *From Feasting to Fasting, the Evolution of a Sin: Attitudes to Food in Late Antiquity* (London: Routledge, 1996), pp. 177–181.

66. Gerd Althoff, "Der frieden-, bündnis- und gemeinschaftstiftende Charakter des Mahles im früheren Mittelalter," in *Essen und Trinken im Mittelalter und Neuzeit: Vorträge eines interdisziplinären Symposions vom 10.–13. Juni an der Justus-Liebig-Universität Gießen,* edited by Irmgard Bitsch, Trude Ehlert and Xenja von Ertzdorff (Sigmaringen: Jan Thorbecke Verlag, 1987), pp. 13–25.

67. Gurevich, *Categories of Medieval Culture,* pp. 222–233, 244–248, 272–276.

68. Guy Halsall, *Settlement and Social Organization: The Merovingian Region of Metz* (Cambridge: Cambridge University Press, 1995), pp. 247–248; Bonnie Effros, *Caring for Body and Soul: Burial and the Afterlife in the Merovingian World* (University Park: Pennsylvania State University Press, 2002), pp. 184–187; Édouard Salin, *La civilisation mérovingienne d'après les sépultures, les textes et le laboratoire* 2 (Paris: De Boccard, 1952), pp. 202–212.

69. "Diese feierliche Essen und Trinken, wie es der heidnische Ritus pflegte, hat die Missionskirche wohl dem christlichen Brauch anzupassen versucht, aber dort, wo es nicht unmittelbar mit dem bekämpften Kulten zusammenhing keineswegs völlig beseitigen oder überwinden können." Hauck, "Rituelle Speisegemeinschaft," p. 612.

108 CREATING COMMUNITY WITH FOOD AND DRINK

70. Thus, Abraham had not eaten with the Chaldaeans, Tobias had excluded himself from meals with the Gentiles, and Moses had not partaken of food with the pharaoh. Wasserschleben, ed., *Die irische Kanonensammlung* 40.1–2, p. 153; Mary Douglas, *Natural Symbols: Explorations in Cosmology* (London: Pantheon Books, 1970), pp. 38–41.

71. C. Munier, ed., *Conc. Agathense a.506 c.*40, in *Concilia Galliae a.314-a.506*, CCSL 148 (Turnhout: Typographi Brepols editores pontificii, 1963), p. 210; Karl Böckenhoff, *Speisesatzungen mosaïscher Art in mittelalterlichen Kirchenrechtsquellen des Morgen und Abendlandes* (Münster: Druck und Verlag der Aschendorffschen Buchhandlung, 1907), pp. 53–54.

72. De Clercq, ed., *Conc Epaonense a.517 c.*15, in *Concilia Galliae,* CCSL 148a, pp. 27–28; Ralph W. Mathisen, "Barbarian Bishops and the Churches 'in barbaricis gentibus' during Late Antiquity," *Speculum* 72 (1997), pp. 693–694.

73. Walter Goffart, *The Narrators of Barbarian History (A. D. 500–800): Jordanes, Gregory of Tours, Bede and Paul the Deacon* (Princeton: Princeton University Press, 1988), pp. 213–220.

74. Martin Heinzelmann, *Gregor von Tours (538–594): 'Zehn Bücher Geschichte.' Historiographie und Gesellschaftskonzept im 6. Jahrhundert* (Darmstadt: Wissenschaftliche Buchgesellschaft, 1994), pp. 150–157.

75. Mathisen, "Barbarian Bishops," pp. 693–694.

76. Gregory of Tours, *Liber in gloria martyrum* 79, edited by Bruno Krusch, in MGH: SRM 1.2 (Hanover: Impensis bibliopolii Hahniani, 1885), pp. 91–92.

77. Caesarius of Arles, *Sermones* 46–47, edited by Morin, CCSL 103, pp. 205–215; William E. Klingshirn, *Caesarius of Arles: The Making of a Christian Community in Late Antique Gaul* (Cambridge: Cambridge University Press, 1994), pp. 196–199; Mary Douglas, *Purity and Danger: An Analysis of the Concepts of Pollution and Taboo* (New York: Praeger, 1966), pp. 129–139.

78. Caesarius of Arles, *Sermones* 188, edited by Germain Morin, in CCSL 104 (Turnhout: Typographi Brepols editores pontificii, 1953), pp. 767–770.

79. Caesarius of Arles, *Sermones* 54, edited by Morin, CCSL 103, pp. 239–240.

80. Leo Cunibert Mohlberg, Leo Eizenhöfer, and Peter Siffrin, eds., *Liber sacramentorum romanae aeclesiae ordinis anni circuli (Cod. Vat. Reg. Lat. 316/ Paris Bibl. Nat. 7193, 41/56) (Gelasian Sacramentary)* 86–87, third edition, in Rerum ecclesiasticarum documenta series maior, fontes 4 (Rome: Casa Editrice Herder, 1960), p. 232.

81. Arbesmann, "Fasting and Prophecy," p. 37.

82. Gerd Theissen, *The Social Setting of Pauline Christianity: Essays on Corinth,* edited and translated by John Schütz (Philadelphia: Fortress Press, 1975), pp. 121–143.

83. Of Paradise, Avitus noted:

"Tellus prompta cibos: fruticis quin alter opimi
Sumiter adsiduus tenui de caespite fructus.
At si curvati fecundo pondere rami
Mitia submittunt sublimi ex arbore poma,

NOTES   109

Protenus in florem vacuus turgescere palmes
Incipit in que novis fetum promittere gemmis.

. . . .

Sic epulas tamen hi capiunt escamque requirunt,
Conpellit quod nulla fames nec lassa fovendo
Indigus hortatur conpleri viscera venter."

Avitus of Vienne, *Poematum libri VI* 2.4–16, edited by Rudolf Peiper, in
MGH: AA 6.2 (Berlin: Apud Weidmannos, 1883), p. 212.

84. Avitus of Vienne, *Poematum libri VI* 4.21–27, in MGH: AA 6.2, pp. 236;
    Böckenhoff, *Speisesatzungen mosaïscher Art,* p. 79. Translation taken from
    George W. Shea, *The Poems of Alcimus Ecdicius Avitus: Translation and Intro-
    duction,* Medieval and Renaissance Texts and Studies 172 (Tempe: Medieval
    and Renaissance Texts and Studies, 1997), p. 100.
85. Numbers 19.15–18 also made reference to furnishings found in the tent in
    which someone had died. Sentiment that the Old Testament had lost au-
    thority on matters of purity (such as those related to Kashrut) seems to
    have been stronger in papal custom than in regional traditions such as the
    Irish penitentials. Resistance to measures echoing Judaic law grew stronger
    by the ninth century. Böckenhoff, *Speisesatzungen mosaïscher Art,* esp. pp.
    21–28, 50–53.
86. Böckenhoff, *Speisesatzungen mosaïscher Art,* pp. 87–89.
87. Mary Douglas, "Sacred Contagion," in *Reading Leviticus: A Conversation
    with Mary Douglas,* edited by John F. A. Sawyer, Journal for the Study of the
    Old Testament, Supplement Series 227 (Sheffield: Sheffield Academic Press
    Ltd., 1996), pp. 101–106.
88. On food regulations in the penitentials, see: Meens, "Pollution," pp. 8–9;
    Bonnassie, "Consommation d'aliments," pp. 1036–1043; Aron I. Gurevich,
    Medieval Popular Culture: Problems of Belief and Perception, translated by Janos
    M. Bak and Paul A. Hollingsworth, in Cambridge Studies in Oral and Lit-
    erate Culture 14 (Cambridge: Cambridge University Press, 1988), pp.
    91–93; and Douglas, *Purity and Danger,* pp. 60–61.
89. Paul Willem Finsterwalder dates the U-version of the penitential to the
    early eighth century. Eighth-century copies survive from Northern France
    (Corbie or St. Ricquier?), Würzburg and possibly Fulda or Mainz. Finster-
    walder, ed., *Die Canones Theodori Cantuariensis,* pp. 177–178, 224.
90. Finsterwalder, ed., *Die Canones Theodori Cantuariensis* U 7.3 and 7.6–10.
91. In 541, the Council of Orléans, canon 15, directed: "Si quis post accep-
    tum baptismi sacramentum ad immolata daemonibus, tanquam ad vom-
    itum, sumenda revertitur, si commonitus a sacerdote se corregere ex hac
    praevaricatione noluerit, a communione catholica pro emendatione sac-
    rilegii suspendatur." In 567, the Council of Tours, canon 23, likewise
    forbade the consumption of pagan offerings, as did the Council of
    Clichy, canon 16, in 626–627. De Clercq, ed., *Concilia Galliae,* CCSL
    148a, p. 136, 191, 294.

110 CREATING COMMUNITY WITH FOOD AND DRINK

92. "Et qui non signaverit coclear quo lambit [sex percussionibus]. . . ." Columbanus, *Regula coenobialis*, edited and translated G. S. M. Walker, in *Sanctus Columbanus, Opera*, Scriptores latini Hiberniae 2 (Dublin: The Dublin Institute for Advanced Studies, 1957), pp. 146–147.

93. Jonas of Bobbio, *Vitae Columbani abbatis discipulorumque eius, libri II* 2.9, edited by Bruno Krusch, in MGH: SRM 37 (Hanover: Impensis bibliopolii Hahniani, 1905), pp. 246–251.

94. "Si comederit uel biberit non petens benedictionem et non responderit Amen, sex percussionibus; et quae non signauerit coclear quo lambit, sex. . . ." Adalbert de Vogüé, "La régle de Donat pour l'abbesse Gauthstrude," *Benedictina* 25 (1978), c.25, p. 268.

95. Paul Connerton, *How Societies Remember* (Cambridge: Cambridge University Press, 1989), pp. 82–84.

96. Gregory the Great, *Dialogi* 2.3.3–5, edited by Adalbert de Vogüé, SC 260 (Paris: Les Éditions du CERF, 1979), pp. 140–143.

97. Gregory the Great, *Dialogi* 3.5.3–4, edited by de Vogüé, SC 260, pp. 272–277.

98. E. A. Lowe, ed., *The Bobbio Missal: A Gallican Mass-Book (Ms. Paris. Lat. 13246)* 2.554, Henry Bradshaw Society 58 (London: Harrison and Sons, Ltd., 1920), p. 169.

99. Mohlberg, Eizenhöfer, and Siffrin, eds., *Liber sacramentorum* 75–76, pp. 224–227.

100. Jonas of Bobbio, *Vitae Columbani abbatis et discipulorumque eius* 1.19, edited by Krusch, in MGH: SRM 37, pp.187–189.

101. Van Uytfanghe, *Stylisation biblique*, pp. 102–110. Likewise, in Gaul in 587, Gregory of Tours reported among other portents: "Prodigia quoque multa dehinc apparuerunt. Nam vasa per domus diversorum signis, nescio quibus, caraxata sunt, quae res nullo umquam modo aut eradi potuit aut deleri." Gregory of Tours, *Libri historiarum X* 9.5, edited by Bruno Krusch, MGH: SRM 1.1, revised edition (Hanover: Impensis bibliopolii Hahniani, 1951), p. 416.

102. Dietrich Claude, *Untersuchungen zu Handel und Verkehr der vor- und frühgeschichtlichen Zeit im Mittel- und Nordeuropa, 2: Der Handel im westlichen Mittelmeer während des Frühmittelalters,* Abhandlungen der Akademie der Wissenschaften in Göttingen, philologisch-historische Klasse, third series, vol. 144 (Göttingen:Vandenhoeck & Ruprecht, 1985), pp. 80–81.

103. Bruno Krusch, ed. *Vita Genovefae virginis Parisiensis* 48, in MGH: SRM 3 (Hanover: Impensis bibliopolii Hahniani, 1896), p. 235; Martin Heinzelmann and Joseph-Claude Poulin, "Genovefa," in *Lexikon des Mittelalters* 4 (Munich: Artemis Verlag, 1989), p. 1237.

104. Peter Brown, "Sorcery, Demons, and the Rise of Christianity from Late Antiquity into the Middle Ages," in *Witchcraft: Confessions and Accusations,* edited by Mary Douglas (London: Tavistock Publications, 1970), pp. 28–29; Mathisen, "Crossing the Supernatural," pp. 309–320.

105. Matthias Hardt, "Silbergeschirr als Gabe im Frühmittelalter," *Ethnographisch-Archäologische Zeitschrift* 37 (1996), pp. 431–444; Matthias Hardt,

NOTES   111

"Silverware in Early Medieval Gift Exchange: *Imitatio Imperii* and Objects of Memory," in *Franks and Alamanni in the Merovingian Period: An Ethnographic Perspective,* edited by Ian Wood, Studies in Historical Archaeoethnology 3 (Woodbridge: Boydell, 1998), pp. 317–326; Enright, *Lady with a Mead Cup,* pp. 49–52.

106. Mechtild Schulze, "Diskussionsbeitrag zur Interpretations früh- und hochmittelalterlicher Flußfunde," *FS* 18 (1984), pp. 222–248; François Baratte, "Remarques préliminaires à un inventaire de la vaisselle d'argent trouvée en Gaule," in his *Argenterie romaine et byzantine: Actes de la table ronde, Paris 11–13 octobre 1983* (Paris: De Boccard, 1988), pp. 85–95; Lotte Hedeager, *Iron-Age Societies: From Tribe to State in Northern Europe, 500 BC to AD 700,* translated by John Hines (Oxford: Blackwell, 1992), pp. 32–35, 66–81.

107. Bruno Judic, "Les 'manières de table' de Grégoire le Grand: Les cuillers envoyées de Lérins à Rome," *Le moyen âge* 106 (2000), pp. 49–62.

108. The vessel in question was an "argenteus discus." Bruno Krusch, ed., *Vitae Caesarii episcopi Arelatensis libri duo* 1.37, in MGH: SRM 3 (Hanover: Impensis bibliopolii Hahniani, 1896), p. 471.

109. Gregory of Tours, *Libri historiarum X* 8,3, edited by Krusch, MGH: SRM 1.1, pp. 372–373; Matthias Hardt, "Verborgene Schätze nach schriftlichen Quellen der Völkerwanderungszeit und des frühen Mittelalters," in *Archäologisches Zellwerk: Beiträge zur Kulturgeschichte in Europa und Asien. Festschrift für Helmut Roth zum 60. Geburtstag,* edited by Ernst Pohl, Udo Recker, and Claudia Theune (Rahden: Verlag Marie Leidorf GmbH, 2001), pp. 256–257.

110. Marcel Mauss, *The Gift: Forms and Functions of Exchange in Archaic Society,* edited by Ian Cunnison (New York: W. W. Norton & Company, Inc., 1967), pp. 41–43.

111. Dominic Janes, "Treasure Bequest: Death and Gift in the Early Middle Ages," in *The Community, the Family and the Saint: Patterns of Power in Early Medieval Europe. Selected Proceedings of the International Medieval Congress, University of Leeds, 4–7 July 1994, 10–13 July 1995,* edited by Joyce Hill and Mary Swan (Turnhout: Brepols, 1998), pp. 368–370.

112. Jean-Marie Pardessus, ed. *Charta qua Leodebodus, abbas Sancti Aniani plurima dona confert monasteriis Sancti Aniani et Sancti Petri Floriacensis (Ann. 667),* in *Diplomata: Chartae, epistolae, leges aliaque instrumenta ad res Gallo-Francicas spectantia* 2.358, reprint edition (Aalen: Scientia Verlag, 1969), pp. 142–145.

113. Jean-Pierre Laporte, "Pour une nouvelle datation du testament d'Erminethrude," *Francia* 14 (1986), p. 577. This estimate antedates the era long thought to be most accurate. Ulrich Nonn, "Erminethrud-Eine vornehme neustrische Dame um 700," *HJ* 102 (1982), pp. 135–143.

114. Hartmut Atsma and Jean Vezin, eds., "Testament d'Erminethrude," in *Chartae latinae antiquiores* 14.592 (Dietikon-Zurich: URS Graf Verlag, 1982), pp. 72–75.

115. Bailey K. Young, "Paganisme, christianisation et rites funéraires mérovingiens," *AM* 7 (1977), pp. 37–40.

112   CREATING COMMUNITY WITH FOOD AND DRINK

116. Sulpicius Severus, *Dialogi* 3, in CSEL 1, pp. 200–201.
117. The ascetic man's power was thereby described as having been miraculously extended "lebetem ligneam." Gregory of Tours, *Liber in gloria confessorum* 96, in MGH: SRM 1.2, new edition (Hanover: Impensis bibliopolii Hahniani, 1885), pp. 359–360; De Nie, *Views,* p. 111.
118. Hen notes that there might have been as many as forty-eight feasts a year at the monastery of Chelles, indeed a very busy schedule. Likewise, at Auxerre, there were approximately thirty feasts celebrated in honor of thirty-two saints by the sixth century. Hen, *Culture and Religion,* pp. 96–99.
119. Peter Cramer, *Baptism and Change in the Early Middle Ages c.200-c.1150* (Cambridge: Cambridge University Press, 1993), pp. 130–136; Peter Brown, "The Rise and Function of the Holy Man in Late Antiquity," in his *Society and the Holy in Late Antiquity* (Berkeley: University of California Press, 1982), pp. 123–126.

Notes to Chapter 2

1. Ralph W. Mathisen, *Roman Aristocrats in Barbarian Gaul: Strategies for Survival in an Age of Transition* (Austin: University of Texas Press, 1993), pp. 13–25, 50–53.
2. Aron J. Gurevich, *Categories of Medieval Culture,* translated by G. L. Campbell (London: Routledge & Kegan Paul, 1985), pp. 221–233.
3. Gerd Athoff, "Der frieden-, bündnis- und gemeinschaftstiftende Charakter des Mahles im früheren Mittelalter," in *Essen und Trinken im Mittelalter und Neuzeit: Vorträge eines interdisziplinären Symposions vom 10.–13. Juni 1987 an der Justus-Liebig-Universität Gießen,* edited by Irmgard Bitsch, Trude Ehlert, and Xenja von Ertzdorff (Sigmaringen: Jan Thorbecke Verlag, 1987), pp. 14–15.
4. Wolfgang Fritze, "Die fränkische Schwurfreundschaft der Merowingerzeit: Ihr Wesen und ihre politische Funktion," *Zeitschrift der Savigny-Stiftung für Rechtsgeschichte,* germanistische Abteilung 71 (1954), p.121.
5. Hans-Werner Goetz, "'Beatus homo qui invenire amicum.' The Concept of Friendship in Early Medieval Letters of the Anglo-Saxon Tradition on the Continent (Boniface, Alcuin)," in *Friendship in Medieval Europe,* edited by Julian Haseldine (Phoenix Mill: Sutton Publishing, 1999), pp. 124–136.
6. Robert A. Markus, *The End of Ancient Christianity* (Cambridge: Cambridge University Press, 1990), pp. 14–17.
7. Arnaldo Momigliano, "Popular Religious Beliefs and the Late Roman Historians," in *Popular Belief and Practice. Papers Read at the Ninth Summer Meeting and Tenth Winter Meeting of the Ecclesiastical History Society,* edited by G. J. Cuming and Derek Baker, Studies in Church History 8 (Cambridge: Cambridge University Press, 1972), pp. 12–18.
8. Giles Constable, *Letters and Letter Collections,* Typologie des sources du moyen âge Occidental 17 (Turnhout: Éditions Brepols, 1976), pp. 11–16, 27–30.
9. Dag Norberg, "Remarques sur les lettres de Saint Didier de Cahors," in *Classical, Medieval and Renaissance Studies in Honor of Berthold Louis Ullman*

NOTES 113

1, edited by Charles Henderson (Rome: Edizioni di storia e letteratura, 1964), pp. 277–279.

10. Desiderius of Cahors, *Epistulae* 1.10, edited by Wilhelm Arndt, in CCSL 117 (Turnhout: Typographi Brepols editores pontificii, 1967), pp. 319–320; Ian Wood, "Administration, Law and Culture in Merovingian Gaul," in *The Uses of Literacy in Early Medieval Europe,* edited by Rosamond McKitterick (Cambridge: Cambridge University Press, 1990), pp. 68–70.

11. Wilhelm Levison, ed., *Vita Audoini episcopi Rotomagensis* 4, in MGH: SRM 5 (Hanover: Impensis bibliopolii Hahniani, 1910), p. 556; Fritze, "Die fränkische Schwurfreundschaft," pp. 105–106.

12. Raymond Van Dam, *Leadership and Community in Late Antique Gaul* (Berkeley: University of California Press, 1985), pp. 141–156; Wood, "Administration, Law and Culture," pp. 76–78.

13. Nancy Gauthier, "Le réseau de pouvoirs de l'évêque dans la Gaule du haut moyen-âge," in *Towns and their Territories between Late Antiquity and the Early Middle Ages,* edited by Gian Pietro Brogiolo, Nancy Gauthier, and Neil Christie, TRW 9 (Leiden: E. J. Brill, 2000), pp. 173–178, 182–201.

14. John Percival, "Villas and Monasteries in Late Roman Gaul," *Journal of Ecclesiastical History* 48 (1997), pp. 1–21.

15. Leopold Hellmuth, *Gastfreundschaft und Gastrecht bei den Germanen,* Österreichische Akademie der Wissenschaften, philosophisch-historische Klasse Sitzungsberichte 440 (Vienna: Verlag der Österreichischen Akademie der Wissenschaften, 1984), pp. 25–26.

16. Avitus of Vienne, *Epistolarum ad diversos libri tres* 74, edited by Rudolf Peiper, in MGH: AA 6.2 (Berlin: Apud Weidmannos, 1883), p. 91; Danuta Shanzer, "Bishops, Letters, Fast, Food and Feast in Later Roman Gaul," in *Revisiting Late Roman Gaul,* edited by Ralph Mathisen and Danuta Shanzer (London: Ashgate, 2001), pp. 229–231. I am thankful to Danuta Shanzer for allowing me to see this manuscript in advance of its publication.

17. Jürgen Hannig, "*Ars donandi:* Zur Ökonomie des Schenkens im früheren Mittelalter," in *Armut, Liebe, Ehre: Studien zur historischen Kulturforschung,* edited by Richard van Dülmen (Frankfurt: Fischer Taschenbuch Verlag, 1988), pp. 11–13.

18. Danuta Shanzer, "Two Clocks and a Wedding: Theodoric's Diplomatic Relations with the Burgundians," *Romanobarbarica* 14 (1996–1997), pp. 225–258; Janet L. Nelson, "Monks, Secular Men and Masculinity, c.900," in *Masculinity in Medieval Europe,* edited by Dawn M. Hadley (London: Longman, 1999), pp. 121–123.

19. Ian Wood, "The Frontiers of Western Europe: Developments East of the Rhine in the Sixth Century," in *The Sixth Century: Production, Distribution and Demand,* edited by Richard Hodges and William Bowden, TRW 3 (Leiden: E. J. Brill, 1998), pp. 247–249.

20. Charles de Clercq, ed., *Conc. Matisconense a.581–583* c.5, in *Concilia Galliae a.511–a.695,* CCSL 148a (Turnhout: Typographi Brepols editores pontificii, 1963), p. 224.

114 CREATING COMMUNITY WITH FOOD AND DRINK

21. De Clercq, ed., *Conc. Burdigalense a.662–675* c.1, in *Concilia Galliae*, CCSL 148a, p. 312. See also the second canon of a council held at Saint-Jean-de-Losne, Côte-d'Or, in 673–675. De Clercq, ed., *Conc. Latunense a.673–675* c.2, in *Concilia Galliae*, CCSL 148a, p. 315.

22. Simon Coates, "Venantius Fortunatus and the Image of Episcopal Authority in Late Antique and Early Merovingian Gaul," *English Historical Review* 115 (2000), pp. 1109–1115, 1136–1137.

23. Burnam W. Reynolds, "*Familia sancti Martini: Domus ecclesiae* on Earth as It Is in Heaven," *Journal of Medieval History* 11 (1985), pp. 137–143.

24. Gauthier, "Le réseau de pouvoirs de l'évêque," pp. 178–182.

25. Guy Halsall, "Violence and Society in the Early Medieval West: An Introductory Survey," in his *Violence and Society in the Early Medieval West* (Woodbridge: Boydell & Brewer, 1998), pp. 12–13.

26. Gregory of Tours, *Libri historiarum X* 8.3–8.5, edited by Bruno Krusch, MGH: SRM 1.1, revised edition (Hanover: Impensis bibliopolii Hahniani, 1951), pp. 372–374; Isabel Moreira, *Dreams, Visions and Spiritual Authority in Merovingian Gaul* (Ithaca: Cornell University Press, 2000), pp. 96–97.

27. Jill Harries, "Christianity and the City in Gaul," in *The City in Late Antiquity,* edited by John Rich, Leicester-Nottingham Studies in Ancient Society 3 (London: Routledge, 1992), pp. 82–96.

28. William E. Klingshirn, *Caesarius of Arles: The Making of a Christian Community in Late Antique Gaul* (Cambridge: Cambridge University Press, 1994), pp. 88–93.

29. Conrad Leyser, *Authority and Asceticism from Augustine to Gregory the Great* (Oxford: Clarendon Press, 2000), pp. 84–85.

30. "Nemo in convivio suo cogat alium amplius bibere quam oportet, ne per ebrietatem et suam et illius animam perdat." Caesarius of Arles, *Sermones* 13.3, edited by Germain Morin, revised edition, CCSL 103 (Turnhout: Typographi Brepols editores pontificii, 1953), p. 66; Michael Richter, *The Formation of the Medieval West: Studies in the Oral Culture of the Barbarians* (Dublin: Four Courts Press, 1994), pp. 35–37.

31. "Qui enim alterum cogit ut se plus quam opus est bibendo inebriet, minus malum ei erat, si carnum eis gladium vulneraret, quam animam eius per ebrietatem occideret." Caesarius of Arles, *Sermones* 46.1, edited by Morin, CCSL 103, p. 205.

32. Caesarius of Arles, *Sermones* 46.4, edited by Morin, CCSL 103, p. 207.

33. Bruno Krusch, ed., *Passio Praeiecti episcopi et martyris Arverni* 7, in MGH: SRM 5 (Hanover: Impensis bibliopolii Hahniani, 1910), p. 229.

34. Krusch, ed., *Passio Praeiecti episcopi et martyris Arverni* 8, in MGH: SRM 5, pp. 229–230.

35. Ian Wood, "Letter and Letter-Collections from Antiquity to the Early Middle Ages: The Prose Works of Avitus of Vienne," in *The Culture of Christendom: Essays in Medieval History in Commemoration of Denis L. T. Bethell,* edited by Marc Anthony Meyer (London: The Hambledon Press, 1993), pp. 29–43.

NOTES   115

36. Venantius Fortunatus, *Vita sancti Germani* 18, edited by Bruno Krusch, in MGH: AA 4.2 (Berlin: Apud Weidmannos, 1885), p. 15; Coates, "Venantius Fortunatus," pp. 1129–1130.

37. Guy Halsall, *Settlement and Social Organization: The Merovingian Region of Metz* (Cambridge: Cambridge University Press, 1995), pp. 79–83; Bonnie Effros, "Skeletal Sex and Gender in Merovingian Mortuary Archaeology," *Antiquity* 74 (2000), pp. 632–639.

38. Kate Cooper and Conrad Leyser, "The Gender of Grace: Impotence, Servitude and Manliness in the Fifth-Century West," *Gender & History* 12 (2000), pp. 536–551.

39. Keith Bradley, "The Roman Family at Dinner," in *Meals in a Social Context: Aspects of the Communal Meal in the Hellenistic World,* edited by Inge Nielsen and Hanne Sigismund Nielsen, Åhrus Studies in Mediterranean Antiquity 1 (Åhrus: Åhrus University Press, 1998), pp. 42–51.

40. John Cassian, *De institutis coenobiorum* 1.11 and 3.12, edited by Michael Petschenig, CSEL 17 (Vienna: F. Tempsky, 1888), pp. 15–16, 45.

41. Ian Wood, "A Prelude to Columbanus: The Monastic Achievement in the Burgundian Territories," in *Columbanus and Merovingian Monasticism,* edited by H. B. Clarke and Mary Brennan, BAR International Series 113 (Oxford: BAR, 1981), p. 4.

42. François Martine, ed. and trans., *Vita sancti Romani abbatis* 36–39, in SC 142 (Paris: Les Éditions du CERF, 1968), pp. 278–283. On the reliability of the hagiographical collection, see: François Masai, "La 'Vita patrum iurensium' et les débuts du monachisme à Saint-Maurice-d'Agaune," in *Festschrift Bernhard Bischoff zu seinem 65. Geburtstag,* edited by Johanne Autenrieth and Franz Brunhölzl (Stuttgart: Anton Hierseman, 1971), pp. 48–49, 58–59.

43. François Martine, ed. and trans., *Vita sancti Lupicini abbatis* 71–78, in SC 142, pp. 318–325.

44. Venantius Fortunatus, *Vita sancti Germani* 10–12, edited by Krusch, in MGH: AA 4.2, p. 12; John Kitchen, *Saints' Lives and the Rhetoric of Gender: Male and Female in Merovingian Hagiography* (New York: Oxford University Press, 1998), p. 42.

45. Benedict of Nursia, *Regula* 56, edited by Rudolph Hanslik, revised edition, CSEL 75 (Vienna: Hoelder-Pichler Tempsky, 1977), p. 144.

46. "Vivant enim solis oleribus, et leguminibus, raroque pisciculis fluvialibus, vel marinis: et hoc ipsum quoties se opportunitas fratrum, vel festivitas solemnitatis dederit alicuius, servata in his et similibus causis discretione maiores." Fructuosus of Braga, *Regula monachorum* 5, edited by Jacques-Paul Migne, in PL 87, reprint edition (Turnhout: Brepols, 1982), p. 1102.

47. These emendations were copied into the eighth-century manuscript now known as BN Ms. Lat. 10318. Bruno Laurioux, "Cuisiner à l'antique: Apicius au moyen âge," *Médiévale* 26 (1994), pp. 18–22.

48. Simon T. Loseby, "Marseilles and the Pirenne Thesis, I: Gregory of Tours, the Merovingian Kings, and 'un grand port,'" in *The Sixth Century: Production,*

116   CREATING COMMUNITY WITH FOOD AND DRINK

Distribution and Demand, edited by Richard Hodges and William Bowden, pp. 218–221.

49. Léon Levillain, *Examen critique des chartes mérovingiennes et carolingiennes de l'abbaye de Corbie* 15, Mémoires et documents publiés par la Société de l'École des chartes 5 (Paris: A. Picard et Fils, Éditeurs, 1902), pp. 235–237; Simon T. Loseby, "Marseilles and the Pirenne Thesis, II: 'Ville morte,'" in *The Long Eighth Century,* edited by Inge Lyse Hansen and Chris Wickham, TRW 11 (Leiden: E. J. Brill, 2000), pp. 178–179.

50. Karl Zeumer, ed., *Marculfi formulae* 1.11, in MGH: Formulae 1 (Hanover: Impensis bibliopolii Hahniani, 1886), p. 495; Dietrich Claude, *Untersuchungen zu Handel und Verkehr der vor- und frühgeschichtlichen Zeit in Mittel- und Nordeuropa, 2: Der Handel im westlichen Mittelmeer während des Frühmittelalters,* Abhandlungen der Akademie der Wissenschaften in Göttingen, philologisch-historische Klasse, third series, vol. 144 (Göttingen: Vandenhoeck & Ruprecht, 1985), pp. 71–84.

51. Gregory of Tours, *Liber vitae patrum* 9.1, edited by Bruno Krusch, in MGH: SRM 1.2 (Hanover: Impensis bibliopolii Hahniani, 1885), pp. 252–253; Kitchen, *Saints' Lives,* pp. 93–94.

52. Venantius Fortunatus, *Vita sancti Paterni* 9, edited by Bruno Krusch, in MGH: AA 4.2 (Berlin: Apud Weidmannos, 1885), p. 35; Kitchen, *Saints' Lives,* pp. 46–67.

53. Sulpicius Severus, *Vita sancti Martini* 9.3, edited by Karl Halm, in CSEL 1 (Vienna: Apud C. Geroldi Filium, 1866), p. 119; Venantius Fortunatus, *Vita sancti Martini* 2.447–2.479, and 3.518–3.528, in MGH: AA 4.2, pp. 328–329, 347; Raymond Van Dam, *Saints and their Miracles in Late Antique Gaul* (Princeton: Princeton University Press, 1993), pp. 13–28; Coates, "Venantius Fortunatus," pp. 1117–1118.

54. Conrad Leyser, "'This Sainted Isle': Panegyric, Nostalgia, and the Invention of Lerinian Monasticism," in *The Limits of Ancient Christianity: Essays on Late Antique Thought and Culture in Honor of R. A. Markus,* edited by William E. Klingshirn and Mark Vessey (Ann Arbor: University of Michigan Press, 1999), pp. 188–206.

55. Jerome, *Epistulae* 3.125, edited by Isidore Hilberg, CSEL 56, revised edition (Vienna: Verlag der Österreichischen Akademie der Wissenschaften, 1996), pp. 124–131; Arbesmann, "Fasting and Prophecy," pp. 38–39; Veronika E. Grimm, *From Feasting to Fasting, the Evolution of a Sin: Attitudes to Food in Late Antiquity* (London: Routledge, 1996), pp. 171–178.

56. Aline Rousselle, "Abstinence et continence dans les monastères de Gaule méridionale à la fin de l'antiquité et au début du moyen age: Étude d'un régime alimentaire et de sa fonction," in *Hommage à André Dupont (1987–1972): Études médiévales languedociennes* (Montpellier: Féderation historique du Languedoc méditerranéen et du Roussillon, 1974), pp. 239–254.

57. Conrad Leyser, "Masculinity in Flux: Nocturnal Emission and the Limits of Celibacy in the Early Middle Ages," in *Masculinity in Medieval Europe,* edited by Dawn M. Hadley (London: Longman, 1999), pp. 103–120.

NOTES 117

58. Regarding Patroclus, Gregory stated: "Vinum, sicera uel omne quod inebriare potest non bibebat praeter aquam parumper melle linitam; sed nec pulmentum aliquod utebatur. Cuius uictus erat panis in aqua infusus atque sale respersus." Gregory of Tours, *Libri historiarum X* 5.10, edited by Krusch, MGH: SRM 1.1, p. 204; Gregory of Tours, *Liber vitae patrum* 13.1, edited by Krusch, in MGH: SRM 1.2, pp. 265–266; Walter Guelphe, "L'éretisme dans le sud-ouest de la Gaule à l'époque mérovingienne," *Annales du Midi* 98 (1986), p. 311.

59. Gregory of Tours, *Liber vitae patrum* 12.1 and 14.2, edited by Krusch, in MGH: SRM 1.2, pp. 262, 268–269.

60. Gregory of Tours, *Liber vitae patrum* 11.1, edited by Krusch, in MGH: SRM 1.2, pp. 259–260; Kitchen *Saints' Lives,* pp. 84–87.

61. Gregory of Tours, *Liber vitae patrum* 9.1, edited by Krusch, in MGH: SRM 1.2, pp. 252–253.

62. Coates, "Venantius Fortunatus," pp. 1124–1126.

63. Bruno Krusch, ed., *Vita Carileffi abbatis Anisolensis* 7–8, in MGH: SRM 3 (Hanover: Impensis bibliopolii Hahniani, 1896), pp. 391–392. Massimo Montanari, by contrast, reads this miracle story as symptomatic of Germanic resistance to wine as opposed to beer. Massimo Montanari, *The Culture of Food,* translated by Carl Ipsen (Oxford: Blackwell, 1994), pp. 18–19.

64. Gregory of Tours, *De virtutibus beati Martini episcopi* 3.1, edited by Krusch, in MGH: SRM 1.2, p. 182; Edward James, "A Sense of Wonder: Gregory of Tours, Medicine and Science," in *The Culture of Christendom: Essays in Commemoration of Denis L. T. Bethell,* p. 54.

65. Marc Van Uytfanghe, *Stylisation biblique et condition humaine dans l'hagiographie mérovingienne (650–750),* Verhandelingen van de Koninklijke Academie voor Wetenschnappen, Letteren en Schone Kunsten van België, Klasse der Letteren, 49, vol. 120 (Brussels: Paleis der Academiën, 1987), pp. 102–110.

66. Gregory of Tours, *Liber vitae patrum* 5, edited by Krusch, in MGH: SRM 1.2, pp. 227–229.

67. Jonas of Bobbio, *Vitae Columbani abbatis et discipulorumque eius, libri II* 1.19, edited by Bruno Krusch, in MGH: SRM 37 (Hanover: Impensis bibliopolii Hahniani, 1905), pp. 187–189.

68. On the more effective expression and manipulation of anger in another Merovingian *vita,* see: Catherine Peyroux, "Reading Anger in an Early Medieval Saint's Life," in *Anger's Past: The Social Uses of Emotion in the Middle Ages,* edited by Barbara Rosenwein (Ithaca: Cornell University Press, 1998), pp. 36–55.

69. Paul Veyne, *Bread and Circuses: Historical Sociology and Political Pluralism,* abridged with an introduction by Oswyn Murray, translated by Brian Pearce (London: Penguin Books, 1990), pp. 24–33.

70. Nancy Gauthier, "La topographie chrétienne entre idéologie et pragmatisme," in *The Idea and Ideal of the Town between Late Antiquity and the Early Middle Ages,* edited by Gian Pietro Brogiolo and Bryan Ward-Perkins, TRW 4 (Leiden: E. J. Brill, 1999), pp. 195–209.

118   CREATING COMMUNITY WITH FOOD AND DRINK

71. Simon T. Loseby, "Arles in Late Antiquity: *Gallula Roma Arelas* and *Urbs Genesii*," in *Towns in Transition: Urban Evolution in Late Antiquity and the Early Middle Ages,* edited by Neil Christie and Simon T. Loseby (Aldershot: Scolar Press, 1996), pp. 58–67.

72. Hans-Werner Goetz, "Der kirchliche Festtag im frühmittelalterlichen Alltag," in *Feste und Feiern im Mittelalter: Paderborner Symposion des Mediävistenverbandes,* edited by Detlef Altenburg, Jörg Jarnut and Hans-Hugo Steinhoff (Sigmaringen: Jan Thorbecke Verlag, 1991), pp. 53–54.

73. Gregory of Tours, *Libri historiarum X* 2.23, edited by Krusch, MGH: SRM 1.1, pp. 68–69.

74. Gregory of Tours, *Liber vitae patrum* 6.3–4, edited by Krusch, in MGH: SRM 1.2, pp. 232–233; Charles Pietri, "L'espace chrétien dans la cité: Le *vicus christianorum* et l'espace chrétien de la cité arverne (Clermont)," *Revue d'histoire de l'église de France* 66 (1980), pp. 185–186.

75. Gregory of Tours, *Liber de virtutibus sancti Juliani* 34–36, edited by Krusch, in MGH: SRM 1.2, pp. 138–139; Giselle de Nie, *Views from a Many-Windowed Tower. Studies of Imagination in the Works of Gregory of Tours,* Studies in Classical Antiquity 7 (Amsterdam: Rodopi, 1987), pp. 112–113.

76. Sidonius Apollinaris, *Epistulae* 5.14 and 7.15, edited by Christian Luetjohann, MGH: AA 8 (Berlin: Apud Weidmannos, 1887), pp. 87–88, 122.

77. Harries, "Christianity and the City," pp. 77–98.

78. Ian Wood, "Topographies of Holy Power in Sixth-Century Gaul," in *Topographies of Power in the Early Middle Ages,* edited by Mayke de Jong and Frans Theuws, TRW 6 (Leiden: E. J. Brill, 2001), pp. 150–153.

79. C. Munier, ed., *Conc. Agathense a. 506* c.21, in *Concilia Galliae a. 314-a. 506,* CCSL 148 (Turnhout: Typographi Brepols editores pontificii, 1963), pp. 202–203; Coates, "Venantius Fortunatus," pp. 1119–1120.

80. "Vt nulli ciuium pascae, natalis Domini uel quinquaginsimae sollemnitatem in uilla leceat celebrare, nisi quem infirmitas probabitur tenuisse." De Clercq, ed., *Conc. Aurelianense a. 511* c.25, in *Concilia Galliae,* CCSL 148a, p. 11.

81. De Clercq, ed., *Conc. Aurelianense a. 541* c.3, CCSL 148a, pp. 132–133.

82. Ian Wood, "Early Merovingian Devotion in Town and Country," in *The Church in Town and Countryside: Papers Read at the Seventeenth Summer Meeting and the Eighteenth Winter Meeting of the Ecclesiastical History Society,* edited by Derek Baker, Studies in Church History 16 (Oxford: Basil Blackwell, 1979), pp. 61–68, 71.

83. Paul Fouracre, "The Work of Audoenus of Rouen and Eligius of Noyon in Extending Episcopal Influence from the Town to the Country in Seventh-Century Neustria," in *The Church in Town and Countryside,* pp. 77–81.

84. Simon T. Loseby, "Gregory's Cities: Urban Functions in Sixth-Century Gaul," in *Franks and Alamanni in the Merovingian Period: An Ethnographic Perspective,* edited by Ian Wood, Studies in Archaeoethnology 3 (Woodbridge: The Boydell Press, 1998), pp. 252–257.

85. Donald A. Bullough, "Social and Economic Structure and Topography of the Early Medieval City," in *Topografia urbana et vita cittadina nell'alto medio-*

NOTES 119

evo in Occidente, 26 aprile–1 maggio 1973 1, Settimane di studio del Centro italiano di studi sull'alto medioevo 21 (Spoleto: Presso la sede del Centro, 1974), pp. 369–370.

86. Walther Schönfeld, "Die Xenodochien in Italien und Frankreich im frühen Mittelalter," *Zeitschrift der Savigny-Stiftung für Rechtsgeschichte,* kanonistische Abteilung 12 (1922), pp. 5–18.

87. See for instance: De Clercq, ed., *Conc. Aurelianense a.549* c.13, in *Concilia Galliae,* CCSL 148a, p. 152.

88. Sidonius Apollinaris, *Epistulae* 6.12, edited by Luetjohann, MGH:AA 8, p. 101; Harries, "Christianity and the City," p. 91.

89. Venantius Fortunatus, *Opera poetica* 3.13, edited by Friedrich Leo, MGH: AA 4.1 (Berlin: Apud Weidmannos, 1881), pp. 65–66; Coates, "Venantius Fortunatus," pp. 1120–1121. Translation taken from Venantius Fortunatus, *Personal and Political Poems,* translated by Judith George, Translated Texts for Historians 23 (Liverpool: Liverpool University Press, 1995), pp. 1–2.

90. "Volumus igitur, quod episcopalis domus, quae ad hoc Deo fauente instituta est, ut sine personarum acceptione omnes in hospitalitate recipiat, canes non habeat, ne forte hii, qui in ea meseriarum suarum leuamen habere confidunt, dum infestorum canum morsibus laniantur, detrimentum uersa uice suorum susteneant corporum." De Clercq, ed., *Conc Matisconense a.585* c.13, in *Concilia Galliae,* CCSL 148a, p. 245; Loseby, "Gregory's Cities," p. 257.

91. Augustine of Hippo, *Confessionum libri XIII* 10.31, edited by Lucas Verheijen, CCSL 27 (Turnhout: Typographi Brepols editores pontificii, 1981), pp. 177–180; Grimm, *From Feasting to Fasting,* pp. 181–182.

Notes to Chapter 3

1. Lynda L. Coon, *Sacred Fictions: Holy Women and Hagiography in Late Antiquity* (Philadelphia: University of Pennsylvania press, 1997), pp. 43–44.

2. Jo Ann McNamara, "The Need to Give: Suffering and Female Sanctity in the Early Middle Ages," in *Images of Sanctity in Medieval Europe,* edited by Renate Blumenfeld-Kosinski and Timea Szell (Ithaca: Cornell University Press, 1991), pp. 199–202.

3. John Kitchen, *Saints' Lives and the Rhetoric of Gender: Male and Female in Merovingian Hagiography* (New York: Oxford University Press, 1998), pp. 13–15; Françoise Thelamon, "Ascèse et sociabilité. Les conduites alimentaires des moines d'Egypte au IVᵉ siècle," *Revue des études augustiniennes* 38 (1992), pp. 314–318.

4. Avitus of Vienne, *Poematum libri VI* 6.636–647, edited by Rudolf Peiper, in MGH:AA 6.2 (Berlin: Apud Weidmannos, 1883), p. 293.

5. Although Régine le Jan refers specifically to seventh-century Francia, the vulnerability of convents to military violence and civil unrest must have represented a similar concern to bishops in southern Gaul during the previous century as well. Régine Le Jan, "Convents, Violence and Competition

120   CREATING COMMUNITY WITH FOOD AND DRINK

for Power in Seventh-Century Francia," in *Topographies of Power in the Early Middle Ages,* edited by Mayke de Jong and Frans Theuws, TRW 6 (Leiden: E. J. Brill, 2001), pp. 243–269.

6. G. Sartory, "In der Arena der Askese. Fasten im frühen Christentum," in *Speisen, Schlemmen, Fasten. Eine Kulturgeschichte des Essens,* edited by Uwe Schultz, (Frankfurt: Insel, 1993), pp. 71–82; Susanna Elm, *"Virgins of God": The Making of Asceticism in Late Antiquity* (Oxford: Clarendon Press, 1994), pp. 253–282.

7. Massimo Montanari, *The Culture of Food,* translated by Carl Ipsen (Oxford: Blackwell, 1994), pp. 23–25.

8. Keith Bradley, "The Roman Family at Dinner," in *Meals in a Social Context: Aspects of the Communal Meal in the Hellenistic World,* edited by Inge Nielsen and Hanne Sigismund Nielsen, Åhrus Studies in Mediterranean Antiquity 1 (Åhrus: Åhrus University Press, 1998), pp. 43–44.

9. See for instance, Jerome's praise for extreme forms of fasting in his letter to Furia: Jerome, *Epistulae* 1.54, edited by Isidore Hilberg, CSEL 54, revised edition (Vienna: Verlag der Österreichischen Akademie der Wissenschaften, 1996), pp. 466–479; Veronika E. Grimm, *From Feasting to Fasting, The Evolution of a Sin: Attitudes to Food in Late Antiquity* (London: Routledge, 1996), pp. 162–196.

10. Caesarius of Arles, *Ad regulam virginum* 67, edited by Germain Morin, in *Sanctus Caesarius episcopus Arelatensis, Opera omnia* 2 (Brugges: Jos. Van der Meersch, 1942), p. 120.

11. Venantius Fortunatus, *De vita sanctae Radegundis* 1.15 and 1.21, edited by Bruno Krusch, in MGH: SRM 2, new edition (Hanover: Impensis bibliopolii Hahniani, 1956), pp. 369, 371; Bruno Krusch, ed., *Vita Rusticulae sive Marciae abbatissae Arelatensis* 7, in MGH: SRM 4 (Hanover: Impensis bibliopolii Hahniani, 1902), p. 343.

12. Gregory of Tours, *Liber vitae patrum* 19.1, edited by Bruno Krusch, in MGH: SRM 1.2 (Hanover: Impensis bibliopolii Hahniani, 1885), pp. 286–287; Kitchen *Saints' Lives,* pp. 101–108, 113.

13. Benedicta Ward, "Pelagia: Beauty Riding By," in her *Harlots of the Desert: A Study of Repentance in Early Monastic Sources* (Kalamazoo: Cistercian Publications, Inc., 1987), pp. 57–75.

14. Grimm, *From Feasting to Fasting,* pp. 162–171.

15. Aline Rousselle, "Abstinence et continence dans les monastères de Gaule méridionale à la fin de l'antiquité et au début du moyen age: Étude d'un régime alimentaire et de sa fonction," in *Hommage à André Dupont (1897–1972): Études médiévales languedociennes* (Montpellier: Féderation historique du Languedoc méditerranen et du Roussillon, 1974), pp. 239–242; Rudolph Arbesmann, "Fasting and Prophecy in Pagan and Christian Antiquity," *Traditio* 7 (1949), pp. 35–36; Grimm, *From Feasting to Fasting,* pp. 171–196.

16. "Qui dominica ieiunat, peccat." Caesarius of Arles, *Regula monachorum,* edited by Germain Morin, in *Sanctus Caesarius episcopus Arelatensis, Opera omnia* 2, p. 153.

17. Venantius Fortunatus, *Opera poetica* Appendix 29, edited by Friedrich Leo, MGH: AA 4.1 (Berlin: Apud Weidmannos, 1961), p. 290; Judith W. George,

NOTES 121

Venantius Fortunatus: A Latin Poet in Merovingian Gaul (Oxford: Clarendon Press, 1992), pp. 173–174.

18. Ferreolus of Uzès, *Regula ad monachos* 35, edited by Jacques-Paul Migne, in *PL* 66 (Paris: Apud J.-P. Migne, Editorem, 1866), p. 972.

19. Avitus of Vienne, *Poematum libri VI* 2.204–276, edited by Peiper, in MGH: AA 6.2, pp. 217–219.

20. Marc van Uytfanghe, *Stylisation biblique et condition humaine dans l'hagiographie mérovingienne (650–750),* Verhandelingen van de Koninklijke Academie voor Wetenschnappen, Letteren en Schone Kunsten van België, Klasse der Letteren 49, vol. 120 (Brussels: Paleis der Academiën, 1987), pp. 161–169; Michael J. Enright, *Lady with a Mead Cup: Ritual, Prophesy and Lordship in the European Warband from La Tène to the Viking Age* (Dublin: Four Courts Press, 1996), pp. 16–17.

21. Bridget Ann Henisch, *Fast and Feast: Food in Medieval Society* (University Park: Pennsylvania State University Press, 1976), pp. 2–10.

22. Walther Schönfeld, "Die Xenodochien in Italien und Frankreich im frühen Mittelalter," *Zeitschrift der Savigny-Stiftung für Rechtsgeschichte, kanonistische Abteilung* 12 (1922), pp. 5–13.

23. Sulpicius Severus, *Dialogi* 12, edited by Karl Halm, in CSEL 1 (Vienna: Apud C. Geroldi Filium Bibliopolam Academiae, 1866), p. 194; René Metz, "Les vièrges chrétiennes en Gaule au IVe siècle," in *Saint Martin et son temps: Memorial au XVIe centenaire des débuts du monachisme en Gaule 361–1961,* Studia anselmiana 46 (Rome: Herder, 1961), pp. 119–120.

24. Krusch, ed., *Vita Rusticulae sive Marciae abbatissae Arelatensis* 4, in MGH: SRM 4, p. 341. On the authenticity of this Merovingian *vita,* see: Pierre Riché, "Note d'hagiographie mérovingienne: La vita S. Rusticulae," *Analecta bollandiana* 72 (1954), pp. 369–377.

25. D.C. Lambot, "Le prototype des monastères cloîtrés de femmes: L'abbaye Saint-Jean d'Arles (VIe siècle)," *Revue liturgique et monastique* 23 (1937–1938), pp. 170–174.

26. David G. Hunter, "Clerical Celibacy and the Veiling of Virgins: New Boundaries in Late Ancient Christianity," in *The Limits of Ancient Christianity: Essays on Late Antique Thought and Culture in Honor of R. A. Markus,* edited by William E. Klingshirn and Mark Vessey (Ann Arbor: University of Michigan Press, 1999), pp. 142–144.

27. Metz, "Les vièrges chrétiennes," pp. 109–132.

28. Caesarius of Arles, *Ad regulam virginum* 1, edited by Morin, in *Sanctus Caesarius episcopus Arelatensis, Opera omnia* 2, pp. 101–102. On the manuscript tradition of this *Rule,* see: Germain Morin, "Problèmes relatifs à la règle de S. Césaire d'Arles pour les moniales," *Revue bénédictine* 44 (1932), pp. 5–20.

29. William E. Klingshirn, *Caesarius of Arles: The Making of a Christian Community in Late Antique Gaul* (Cambridge: Cambridge University Press, 1994), pp. 104–107, 117–123.

30. "Si quas parentibus suis saeculo renuntiare et sanctum ovile voluerit introire, ut spiritalium luporum faucibus deo adiuvante possit evadere, usque

ad mortem suam non egrediatur, nec in basilicam, ob ostium esse videtur."
Caesarius of Arles, *Ad regulam virginum* 2, edited by Morin, in *Sanctus Caesarius episcopus Arelatensis, Opera omnia* 2, p. 102.

31. Charles de Clercq, ed., *Conc. Aurelianense a.549* c.19, in *Concilia Galliae a.511-a.695,* in CCSL 148a (Turnhout: Typographi Brepols editores pontificii, 1963), p. 155.

32. Augustine of Hippo, *Opera omnia* Ep. 211, edited by Jacques-Paul Migne, in PL 33 (Paris: Apud editorem in via dicta d'Amboise, 1845), pp. 958–965.

33. Ambrose of Milan, *De virginibus libri tres* 3.2 and 3.4, edited by Egnatius Cazzaniga, in Corpus scriptorum latinorum Pravianum (Turin: In aedibus Io. Bapt. Paraviae et sociorum, 1948), pp. 59, 64.

34. John Cassian, *De institutis coenobiorum* 3.8, edited by Michael Petschenig, CSEL 17 (Vienna: F. Tempsky, 1888), pp. 42–43.

35. Friedrich Prinz, *Frühes Mönchtum im Frankenreich: Kultur und Gesellschaft in Gallien, den Rheinlanden und Bayern am Beispiel der monastischen Entwicklung (4. bis 8. Jahrhundert),* second edition (Munich: R. Oldenbourg Verlag, 1988), pp. 72–77.

36. For the problematic dating of the adoption of Caesarius's *Rule* at Poitiers based in part on Gregory of Tours's *Libri historiarum X* 9.40, see: René Aigrain, "Le voyage de Sainte Radegonde à Arles," *Bulletin philologique et historique* (1926–1927), pp. 119–127.

37. Georg Scheibelreiter, "Königstöchter im Kloster: Radegund (+587) und der Nonnenaufstand von Poitiers (589)," *Mitteilungen des Instituts für österreichische Geschichtsforschung* 87 (1979), pp. 14–16; Fernand Benoit, "Topographie monastique d'Arles au VIe siècle," in *Études mérovingiennes: Actes des journées de Poitiers 1er–3 mai 1952* (Poitiers: Éditions A. et J. Picard, 1953), pp. 13–17.

38. Donald Hochstetler gives a basic outline of the implications of claustration on nuns' daily lives, but does not discuss why such stringent requirements were appropriate to women and not to men. Donald Hochstetler, "The Meaning of Monastic Cloister for Women According to Caesarius of Arles," in *Religion, Culture, and Society in the Early Middle Ages. Studies in Honor of Richard E. Sullivan,* edited by Thomas F. X. Noble and John J. Contreni (Kalamazoo: Medieval Institute Publications, 1987), pp. 27–40.

39. D. C. Lambot attributes the need for claustration to abuses by virgins of their freedoms, but does not specify what they were nor does he indicate why the abuses were supposedly evident only among female religious. Lambot, "Le prototype des monastères," pp. 170–174.

40. Klingshirn, *Caesarius of Arles,* pp. 117–123.

41. Roberta Gilchrist, *Gender and Material Culture: The Archaeology of Religious Women* (London: Routledge, 1993), pp. 4–8.

42. Hans-Werner Goetz, "Heiligenkult und Geschlecht: Geschlectsspezifisches Wunderwirken in frühmittelalterliche Mirakelberichten?" *Das Mittelalter* 1 (1996), pp. 89–111; Hans-Werner Goetz, "*Nomen feminile:* Namen und Namengebung der Frauen im frühen Mittelalter," *Francia* 23 (1996), pp.

NOTES

99–134. He points out some of the problematic aspects of studies seeking to incorporate quantitative data, such as: Jane Tibbetts Schulenberg, "Female Sanctity: Public and Private Roles, ca. 500–1100," in *Women and Power in the Middle Ages,* edited by Mary Erler and Maryanne Kowaleski (Athens: University of Georgia Press, 1988), pp. 102–125.

43. Maurice Godelier, *Idéel et le matériel: Pensée, économies, sociétés* (Paris: Librairie Arthème Fayard, 1984), pp. 46–61.

44. Prinz, *Frühes Monchtum,* pp. 76–77; J. Biarne, "Les temps du moine d'après les premières règles monastiques d'Occident (IVe-VIe siècles)," in *Les temps chrétien de la fin de l'antiquité au moyen âge IIIe-XIIIe siècles,* Colloques internationaux du CNRS 604 (Paris: Éditions du CNRS, 1984), p. 101.

45. Caesarius of Arles, *Ad regulam virginum* 71, edited by Morin, in *Sanctus Caesarius episcopus Arelatensis, Opera omnia* 2, p. 123; Caesarius of Arles, *Regula monachorum,* edited by Morin, in *Sanctus Caesarii episcopus Arelatensis, Opera omnia* 2, p. 154.

46. Caesarius of Arles, *Ad regulam virginum* 14 and 30, edited by Morin, in *Sanctus Caesarius episcopus Arelatensis, Opera omnia* 2, pp. 104, 108–109.

47. Caesarius of Arles, *Regula monachorum,* edited by Morin, in *Sanctus Caesarius episcopus Arelatensis, Opera omnia* 2, pp. 150–154.

48. Rousselle, "Abstinence et continence," pp. 242–246.

49. Caesarius of Arles, *Regula monachorum,* edited by Morin, in *Sanctus Caesarius episcopus Arelatensis, Opera omnia* 2, pp. 153–154.

50. Caesarius of Arles, *Ad regulam virginum* 67, edited by Morin, in *Sanctus Caesarius episcopus Arelatensis, Opera omnia* 2, p. 120.

51. Caesarius of Arles, *Sanctae sorori Caesariae abbatissae* 3, edited by Morin, in *Sanctus Caesarius episcopus Arelatensis, Opera omnia* 2, p. 136.

52. "Convivium etiam his personis, hic est, episcopis, abbatibus, monachis, clericis, saecularibus viris, mulieribus in habitu saeculari, nec abbatissae parentibus, nec alicuius sanctimonialis numquam, nec in monasterio, vel extra monasterium praeparetis: sed nec episcopo huius civitatis, nec provisori quidem ipsius monasterii convivium fiat. De civitate vero nec religiosae feminae, nisi forte sint magnae conversationis et quae monasterium satis honorent; et hoc rarissime fiat." Caesarius of Arles, *Ad regulam virginum* 39, edited by Morin, in *Sanctus Caesarius episcopus Arelatensis, Opera omnia* 2, p. 112.

53. "Si qua tamen de alia civitate ad requirendam filiam suam, aut ad visitandum monasterium venerit, si religiosa est, et abbatissae visum fuerit, debet ad convivium revocari, reliquae populo debent orare, quam corporalia convivia praeparare. Si quis vero germanam suam, vel filia, aut quamlibet parentem, aut sibi cognatam videre voluerit, praesente formaria vel qualibet seniore ei conloquium non negetur." Caesarius of Arles, *Ad regulam virginum* 40, edited by Morin, in *Sanctus Caesarius episcopus Arelatensis, Opera omnia* 2, p. 112.

54. Caesarius of Arles, *Ad regulam virginum* 53, edited by Morin, in *Sanctus Caesarius episcopus Arelatensis, Opera omnia* 2, p. 116; Morin, "Problèmes relatifs," pp. 12–15.

124   CREATING COMMUNITY WITH FOOD AND DRINK

55. Adalbert de Vogüé, "La règle de Donat pour l'abbesse Gauthstrude," *Benedictina* 25 (1978), c.58, pp. 294–295.

56. Charles de Clercq, *La législation religieuse franque de Clovis à Charlemagne. Études sur les actes de conciles et les capitulaires, les statuts diocésaines et les règles monastiques 507–814* (Louvain: Bibliothèque de l'Université, 1936), pp. 85–87; Prinz, *Frühes Mönchtum*, p. 80.

57. Benedict of Nursia, *Regula* 56, edited by Rudolph Hanslik, CSEL 75, revised edition (Vienna: Hoelder-Pichler Tempsky, 1977), p. 144.

58. Aurelian of Arles, *Regula ad monachos* 48, edited by Jacques-Paul Migne, in PL 68 (Paris: Apud editorem in via dicta d'Amboise, 1847), p. 392.

59. Aurelian of Arles, *Regula ad virgines,* edited by Jacques-Paul Migne, in PL 68, pp. 397–408.

60. De Vogüé, "La règle de Donat," c.58, p. 295.

61. Leander of Seville, *Liber de institutione virginum et contemptu mundi ad Florentinam sororem* 4, 8, 9 and 15, edited by Jacques-Paul Migne, in PL 72 (Paris: Paul Garnier fratres, editores, 1878), pp. 882–885, 889.

62. Venantius Fortunatus and Baudonivia, *De vita sanctae Radegundis libri II,* new edition, edited by Krusch, in MGH SRM 2, pp. 358–395; Gregory of Tours, *Liber in gloria confessorum* 104, edited by Bruno Krusch, in MGH: SRM 1.2 (Hanover: Impensis bibliopolii Hahniani, 1885), pp. 814–816; Gregory of Tours, *Liber in gloria martyrum* 5, edited by Bruno Krusch, in MGH: SRM 1.2, pp. 489–492; Gregory of Tours, *Libri historiarum X* 3.7, 9.2; 9.39–43; 10.15–17, edited by Bruno Krusch, MGH: SRM 1.1, revised edition (Hanover: Impensis bibliopolii Hahniani, 1951), pp. 103–105, 415, 460–475, 501–509.

63. Venantius Fortunatus, *Opera poetica,* edited by Leo, in MGH: AA 4.1.

64. Dick Harrison, *The Age of Abbesses and Queens: Gender and Political Culture in Early Medieval Europe* (Lund: Nordic Academic Press, 1998), pp. 94–95.

65. De Clercq, ed., *Conc. Aurelianense a.511* c.19 and 22, in *Concilia Galliae,* CCSL 148a, pp. 10–11.

66. De Clercq, ed., *Conc. Aurelianense a.533* c.21, in *Concilia Galliae,* CCSL 148a, pp. 102.

67. De Clercq, ed., *Conc. Arelatense a.554* c.2, in *Concilia Galliae,* CCSL 148a, pp. 171–172.

68. Scheibelreiter, "Königstöchter," pp. 1–5, 10; Brian Brennan, "St. Radegund and the Early Development of her Cult at Poitiers," *Journal of Religious History* 13 (1985), pp. 340–346.

69. Étienne Delaruelle, "Sainte Radegonde, son type de sainteté et la chrétienté de son temps," in *Études mérovingiennes,* pp. 65–72.

70. Bonnie Effros, "Symbolic Expressions of Sanctity: Gertrude of Nivelles in the Context of Merovingian Mortuary Custom," *Viator* 27 (1996), pp. 1–10.

71. Sabine Gäbe, "Radegundis: Sancta, Regina, Ancilla. Zum Heiligskeitideal der Radegundsviten von Fortunat und Baudonivia," *Francia* 16(1989), pp. 2–4; Delaruelle, "Sainte Radegonde," pp. 69–70.

NOTES

72. Gregory of Tours, *Libri historiarum X* 3.7, edited by Krusch, MGH: SRM 1.1, p. 105.
73. George, *Venantius Fortunatus,* pp. 169–173.
74. Brennan, "St. Radegund," pp. 341–342; Jo Ann McNamara and John E. Halborg, trans., *Sainted Women of the Dark Ages* (Durham: Duke University Press, 1992), p. 63; Maria Caritas McCarthy, trans., *The Rule for Nuns of Caesarius of Arles: A Translation with a Critical Introduction,* Catholic University of America, Studies in Mediaeval History, new series 16 (Washington, D.C.: Catholic University of America, 1960), p. 160.
75. Caroline Walker Bynum, *Holy Feast and Holy Fast: The Religious Significance of Food to Medieval Women* (Berkeley: University of California Press, 1987), pp. 78–84.
76. Aline Rousselle, *Porneia: On Desire and the Body in Antiquity,* translated by Felicia Pheasant (Cambridge: Blackwell, 1988), pp. 160–173.
77. For the use of asceticism, in particular sexual asceticism, to advance clerical authority in late antiquity, see: Kate Cooper, *The Virgin and the Bride: Idealized Womanhood in Late Antiquity* (Cambridge: Harvard University Press, 1996), pp. 55–59.
78. Simon Coates, "Regendering Radegund? Fortunatus, Baudonivia and the Problem of Female Sanctity in Merovingian Gaul," in *Gender and Christian Religion: Papers Read at the 1996 Summer Meeting and the 1997 Winter Meeting of the Ecclesiastical History Society,* edited by R. N. Swanson, Studies in Church History 34 (Woodbridge: The Boydell Press, 1998), pp. 40–42.
79. Venantius Fortunatus, *De vita sanctae Radegundis* 1.15 and 1.21, edited by Krusch, in MGH: SRM 2, pp. 369, 371.
80. Wilhelm Gundlach, ed., *Epistolae aevi Merovingicae collectae* 11, in MGH: Epistolae 1 (Berlin: Apud Weidmannos, 1892), p. 452.
81. Venantius Fortunatus wrote:

> *Fortunatus agens, Agnes quoque versibus orant,*
> *Ut lassata nimis vina benigna bibas.*
> . . . .
> *non gula vos, sed causa trahat modo sumere vina,*
> *talis enim potus viscera lassa iuvat.*
> *sic quoque Timotheum Paulus, tuba gentibus una*
> *ne stomachum infirmet sumere vina iubet.*

Venantius Fortunatus, *Opera poetica* 11.4, edited by Leo, MGH: AA 4.1, p. 269; George, *Venantius Fortunatus,* p. 172.
82. Baudonivia, *De vita sanctae Radegundis libri II* 2.7–8, edited by Krusch, in MGH: SRM 2, pp. 382–383.
83. Jacques Fontaine, "Hagiographie et politique, de Sulpice Sévère à Venance Fortunat," *Revue historique écclesiastique en France* 62 (1976), pp. 113–140. There is no concrete reason to doubt Baudonivia's authorship of the latter

vita. Louise Coudanne, "Baudonivie, moniale de Sainte-Croix et biographe de Sainte-Radegonde," in *Études mérovingiennes*, pp. 45–49.

84. George, *Venantius Fortunatus*, pp. 161–168.

85. Bonnie Effros, "Images of Sanctity: Contrasting Descriptions of Radegund by Venantius Fortunatus and Gregory of Tours," *UCLA Historical Journal* 10 (1990), pp. 38–58.

86. Baudonivia, *De vita sanctae Radegundis libri II* 2.16, edited by Krusch, in MGH: SRM 2, p. 388; Gregory of Tours, *Liber in gloria martyrum* 5, edited by Krusch, in MGH: SRM 1.2, p. 489; Gäbe, "Radegundis," pp. 5–15; Suzanne Fonay Wemple, *Women in Frankish Society: Marriage and the Cloister 500–900* (Philadelphia: University of Pennsylvania Press, 1981), pp. 181–185.

87. Gregory of Tours, *Libri historiarum X* 10.16, edited by Krusch, MGH: SRM 1.1, p. 506. For commentary on this incident: McNamara and Halborg, trans., *Sainted Women of the Dark Ages*, pp. 64–65.

88. Caesarius of Arles, *Ad regulam virginum* 14, 30, 71, edited by Morin, in *Sanctus Caesarius episcopus Arelatensis, Opera omnia* 2, pp. 104, 108–109, 123. McCarthy notes that these measures were derived from Cassian's *Rule* for monks. McCarthy, ed., *The Rule for Nuns*, pp. 174, 180, 202–204.

89. Venantius Fortunatus, *De vita sanctae Radegundis* 1.17, 1.20, 1.24, edited by Krusch, in MGH: SRM 2, pp. 370–372; Kitchen, *Saints' Lives*, pp. 144–145.

90. For specific references to *convivia* in the poetry of Fortunatus, see: Venantius Fortunatus, *Opera poetica* 11.22, 11.22a, 11.23, 11.23a, edited by Leo, MGH: AA 4.1, pp. 267–268. Fortunatus's descriptions of food were not merely symbolic but acknowledged the nuns' patronage in poems such as "Pro ovis et prunis." Venantius Fortunatus, *Opera poetica* 11.20, edited by Leo, MGH AA 4.1, p. 266.

91. Venantius Fortunatus, *De vita sanctae Radegundis* 1.31, 2.10, edited by Krusch, in MGH: SRM 2, pp. 374, 384–385; Kitchen, *Saints' Lives*, pp. 152–153.

92. Bruno Krusch, ed., *Vita Genovefae virginis Parisiensis* 21, in MGH: SRM 3 (Hanover: Impensis bibliopolii Hahniani, 1896), p. 18; Giselle de Nie, *Views from a Many-Windowed Tower: Studies of Imagination in the Works of Gregory of Tours* (Amsterdam: Rodopi, 1987), pp. 112–113.

93. Jo Ann McNamara, "A Legacy of Miracles: Hagiography and Nunneries in Merovingian Gaul," in *Women of the Medieval World*, edited by Julius Kirshner and Suzanne F. Wemple (Oxford: Basil Blackwell, 1985), pp. 45–46.

94. Caesarius of Arles, *Ad regulam virginum* 39–41, 53, edited by Morin, in *Sanctus Caesarius episcopus Arelatensis, Opera omnia* 2, pp. 112, 116; Hochstetler, "The Meaning of Monastic Cloister," pp. 28–31.

95. Claustration appears to have been regularly ignored prior to the ninth century. I thank the participants in Working Group 1 of the European Science Foundation "Transformation of the Roman World Project" for their comments at Barcelona, 31 October 1997.

96. Jo Ann McNamara, "*Imitatio Helenae:* Sainthood as an Attribute of Queenship," in *Saints: Studies in Hagiography*, edited by Sandro Sticca, Medieval &

NOTES 127

Renaissance Texts & Studies 141 (Binghamton: SUNY Center for Medieval and Early Renaissance Studies, 1996), pp. 63–66.

97. Arbesmann, "Fasting and Prophecy," pp. 9–20.

98. Isabel Moreira, "*Provisatrix optima:* St. Radegund of Poitiers' Relic Petitions to the East," *Journal of Medieval History* 19 (1993), pp. 285–290, 298–305; George, *Venantius Fortunatus,* pp. 165–167.

99. Venantius Fortunatus, *De vita sanctae Radegundis libri II* 2.16, edited by Krusch, in MGH: SRM 2, pp. 387–389.

100. Gregory of Tours, *Libri historiarum X* 9.40, edited by Krusch, MGH: SRM 1.1, p. 464; Scheibelreiter, "Königstöchter," pp. 12–13.

101. Peter Brown, "Relics and Social Status in the Age of Gregory of Tours," in his *Society and the Holy in Late Antiquity* (London: Faber & Faber, Ltd., 1982), pp. 247–249. The event was in fact presented by Baudonivia as a re-enactment of the passion of Christ. Moreira, *"Provisatrix optima,"* pp. 302–303.

102. Venantius Fortunatus, *Opera poetica* Appendix 2, edited by Leo, MGH: AA 4.1, pp. 275–278; E. Gordon Whatley, "An Early Literary Quotation from the *Inventio S. Crucis:* A Note on Baudonivia's *Vita S. Radegundis* (BHL 7049)," *Analecta bollandiana* 111 (1993), pp. 81–91; Gäbe, "Radegundis," pp. 16–18.

103. Krusch, ed., *Vita Rusticulae sive Marciae abbatissae Arelatensis* 7, in MGH: SRM 4, p. 343; Susanne Wittern, *Frauen, Heiligkeit und Macht. Lateinische Frauenviten aus dem 4. bis 7. Jahrhundert,* Ergebnisse der Frauenforschung 33 (Stuttgart: Verlag J.B. Metzler, 1994), pp. 90–91.

104. Krusch, ed., *Vita Rusticulae sive Marciae abbatissae Arelatensis* 16, 19, 26, 27, in MGH: SRM 4, pp. 346–347, 350–351.

105. This *Rule* is no longer thought to have been written by Waldebert, one of Columbanus's successors at Luxeuil. Felice Lifshitz, "Is Mother Superior? Towards a History of Feminine Amtscharisma," in *Medieval Mothering,* edited by John Carmi Parsons and Bonnie Wheeler (New York: Garland Publishing, Inc., 1996), p. 126. On Burgundofara in general, see: Alexander Bergengruen, *Adel und Grundherrschaft im Merowingerreich,* Vierteljahrschrift für Sozial- und Wirtschaftsgeschichte, Beihefte 41 (Wiesbaden: Franz Steiner Verlag GmbH, 1958), pp. 65–76.

106. Prinz, *Frühes Mönchtum,* pp. 81–82.

107. Jacques-Paul Migne, ed., *Regula cuiusdam patris ad virgines* 3, in PL 88 (Paris: J.-P. Migne editorem, 1862), pp. 1054–1055.

108. Jonas of Bobbio, *Vitae Columbani abbatis discipulorumque eius, libri II* 2.22, edited by Bruno Krusch, in MGH: SRG 37 (Hanover: Impensis bibliopolii Hahniani, 1905), pp. 277–279.

Notes to Chapter 4

1. At the cemetery of Frénouville (Normandy), archaeologists founds remains of a herniary brace in grave no. 500. From accompanying goods,

128 CREATING COMMUNITY WITH FOOD AND DRINK

Christian Pilet judged the device to date from the mid-seventh century, and thus fairly late evidence for the survival of medical practice even on the frontiers of Merovingian Gaul. Christian Pilet, *La nécropole de Frénouville: Étude d'une population de la fin du IIIe à la fin du VIIe siècle* 1, BAR International series 83(i) (Oxford: BAR, 1980), pp. 145–147.

2. Katharine Park, "Medicine and Society in Medieval Europe, 500–1500," in *Medicine in Society: Historical Essays,* edited by Andrew Wear (Cambridge: Cambridge University Press, 1992), pp. 65–70.

3. Marcellus, *De medicamentis liber,* edited by Max Niedermann, translated by Julia Kollesch and Diethard Nickel, Corpus medicorum latinorum 5 (Berlin: Akademie Verlag, 1968), pp. 2–4; Katherine Fischer Drew, "Marcellus Empiricus," in *Lexikon des Mittelalters* 6 (Munich: Artemis Verlag, 1993), pp. 221–222.

4. Richard Kieckhefer, *Magic in the Middle Ages* (Cambridge: Cambridge University Press, 1989), pp. 21–24; John M. Riddle, "Pharmacy," in *Late Antiquity: A Guide to the Postclassical World,* edited by G.W. Bowersock, Peter Brown, and Oleg Grabar (Cambridge: Harvard University Press, 1999), pp. 641–642.

5. Danielle Gourevitch, "Présence de la médecine rationelle gréco-romaine en Gaule," in *La médecine en Gaule: Villes d'eaux, sanctuaires des eaux,* edited by André Pelletier (Paris: Picard, Éditeur, 1985), pp. 74–81.

6. Gerhard Baader, "Early Medieval Latin Adaptations of Byzantine Medicine in Western Europe," in *Symposium on Byzantine Medicine,* edited by John Scarborough, Dumbarton Oaks Papers 38 (Washington, D.C.: Dumbarton Oaks Research Library and Collection, 1984), pp. 251–256; Gerhard Baader, "Die Entwicklung der medizinischen Fachsprache in der Antike und im frühen Mittelalter," in *Medizin im mittelalterlichen Abendland,* edited by Gerhard Baader and Gundolf Keil, Wege der Forschung 363 (Darmstadt: Wissenschaftliche Buchgesellschaft, 1982), pp. 423–426.

7. André Finot, "Les médecins des rois mérovingiens et carolingiens," *Histoire des sciences médicales* 4 (1970), pp. 41–42.

8. Klaus-Dietrich Fischer, "Zur Entwicklung des ärztlichen Standes im römischen Kaisserriech," *Medizin-historisches Journal* 14 (1979), pp. 169–170; Rebecca Flemming, *Medicine and the Making of Roman Women: Gender, Nature and Authority from Celsus to Galen* (Oxford: Oxford University Press, 2000), pp. 35–50.

9. John M. Riddle, "Theory and Practice in Medieval Medicine," *Viator* 5 (1974), pp. 158–168.

10. Bruno Krusch, ed., *Vitae Caesarii episcopi Arelatensis libri duo* 1.41, in MGH: SRM 3 (Hanover: Impensis bibliopolii Hahniani, 1896), p. 473.

11. Gregory of Tours, *Libri historiarum X* 10.15, edited by Bruno Krusch, MGH: SRM 1.1, revised edition (Hanover: Impensis bibliopolii Hahniani, 1937), p. 504; Gerhard Baader, "Gesellschaft, Wirtschaft und ärztlicher Stand im frühen und hohen Mittelalter," *Medizin-historisches Journal* 14 (1979), pp. 178–179.

NOTES 129

12. Marcellus of Bordeaux noted that he wrote for both the sake of good health and to heighten others' opinions of him: particularly that of the emperor: "In summa me haec benigne parasse et tamen super his monuisse sufficiet; vos perinde sanitati vestrae atque opinioni meae consuluisse conveniet." Marcellus, *De medicamentis liber,* introduction, p. 4.

13. Gregory of Tours, *Libri historiarum X* 7.25, edited by Krusch, MGH: SRM 1.1, pp. 344–345; Valerie I. J. Flint, "The Early Medieval 'Medicius,' the Saint—and the Enchanter," *Social History of Medicine* 2 (1989), p. 133.

14. "Si quis medicus infirmum ad placitum susceperit, cautionis emisso vinculo, infirmum restituat sanitati. Certe si periculum contigerit mortis, mercedem placiti penitus non requirat; nec ulla exinde utrique parti calumnia moveatur." Karl Zeumer, ed., *Leges visigothorum* 11.1.4, MGH: Leges 1 (Hanover: Impensis bibliopolii Hahniani, 1902), pp. 401–402; Darrel W. Amundsen, "Visigothic Medical Legislation," *Bulletin of the History of Medicine* 40 (1971), pp. 553–565.

15. "Rex vero, peracto ex more iusticio, oppressus iniquae coniugis iuramento, implevit praeceptum iniquitatis. Nam duos medicos, qui ei studium adhibuerant, gladio ferire praecepit; quod non sine peccato facto fuisse, multorum censit prudentia." Gregory of Tours, *Libri historiarum X* 5.35, edited by Krusch, MGH: SRM 1.1, pp. 241–242; Park, "Medicine and Society," p. 67.

16. Flint, "The Early Medieval 'Medicus,'" pp. 131–133.

17. J.-N. Biraben and Jacques Le Goff, "The Plague in the Early Middle Ages," in *Biology of Man in History: Selections from the "Annales: Économies, sociétés, civilisations,"* edited by Robert Forster and Orest Ranum (Baltimore: Johns Hopkins University Press, 1975), pp. 57–77.

18. Valerie I. J. Flint, *The Rise of Magic in Early Medieval Europe* (Princeton: Princeton University Press, 1991), pp. 252–253.

19. "Et atque utinam ipsam sanitatem vel de simplici medicorum arte conquirerent. Sed dicunt sibi: Illum ariolum vel divinum, illum sortilegum, illam erbariam consulamus. . . ." Caesarius of Arles, *Sermones* 52.5, edited by Germain Morin, revised edition, CCSL 103 (Turnhout: Typographi Brepols editores pontificii, 1953), p. 232.

20. "Quoniam non oportet ministros altaris aut clericos magos aut incantatores esse, aut facere quae dicuntur phylacteria, quae sunt magna obligamenta animarum: hos autem, qui talibus utuntur, proici ab ecclesia iussimus." C. Munier, ed., *Conc. Agathense a.506* c.68, in *Concilia Galliae a.314-a.506,* CCSL 148 (Turnhout: Typographi Brepols editores pontificii, 1963), p. 228; Frederick S. Paxton, "Anointing the Sick and the Dying in Christian Antiquity and the Early Medieval West," in *Health, Disease and Healing in Medieval Culture,* edited by Sheila Campbell, Bert Hall, and David Klausner (New York: St. Martin's Press, 1992), p. 94.

21. Gregory of Tours, *Libri historiarum X* 9.6, edited by Krusch, MGH: SRM 1.1, pp. 417–418; Flint, "The Early Medieval 'Medicus,'" pp. 137–143.

22. Although slightly later than the rest of our discussion, a one-page treatise inserted in Dioscorides's *De materia medica* (BN Ms. Lat. 9332) circa 800,

130 CREATING COMMUNITY WITH FOOD AND DRINK

demonstrates how blurred the line between medicine and magic was. Derived mostly from Pliny the Elder, the piece indicated a variety of applications for the corpse of a vulture. Loren C. MacKinney, "An Unpublished Treatise on Medicine and Magic from the Age of Charlemagne," *Speculum* 18 (1943), pp. 494–496.

23. Richard Kieckhefer, "The Specific Rationality of Medieval Magic," *American Historical Review* 99 (1994), pp. 818–819.

24. "Illi vero qui tali iniquitate repleti sunt et sortes et divinationes faciunt et populum prevaricando seducunt, ubi inventi vel invente fuerint seu liberi seu servi vel ancille sint, gravissime publice fustigentur et venundentur, et pretia ipsorum pauperibus erogentur." Charles de Clercq, ed., *Conc. Narbonense a.589* c.14, in *Concilia Galliae a.511-a.695*, CCSL 148a (Turnhout: Typographi Brepols editores pontificii, 1963), pp. 256–257.

25. Desiderius of Bordeaux, for instance, allegedly boasted of being able to heal more effectively than Saint Martin himself. This rumor must have aggravated Gregory of Tours to no end. Gregory of Tours, *Libri historiarum X* 9.6, edited by Krusch, MGH: SRM 1.1, p. 417.

26. Benedict of Nursia, *Regula* 36, edited by Rudolph Hanslik, CSEL 75 (Vienna: Hoelder-Pichler-Tempsky, 1977), pp. 104–105.

27. Loren C. MacKinney, "Medical Ethics and Etiquette in the Early Middle Ages: The Persistence of Hippocratic Ideals," *Bulletin of the History of Medicine* 26 (1952), pp. 3–5.

28. Venantius Fortunatus, *Opera poetica* 4.1, edited by Friedrich Leo, MGH: AA 4.1 (Berlin: Apud Weidmannos, 1881), pp. 79–80; Baader, "Gesellschaft, Wirtschaft," p. 179.

29. Cassiodorus, *Institutiones* 1.31, edited by R. A. B. Mynors (Oxford: Clarendon Press, 1937), pp. 78–79; Loren C. MacKinney, *Early Medieval Medicine, with Special Reference to France and Chartres* (Baltimore: The Johns Hopkins Press, 1937), pp. 42–44.

30. "Quod si nec ita correxerit aut forte, quod absit, in superbia elatus etiam defendere voluerit opera sua, tunc abbas faciat, quod sapiens medicus. . . ." Benedict of Nursia, *Regula* 28.2, edited by Hanslik, CSEL 75, p. 92; Einar Molland, "*Ut sapiens medicus:* Medical Vocabulary in St. Benedict's *Regula monachorum,*" *Studia monastica* 6 (1964), pp. 274–287.

31. Caesarius of Arles, *Sermones* 50.1, edited by Morin, CCSL 103, pp. 224–225; Frederick S. Paxton, "Sickness, Death and Dying: The Legacy of Barbarian Europe in Ritual and Practice," in *Minorities and Barbarians in Medieval Life and Thought,* edited by Susan J. Ridyard and Robert G. Benson (Sewanee: University of the South Press, 1996), pp. 225–227.

32. Antoine Chavasse, *Étude sur l'onction des infirmes dans l'Église latine du IIIe au XIe siècle* 1, doctoral dissertation (Lyon: Faculté de théologie de Lyon, 1942), pp. 40–48, 76–78.

33. Frederick S. Paxton, *Christianizing Death: The Creation of a Ritual Process in Early Medieval Europe* (Ithaca: Cornell University Press, 1990), pp. 50–51.

NOTES   131

34. " . . . sed qui aegrotat, in sola Dei misericordia confidat et eucaristiam corporis ac sanguinis Christi cum fide et devotione accipiat oleumque benedictum fideliter ab ecclesia petat, unde corpus suum in nomine Christi ungeat, et secundum apostolum oratio fidei salvabit infirmum et allevabit eum Dominus; et non solum corporis sed etiam animae sanitatem recipiet. . . ." Bruno Krusch, ed., *Vita Eligii episcopi Noviomagensis* 2.16, in MGH: SRM 4 (Hanover: Impensis bibliopolii Hahniani, 1902), p. 707.

35. Aaron the Presbyter (d. 560), a Monophysite monk, was said by John of Ephesus to have been cured of urinal retention by physicians who successfully inserted a lead catheter. This device enabled him to fulfill his ascetic duties for another twenty years. Peregrine Horden, "The Death of Ascetics: Sickness and Monasticism in the Early Byzantine East," in *Monks, Hermits and the Ascetic Tradition: Papers Read at the 1984 Summer Meeting and the 1985 Winter Meeting of the Ecclesiastical History Society,* edited by W. J. Sheils, Studies in Church History 22 (Oxford: Ecclesiastical History Society, 1985), pp. 41–52.

36. Flint, "The Early Medieval 'Medicus,'" p. 139.

37. He mocked medical manuals by stating: "Porcorum autem et anserum, et gallinarum, phasianorumque adipes quid commodi habeant, omnes medicorum declarant libri: quos si legeris, videbis tot curationes esse in vulture quot membra sunt." Jerome, *Adversus Jovinianum* 2.6, edited by Jacques-Paul Migne, in PL 23, reprint edition (Turnhout: Brepols, 1983), pp. 306–307; Molland, "*Ut sapiens medicus,*" pp. 289–290.

38. Edward James, "A Sense of Wonder: Gregory of Tours, Medicine and Science," in *The Culture of Christendom: Essays in Medieval History in Commemoration of Denis L. T. Bethell,* edited by Mark Anthony Meyer (London: The Hambledon Press, 1993), pp. 52–59.

39. Gregory of Tours, *Libri historiarum X* 5.6, edited by Krusch, MGH: SRM 1.1, p. 203. Some of Gregory's rhetorical venom was directed against the fact that the services of a Jew were preferred to those of a Christian. Peter Brown, "Sorcery, Demons and the Rise of Christianity from Late Antiquity into the Middle Ages," in *Witchcraft, Confessions and Accusations,* edited by Mary Douglas (London: Tavistock Publications, 1970), pp. 35–36.

40. Bruno Krusch, ed., *Vita Iuniani confessoris Commodoliacensis* 6–7, in MGH: SRM 3 (Hanover: Impensis bibliopolii Hahniani, 1896), pp. 378–379; Flint, "The Early Medieval 'Medicius,'" pp. 134–135.

41. Friedrich Prinz, *Frühes Mönchtum im Frankenreich: Kultur und Gesellschaft in Gallien, den Rheinlanden un Bayern am Beispiel der monastischen Entwicklung (4. bis 8. Jahrhundert),* second edition (Darmstadt: Wissenschaftliche Buchgesellschaft, 1988), pp. 274–275.

42. Janet L. Nelson, "Queens as Jezebels: Brunhild and Balthild in Merovingian History," in *Politics and Ritual in Early Medieval Europe* (London: The Hambledon Press, 1986), pp. 17–23; Ian Wood, *The Merovingian Kingdoms 450–751* (London: Longman, 1994), pp. 198–202.

43. "Coepit ipsa domna Balthildis corpore infirmari et viscerum incisione, pessimo infirmitatis vitio, graviter laborare, et nisi medicorum studia

132 CREATING COMMUNITY WITH FOOD AND DRINK

subvenissent, pene deficere. Sed magis ipsa ad caelestem medicum semper fidem habebat de salute sua." Bruno Krusch, ed., *Vita sanctae Balthildis* A.12, in MGH: SRM 2, new edition (Hanover: Impensis bibliopolii Hahniani, 1956), p. 497.

44. " . . . qui [fratres Baronti] psalmodiae cantus recitarent per ordinem, ut caelestis medicus mitteret animam in corpore." Wilhelm Levison, eds., *Visio Baronti monachi Longoretensis* 2, in MGH: SRM 5 (Hanover: Impensis bibliopolii Hahniani, 1910), p. 378.

45. "Universae salutis Deum et universae virtutis Dominum dipraecimor pro fratribus et sororibus nostris, qui secundum carnem diversis aegretudinum generibus insultantur ut his Dominus caeleste medicinae suae munus indulgeat." Leo Cunibert Mohlberg, ed., *Missale Gothicum: Das Gallikanische Sakramentar (Cod. Vatican. Regin. Lat. 317) des VII.-VIII. Jahrhunderts,* Codices liturgici e Vaticanis praesertim delecti phototypice expressi 1.240 (Augsburg: Dr. Benno Filser Verlag GmbH, 1929), f. 159r; Paxton, *Christianizing Death,* pp. 57–59.

46. One nun at the sixth-century monastic foundation of Radegund in Poitiers noted with disgust that the former queen delighted in kissing lepers on the face. Venantius Fortunatus, *De vita sanctae Radegundis libri II* 1.19, edited by Bruno Krusch, in MGH: SRM 2, new edition (Hanover: Impensis bibliopolii Hahniani, 1956), pp. 370–371.

47. Raymond Van Dam, *Saints and their Miracles in Late Antique Gaul* (Princeton: Princeton University Press, 1993), pp. 88–89.

48. Gregory of Tours recounted the tale of a woman who toiled in her field on the feast day of St. John and was punished with a burning sensation in her hands for violating the holy day with labor. Gregory of Tours, *De virtutibus beati Martini episcopi* 2.57, edited by Bruno Krusch, in MGH: SRM 1.2 (Hanover: Impensis bibliopolii Hahniani, 1885), p. 178.

49. Jerome Kroll and Bernard Bachrach, "Sin and the Etiology of Disease in Pre-Crusade Europe," *Journal of the History of Medicine and Allied Sciences* 41 (1986), pp. 405–407.

50. Peter Brown, *The Cult of Saints: Its Rise and Function in Latin Christianity* (Chicago: University of Chicago Press, 1981), pp. 113–120; Peter Brown, "Relics and Social Status in the Age of Gregory of Tours," in his *Society and the Holy in Late Antiquity* (London: Faber & Faber, Ltd., 1982), pp. 228–230.

51. Peter Brown, "The Rise and Function of the Holy Man in Late Antiquity," in his *Society and the Holy in Late Antiquity,* pp. 139–141; Joan M. Petersen, "Dead or Alive? The Holy Man as Healer in East and West in the Late Sixth Century," *Journal of Medieval History* 9 (1983), pp. 91–98.

52. Giselle de Nie, *Views from a Many-Windowed Tower: Studies of Imagination in the Works of Gregory of Tours,* Studies in Classical Antiquity 7 (Amsterdam: Rodopi, 1987), pp. 218–223.

53. Isabel Moreira, *Dreams, Visions and Spiritual Authority in Merovingian Gaul* (Ithaca: Cornell University Press, 2000), pp. 131–135.

NOTES

54. Gregory of Tours, *Liber in gloria confessorum* 78, edited by Bruno Krusch, in MGH: SRM 1.2, pp. 344–346; Biraben and Le Goff, "The Plague in the Early Middle Ages," pp. 60–61.

55. "Nam, si qui nunc frigoritici in eius honore missas devote celebrant eiusque pro requie Deo offerunt oblationem, statim, conpressis tremoribus, restinctis febribus, sanitate praestinae restaurantur." Gregory of Tours, *Liber in gloria martyrum* 74, edited by Bruno Krusch, in MGH: SRM 1.2, p. 87; Frederick S. Paxton, "Power and the Power to Heal: The Cult of St. Sigismund of Burgundy," *EME* 2 (1993), pp. 95–97; Karl Heinrich Krüger, *Königsgrabkirchen der Franken, Angelsachsen und Langobarden bis zur Mitte des 8. Jahrhunderts,* Münstersche Mittelalter-Schriften 4 (Munich: Wilhelm Fink Verlag, 1971), pp. 63–64.

56. On the continuity of use of water sanctuaries for healing well into the Christian period, see: Aline Rousselle, *Croire et guérir: La foi en Gaule dans l'antiquité tardive* (Paris: Librairie Arthème Fayard, 1990), pp. 185–200.

57. Frederick S. Paxton, "Liturgy and Healing in an Early Medieval Saint's Cult: The Mass *in honore sancti Sigismundi* for the Cure of Fevers," *Traditio* 49 (1994), pp. 23–33; Robert Folz, "Zur Frage der heiligen Könige: Heiligkeit und Nachleben in der Geschichte des burgundischen Königtums," *Deutsches Archiv für Erforschung des Mittelalters* 14 (1958), pp. 324–326.

58. Park, "Medicine and Society," pp. 73–74.

59. Aline Rousselle, "La sage-femme et le thaumaturge dans la Gaule tardive: Les femmes ne font pas de miracles," in *La médecine en Gaule: Villes d'eaux, sanctuaires des eaux,* edited by André Pelletier (Paris: Picard, Éditeur, 1985), pp. 249–250.

60. Gregory of Tours, *Liber in gloria confessorum* 24, edited by Krusch, in MGH: SRM 1.2, pp. 313–314; Park, "Medicine and Society," p. 69.

61. When her son Theoderic died of dysentery in 584, Brunhild had a number of Parisian women who had allegedly supplied a healing potion tortured and killed. According to Gregory's grisly account, the queen accused them and their intermediary Mummolus, a prefect in the royal court, of practicing sorcery. Gregory of Tours, *Libri historiarum X* 6.35, edited by Krusch, MGH: SRM 1.1, pp. 305–306.

62. For the last, see: Gregory of Tours, *De virtutibus beati Martini episcopi* 3.43, edited by Bruno Krusch, in MGH: SRM 1.2, p. 193; Gregory of Tours, *Liber de virtutibus sancti Juliani* 45, edited by Bruno Krusch, in MGH: SRM 1.2, p. 131; Petersen, "Dead or Alive?," pp. 93–94.

63. Gregory of Tours, *Libri historiarum X* 7.1, edited by Krusch, in MGH: SRM 1.1, pp. 323–327; Rudolph Arbesmann, "Fasting and Prophecy in Pagan and Christian Antiquity," *Traditio* 7 (1949), pp. 69–70.

64. See Jerome's letter to Eustochium, the daughter of Paula, and its emphasis on the need for restraint in the consumption of food and wine: Jerome, *Epistolae* 22, edited by Isidore Hilberg, CSEL 54 (Vienna: F. Tempsky, 1910), pp. 143–211; Veronika E. Grimm, *From Feasting to Fasting, the Evolution of a*

134   CREATING COMMUNITY WITH FOOD AND DRINK

Sin: Attitudes to Food in Late Antiquity (London: Routledge, 1996), pp. 162–170.

65. Jerome, *Epistolae* 54.9–10, edited by Hilberg, CSEL 54, pp. 474–477; Grimm, *From Feasting to Fasting*, pp. 177–181.

66. Augustine of Hippo, *Opera omnia* Ep. 211.8–9, edited by Jacques-Paul Migne, in PL 33 (Paris: Apud editorem in via dicta d'Amboise, 1845), pp. 960–961.

67. Augustine of Hippo, *De utilitate ieiunii* 1–2, edited by S. D. Ruegg, in CCSL 13.2 (Turnhout: Typographi Brepols editores pontificii, 1969), pp. 231–233; Grimm, *From Feasting to Fasting*, pp. 184–189.

68. Venantius Fortunatus, *Opera poetica* 11.4, edited by Leo, MGH: AA 4.1, p. 269.

69. Riddle, "Theory and Practice," pp. 158–163.

70. "Obscura nimis est hominum salus, temperies ex contrariis umoribus constans: ubi quicquid horum excreverit, ad infirmitatem protinus corpus adducit. hinc est quod sicut aptis cibis valitudo fessa recreatur, sic venenum est, quod incompetenter accipitur." Cassiodorus, *Variarum libri duodecim* 6.19, edited by Theodor Mommsen, MGH: AA 12 (Berlin: Apud Weidmannos, 1894), pp. 191–192.

71. The *Sapientia artis medicinae* is preserved in four manuscript copies, the two elder ones being dated to the ninth or tenth centuries: Codex Hunterianus T. 4.13, f. 53r–54v and Codex Sangallensis 751, pp. 446–447, 453–455. M. Wlaschky believed the original text to be much older, likely dating from the sixth century, but offered no suggestions as to its provenance. M. Wlaschky, "*Sapientia artis medicinae:* Ein frühmittelalterliches Kompendium der Medizin," *Kyklos* 1 (1928), pp. 103–113.

72. Mark Grant, "Introduction," in *Anthimus, De observatione ciborum* (Blackawton: Prospect Books, 1996), pp. 12–21.

73. Loren MacKinney argues for the successful propagation of Anthimus's treatise solely on the basis of its survival in ninth- and tenth-century copies. MacKinney, *Early Medieval Medicine*, pp. 42–44. The copying of the letter in monastic houses, however, does not necessarily imply that the text found widespread approval in lay circles.

74. S. J. B. Barnish, "Introduction," in *The Variae of Magnus Aurelius Cassiodorus Senator*, Translated Texts for Historians 12 (Liverpool: Liverpool University Press, 1992), pp. xiv–xvii.

75. "Fas est tibi nos fatigare ieiuniis, fas est contra nostrum sentire desiderium et in locum beneficii dictare, quod nos ad gaudia salutis excruciet." Cassiodorus, *Variarum libri duodecim* 6.19, edited by Mommsen, MGH: AA 12, pp. 191–192; MacKinney, *Early Medieval Medicine*, pp. 44–45.

76. Valentin Rose, "Die Diätetik des Anthimus an Theuderich König der Franken," in his *Anecdota graeca et graecolatina: Mitteilungen aus Handschriften zur Geschichte der griechischen Wissenschaft* 2, reprint edition (Amsterdam: Verlag Adolf M. Hakkert, 1963), pp. 49–50.

77. In the *Sapientia artis medicinae,* the anonymous author gave the following example of the consequences of imbalance: "Frenetica passio ex quo hu-

NOTES 135

more contingit? Ex nimio vino et aqua frigida contingit; ex frigore primum humitridiant, ex eo vicio reumatizant illi venae et cerebrum suspenditur, in somnietate patiuntur et alienantur." Wlaschky, "*Sapientia artis medicinae,*" 3.2, p. 108.

78. "Quoniam prima sanitas hominum in cibis congruis constat, id est si bene adhibiti fuerint, bonam digestionem corporis faciunt, si autem non bene fuerint cocti, gravitatem stomacha et ventri faciunt, etiam et crudus homoris generant et acidivas carbunculus et ructus gravissimus faciunt." Anthimus, *De observatione ciborum ad Theodoricum regem francorum epistola,* edited and translated by Eduard Liechtenhan, Corpus medicorum latinorum 8,1 (Berlin: In aedibus academiae scientiarum,1963), p. 1.

79. "Quomodo in fabrica domus parietis si calcem et aquam quis tantum temperaverit quantum ratio poscit ut spissa sit ipsa mixtio, proficit in fabrica, et tenit, si autem satis sicut supra diximus prima sanitas ex cibis bene coctis et bene digestis constat." Anthimus, *De observatione ciborum,* edited by Liechtenhan, p. 2.

80. "Pinguamen ipsius laredi, quod in cibo aliquo supermissum fuerit vel super olera, ubi oleum non fuerit, non nocet." Anthimus, *De observatione ciborum* c.14, edited by Liechtenhan, p. 9; Carl Deroux, "Des traces inconnues de la *Dietétique* d'Anthime dans un manuscrit duVatican (Reg. Lat. 1004)," *Latomus* 33 (1974), p. 685.

81. "Similiter et de butero recentem si acceperit tisecus, sed buter ipsum sale nec penitus non habeat. nam si habuerit sale, peius exterminat. si purum et recentem et mel modicum admixtum fuerit, sic linguat cata modicum et supinus se ponat." Anthimus, *De observatione ciborum* c.77, edited by Liechtenhan, pp. 28–29; Galen, *On the Powers of Food* 3, translated by Mark Grant, in *Galen on Food and Diet* (London: Routledge, 2000), pp. 163–164.

82. Anthimus, *De observatione ciborum* c.15, edited by Liechtenhan, p. 10.

83. "De crudo vero laredo, quod solent, ut audio, domni Franci comedere, miror satis, quis illis ostendit talem medicinam, ut non opus habeant alias medicinas, qui sic crudum illut manducant, quia beneficium grandem et pro antidotus sanitatem illis praestat. . . ." Anthimus, *De observatione ciborum* c.14, edited by Liechtenhan, p. 9.

84. Deroux, "Des traces inconnues," pp. 680–682.

85. Bruno Laurioux, "Cuisiner à l'antique: Apicius au moyen âge," *Médiévales* 26 (1994), pp. 17–23.

86. Jean Lestocquoy, "Épices, médecine et abbayes," in *Études mérovingiennes: Actes des journées de Poitiers, 1ᵉʳ–3 mai 1952* (Paris: A. et J. Picard, 1953), pp. 179–186.

87. Karl Mras, "Anthimus und andere lateinische Ärzte im Lichte der Sprachforschung," *Wiener Studien* 61–62 (1943–1947), pp. 98–117; Gordon M. Messing, "Remarks on Anthimus, *De observatione ciborum,*" *Classical Philology* 37 (1942), pp. 150–158.

88. Wood, *The Merovingian Kingdoms,* pp. 51–54, 164–165; Eugen Ewig, *Die Merowinger und das Frankenreich,* Urban-Taschenbücher 392 (Stuttgart: Verlag W. Kohlhammer, 1988), pp. 34–35.

136 CREATING COMMUNITY WITH FOOD AND DRINK

89. Peter Heather, *The Goths* (Oxford: Blackwell Publishers, 1996), pp .222–227.
90. Gregory of Tours, *Libri historiarum X* 3.5, edited by Krusch, MGH: SRM 1.1, pp. 112–116; Grant, *Anthimus, De observatione ciborum*, pp. 29–30.
91. On this concept among the Ostrogoths in general, see: Patrick Amory, *People and Identity in Ostrogothic Italy 489–554* (Cambridge: Cambridge University Press, 1997), pp. 112–120.
92. Herwig Wolfram, *The Roman Empire and its Germanic Peoples*, translated by Thomas Dunlap (Berkeley: University of California Press, 1997), pp. 218–222; Thomas S. Burns, *A History of the Ostrogoths* (Bloomington: Indiana University Press, 1984), pp. 128–130.
93. Liechtenhan, "Ad lectorem praefatio," in *Anthimi, De observatione ciborum*, pp. ix–xx.
94. Raymond Van Dam, *Saints and their Miracles in Late Antique Gaul* (Princeton: Princeton University Press, 1993), pp. 82–115.
95. Flemming, *Medicine and the Making of Roman Women*, pp. 111–112.

Notes to Chapter 5

1. Auguste Audollent, *Les tombes gallo-romaines à l'inhumation des Martres-de-Veyre (Puy-de-Dôme)*, in Mémoires pres. par div. savants à l'Académie des Inscriptions 13 (Paris: Imprimerie nationale, 1923), pp. 16–38, 53; Édouard Salin, *La civilisation mérovingienne d'après les sépultures, les textes et le laboratoire* 4 (Paris: Éditions A. et J. Picard et Cie., 1959), p. 30.
2. Petronius, *Satyricon* 71, translated by Michael Heseltine, revised by E. H. Warmington (Cambridge: Harvard University Press, 1975), pp. 160–165.
3. On late antique feasting imagery among Christians, see: Paul-Albert Février, "A propos du répas funéraire: Culte et sociabilité," *Cahiers archéologiques* 26 (1977), pp. 29–45.
4. Louis-Vincent Thomas, *Rites de mort: Pour la paix des vivants* (Paris: Fayard, 1985), pp. 238–239.
5. Hayo Vierck, "Hallenfreude: Archäologische Spuren frühmittelalterlicher Trinkgelage und mögliche Wege zur ihrer Deutung," in *Feste und Feiern im Mittelalter: Paderborner Symposion des Mediävistenverbandes*, edited by Detlef Altenburg, Jörg Jarnut and Hans-Hugo Steinhoff (Sigmaringen: Jan Thorbecke Verlag, 1991), pp. 115–122.
6. Nikolaus Kyll, *Tod, Grab, Begräbnisplatz, Totenfeier: Zur Geschichte ihres Brauchtums im Trierer Lande und in Luxemburg unter besonderer Berücksichtigung des Visitationshandbuches des Regino von Prüm (+915)*, Rheinisches Archiv 81 (Bonn: Ludwig Röhrscheid Verlag, 1972), pp. 36–37.
7. Marcel Mauss, *The Gift. Forms and Functions of Exchange in Archaic Societies*, translated by Ian Cunnison (New York: W. W. Norton & Company, Inc., 1967), pp. 10–12.
8. Georges Bataille, "The Notion of Expenditure," in *Visions of Excess: Selected Writings, 1927–1939*, edited and translated by Allan Stoekl, Theory and

NOTES 137

History of Literature 14 (Minneapolis: University of Minnesota Press, 1985), pp. 120–123.

9. Bonnie Effros, *Caring for Body and Soul: Burial and the Afterlife in the Merovingian World* (University Park: Pennsylvania State University Press, 2002), pp. 184–187.

10. Friederike Naumann-Steckner, "Death on the Rhine: Changing Burial Customs in Cologne, 3rd to 7th Century," in *The Transformation of the Roman World AD 400–900,* edited by Leslie Webster and Michelle Brown (London: British Museum Press, 1997), pp. 148–157.

11. Hugh Lindsay, "Eating with the Dead: The Roman Funerary Banquet," in *Meals in Context: Aspects of the Communal Meal in the Hellenistic World,* edited by Inge Nielsen and Hanne Sigismund Nielsen, Åhrus Studies in Mediterranean Antiquity 1 (Åhrus: Åhrus University Press, 1998), pp. 72–75.

12. Valerie I. J. Flint, *The Rise of Magic in Early Medieval Europe* (Princeton: Princeton University Press, 1991), pp. 213–215; Hilda Ellis Davidson, *The Lost Beliefs of Northern Europe* (London: Routledge, 1993), pp. 90ff.

13. Bernhard Kötting, "Die Tradition der Grabkirche," in *Memoria: Der geschichtliche Zeugniswert des liturgischen Gedenkens im Mittelalter,* edited by Karl Schmid and Joachim Wollasch, Münstersche Gedenkens im Mittelalter-Schriften 48 (Munich: Wilhelm Fink Verlag, 1984), pp. 71–73.

14. Arnold Angenendt, "Theologie und Liturgie der mittelalterlichen Toten-Memoria," in *Memoria: Der geschichtliche Zeugniswert des liturgischen Gedenkens im Mittelalter,* pp. 171–172.

15. " . . . nam per triduum hymnis Dominum collaudavimus super sepulcrum ipsius, et redemptionis Sacramenta tertio die obtulimus." Luigi Carrozzi, ed., *Sant'Agostino: Le lettere* 2.158.2, *Opera di Sant'Agostino* 22 (Rome: Nuova biblioteca agostiniana, Citta' nuova editrice, 1971), pp. 640–641.

16. Homeyer, "Der Dreißigste,"in *Abhandlungen der Königlichen Akademie der Wissenschaften zu Berlin, 1864,* philologische und historische Abhandlungen (Berlin: Königliche Akademie der Wissenschaften, 1865), pp. 90ff.

17. Richard Krautheimer, "Mensa-Coemiterium-Martyrium," in his *Studies in Early Christian, Medieval and Renaissance Art* (New York: New York University Press, 1969), pp. 45–46; Franz Cumont, *Lux perpetua* (Paris: Librairie Orientaliste Paul Geuthner, 1949), pp. 29–41.

18. Ramsay MacMullen, *Christianity and Paganism in the Fourth to Eighth Centuries* (New Haven: Yale University Press, 1997), pp. 63–64.

19. Otto Gerhard Oexle, "Mahl und Spende im mittelalterlichen Totenkult," *FS* 18 (1984), pp. 408ff.

20. Augustine of Hippo, *Confessionum libri XIII* 6.2.2, edited by Lucas Verheijen, CCSL 27 (Turnhout: Typographi Brepols editores pontificii, 1981), pp. 74–75; Jean-Paul Jacob and Jean-Régis Mirbeau Gauvin, "Du don au mort à la redemption: Évolution du dépôt funéraire du Bas-Empire à l'apparition du don *pro anima,*" *Revue d'histoire du droit* 48 (1980), pp. 321–322.

21. " . . . miror cur apud quosdam (in)fideles hodie tam perniciosus error increverit, ut super tumulos defunctorum cibos et vina conferant; quasi

138   CREATING COMMUNITY WITH FOOD AND DRINK

egressae de corporibus animae carnales cibos requirant." Augustine of Hippo, *Fragmenta sermonum* 190, edited by Jacques-Paul Migne, in PL 39 (Paris: Apud editorem in via dicta d'Amboise, 1847), p. 2101.

22. Yitzhak Hen, *Culture and Religion in Merovingian Gaul, AD. 481–751* (Leiden: E. J. Brill, 1994), pp. 162–167.

23. Edward James, *The Merovingian Archaeology of South-West Gaul* 1, BAR Supplementary Series 25(i) (Oxford: BAR, 1977), p. 164.

24. Gregory of Tours, *Libri historiarum X* 2.23, edited by Bruno Krusch, MGH SRM 1.1, revised edition (Hanover: Impensis bibliopolii Hahniani, 1951), pp. 68–69; Naumann-Steckner, "Death on the Rhine," p. 157.

25. Isabel Moreira, *Dreams, Visions and Spiritual Authority in Merovingian Gaul* (Ithaca: Cornell University Press, 2000), pp. 90–91.

26. Février, "A propos du répas funéraire," pp. 42–43.

27. " . . . hoc est, maerenti ecclesiae vivificatum reddit, cum peccator admissor crimine, antequam sepeliatur. . . ." Caesarius of Arles, *Sermones* 2.190, edited by Germain Morin, CCSL 104 (Turnhout: Typographi Brepols editores pontificii, 1953), pp. 775–777.

28. Caesarius of Arles, *Sermones* 1.55, edited by Germain Morin, CCSL 103 (Turnhout: Typographi Brepols editores pontificii, 1953), pp. 241–244; Flint, *The Rise of Magic*, p. 269.

29. "Sunt etiam qui in festivitate cathedrae domni Petri intrita mortuis offerunt et post missas redeuntes ad domus proprias ad gentilium revertuntur errores et post corpus domini sacratas daemoni escas accipiunt. . . ." Charles de Clercq, ed., *Conc. Turonense a. 567* c.23(24), in *Concilia Galliae, a. 511–a. 695,* CCSL 148a (Turnhout: Typographi Brepols editores pontificii, 1963), p. 191.

30. Salin, *La civilisation mérovingienne* 4, pp. 36–37; Lindsay, "Eating with the Dead," pp. 74–75.

31. *El Concilio III de Toledo base de la nacionalidad y civilizacion española* c.22 (Madrid: Imprenta de Fortanent, 1891), p. 34; Rachel L. Stocking, *Bishops, Councils and Consensus in the Visigothic Kingdom, 589–633* (Ann Arbor: University of Michigan Press, 2000), pp. 80–85.

32. Alfred Boretius, ed., *Childeberti I. regis praeceptum,* in MGH: Leges 2, Capitularia 1.2 (Hanover: Impensis bibliopolii Hahniani, 1883), pp. 2–3; Hen, *Culture and Religion*, p. 160.

33. "Non liceat Christianis prandia ad defunctorum sepulchra deferre et sacrificare de re mortuorum." Martin of Braga, *Capitula ex orientalium patrum synodis ordinata atque collecta* 69, edited by Claude W. Barlow, in *Martinus episcopus Bracarensis, Opera omnia,* Papers and Monographs of the American Academy in Rome 12 (New Haven: Yale University Press, 1950), p. 140.

34. Eligius of Noyon, *Praedicatio de supremo iudicio* 2, edited by Bruno Krusch, in MGH: SRM 4 (Hanover: Impensis bibliopolii Hahniani, 1902), p. 751.

35. "De genere servorum, qui sepulchris defunctorum pro qualitate ipsius ministerii depotantur, hoc placuit observari, ut, sub qua ab auctoribus fuerint conditione dimissi, sive haeredibus sive ecclesie pro defensione

NOTES   139

fuerint depotati, volutas defuncti circa eos in omnibus debeat conservari. Quod si ecclesia eos de his sanctis functionibus in omni parte defenderit, ecclesiae tam illi quam posteri eorum defensione in omnibus potiantur et occursum impendat." De Clercq, ed., *Conc. Parisiense a.556–573* c.9, in *Concilia Galliae,* CCSL 148a, p. 209.

36. Venantius Fortunatus, *Vita sancti Marcelli* 40–48, edited by Bruno Krusch, in MGH: AA 4.2 (Berlin: Apud Weidmannos, 1885), pp. 53–54.

37. "Nam trigesimo ab eius [Senochi] obitu die, cum ad eius tumulum missa celebraretur Chaidulfus quidam contractus, dum stipem postulat, ad eius sepulturam accedit. Qui dum pallam superpositam osculis veneratur, dissolutis membrorum ligaturis, directus est." Gregory of Tours, *Liber vitae patrum* 15.4, edited by Bruno Krusch, in MGH: SRM 1.2 (Hanover: Impensis bibliopolii Hahniani, 1885), p. 724; Kyll, *Tod, Grab,* p. 185.

38. Gregory of Tours, *Liber in gloria confessorum* 64, edited by Bruno Krusch, in MGH: SRM 1.2, pp. 335–336; Peter Brown, *The Rise of Western Christendom: Triumph and Diversity A.D. 200–1000* (Malden: Blackwell Publishers, 1996), p. 163.

39. Gregory of Tours, *Liber in gloria martyrum* 50, edited by Bruno Krusch, in MGH: SRM 1.2, pp. 522–524; Richard Morris, *The Church in British Archaeology,* CBA Research Report 47 (London: CBA, 1983), p. 26.

40. Gregory the Great, *Registrum epistularum libri VIII-XIV* 8.4, edited by Dag Norberg, CCSL 140a (Turnhout: Typographi editores Brepols pontificii, 1982), p. 521.

41. Patrick J. Geary, "Exchange and Interaction between the Living and the Dead in Early Medieval Society," in his *Living with the Dead in the Middle Ages* (Ithaca: Cornell University Press, 1994), pp. 89–92; Bonnie Effros, "Beyond Cemetery Walls: Early Medieval Funerary Topography and Christian Salvation," *EME* 6 (1997), pp. 1–23.

42. Wilhelm Levison, ed., *Visio Baronti monachi Longoretensis* 14, in MGH: SRM 5 (Hanover: Impensis bibliopolii Hahniani, 1910), p.389; Luce Pietri, "Les sépultures privilégiées en Gaule d'après les sources littéraires," in *L'inhumation privilégiée du IVe au VIIIe siècle en Occident: Actes du colloque tenu à Créteil les 16–18 mars 1984,* edited by Yvette Duval and Jean-Charles Picard (Paris: De Boccard, 1986), p. 135; Moreira, *Dreams, Visions,* p. 163.

43. Leo Cunibert Mohlberg, Leo Eizenhöfer and Petrus Siffrin, eds., *Liber sacramentorum romanae aeclesiae ordinis anni circuli (Codex Vat. Reg. Lat. 316/ Paris Bibl. Nat. 7193, 41/56) (Sacramentarium Gelasianum)* c.1680–1684, 1690–1695, third edition, Rerum ecclesiasticarum documenta, series maior, fontes 4 (Rome: Casa Editrice Herder, 1981), pp. 245–247; Antoine Chavasse, *Le sacramentaire gélasien (Vaticanus Reginensis 316),* in Bibliothèque de théologie, series 4, vol. 1 (Paris: Desclée et Co., 1958), pp. 69–70; Kyll, *Tod, Grab,* p. 186.

44. R. Rau, ed., *Concilium germanicum* (742) c.5, in *Briefe des Bonifatius, Willibalds Leben des Bonifatius, nebst einigen zeitgenössichen Dokumenten,* Ausgewählte Quellen zur deutschen Geschichte des Mittelalters 4b (Darmstadt:

140 CREATING COMMUNITY WITH FOOD AND DRINK

Wissenschaftliche Buchgesellschaft, 1968), p. 380; Hen, *Culture and Religion*, p. 177.

45. "[2.] De sacrilegio super defunctos id est dadsisas." "[9.] De sacrificio quod fit alicui sanctorum." Alfred Boretius, ed., *Indiculus superstitionum et paganiarum*, in MGH: Leges 2, Capitularia 1.108, p. 223; Alain Dierkens, "Superstitions, christianisme et paganisme à la fin de l'époque mérovingienne: A propos de l'*Indiculus superstitionum et paganiarum*," in *Magie, sorcellerie, parapsychologie*, edited by Hervé Hasquin, Laicité série recherches 5 (Brussels: Éditions de l'Université de Bruxelles, 1984), pp. 18–19.

46. Oexle, "Mahl und Spende," pp. 404–405; Flint, *The Rise of Magic*, pp. 269–270.

47. Salin, *La civilisation mérovingienne* 4, pp. 30–35; Edward James, *The Franks* (Oxford: Basil Blackwell Ltd., 1988), p. 141; Otto Doppelfeld, "Die Domgrabung XI. Das fränkische Frauengrab," *Kölner Domblatt* 16–17 (1959), pp. 71–74; Otto Doppelfeld, "Die Domgrabung XII. Totenbett und Stuhl des Knabengrabes," *Kölner Domblatt* 18–19 (1960), p. 88.

48. Frédéric Scuvée, *Le cimetière barbare de Réville (Manche) (VIe-VIIe siècles)* (Caen: Caron et Cie, 1973), pp. 69–76, 159–162.

49. Madeleine Châtelet, Patrice Georges and Paschal Rohmer, *Erstein "beim Limersheimerweg" (Bas-Rhin): Une nécropole mérovingienne du 6e-7e siècle*, unpublished preliminary report (Strasbourg: Service régionale d'archéologie d'Alsace, 2000), pp. 6–11, 16–74. I thank Patrick Périn for allowing me to see this manuscript.

50. Pierre Demolon and Frans Verhaeghe, "La céramique de Veme au Xeme siècle dans le Nord de la France et la Flandre belge: État de la question," in *Travaux du groupe de recherches et d'études sur la céramique dans le Nord-Pas-de-Calais. Actes du colloque d'Outreau (10–12 avril 1992)*, edited by Daniel Piton (Arras: Groupe de recherches et d'études sur la céramique dans le Nord, 1993), pp. 387–388.

51. Michel Colardelle, *Sépulture et traditions funéraires du Ve au VIIIe siècle après J.-C. dans les campagnes des Alpes françaises du Nord (Drôme, Isère, Savoie, Haute-Savoie)* (Grenoble: Publications de la Société alpine du documentation et de recherche en archéologie historique, 1993), pp. 356–358.

52. Jacques Coupry, "Circonscription d'Aquitaine," *Gallia* 29 (1971), p. 333.

53. Bailey K. Young, "Pratiques funéraires et mentalités païennes," in *Clovis: Histoire et mémoire. Le baptême de Clovis, l'événement*, edited by Michel Rouche (Paris: Presses de l'Université de Paris-Sorbonne, 1997), pp. 19–23; Bailey K. Young, "Merovingian Funeral Rites and the Evolution of Christianity: A Study in the Historical Interpretation of Archaeological Material," Ph.D. diss. (University of Pennsylvania, 1975), pp. 180–182.

54. Renate Pirling, "Ein fränkisches Fürstengrab aus Krefeld-Gellep," *Germania* 42 (1964), pp. 204–206, 213–214.

55. Bailey K. Young, "Paganisme, christianisation et rites funéraires mérovingiens," *AM* 7 (1977), pp. 37–40; Young, "Merovingian Funeral Rites," pp. 174–182.

NOTES 141

56. See Alain Dierkens' strongly-worded critique of this methodology in his response included in Bailey K.Young, "Quelques réflexions sur les sépultures privilégiées, leur contexte et leur évolution surtout dans la Gaule de l'Est," in *L'inhumation privilégiée du IVe au VIIIe siècle en Occident*, p. 83.

57. Colardelle, *Sépulture et traditions funéraires*, pp. 356–362.

58. Young, "Paganisme, christianisation," pp. 37–40.

59. Patrick Périn, "Les Ardennes à l'époque mérovingienne: Étude archéologique," *Études ardennaises* 50 (1967), pp. 21–22.

60. Paul-Albert Février, "La tombe chrétienne et l'Au-delà," in *Le tempes chrétien de la fin de l'antiquité au moyen âge IIIe-XIIIe siècles, Paris, 9–12 mars 1981*, Colloques internationaux du CNRS 604 (Paris: Éditions du CNRS, 1984), pp. 171–176.

61. Donald Bullough, *Friends, Neighbors and Fellow-Drinkers: Aspects of Community and Conflict in the Early Medieval West*, Chadwick lecture 1990 (Cambridge: Department of Anglo-Saxon, Norse and Celtic, 1991), pp. 6–8.

62. Young, "Paganisme, christianisation," pp. 37–40;Young, "Merovingian Funeral Rites," pp. 174–182.

63. Bonnie Effros, *Merovingian Mortuary Archaeology and the Making of the Early Middle Ages* (Berkeley: University of California Press, in press).

64. Guy Halsall, "Burial, Ritual and Merovingian Society," in *The Community, the Family and the Saint: Patterns of Power in Early Medieval Europe. Selected Proceedings of the International Medieval Congress, University of Leeds, 4–7 July 1994, 10–13 July 1995*, edited by Joyce Hill and Mary Swan (Turnhout: Brepols, 1998), pp. 327–332.

65. But see: Günter Behm-Blancke, "Trankgaben und Trinkzeremonien im Totenkult der Völkerwanderungszeit," *Alt-Thüringen* 16 (1979), p. 171.

66. Davidson, *The Lost Beliefs*, pp. 91–93; Flint, *The Rise of Magic*, p. 119.

67. David Wilson, *Anglo-Saxon Paganism* (London: Routledge, 1992), pp. 100–102;Young, "Paganisme, christianisation," pp. 57–58.

68. Klaus Kerth, Arno Rettner and Eva Stauch, "Die tierischen Speisebeigaben von zwei merowingerzeitlichen Gräberfeldern in Unterfranken," *AK* 24 (1995), pp. 441–455.

69. Salin, *La civilisation mérovingienne* 4, pp. 19–26.

70. Judith Oexle, "Merowingerzeitliche Pferdebestattungen—Opfer oder Beigaben?" *FS* 18 (1984), pp. 123–150.

71. Amaury Thiérot and Raymond Lantier, "Le cimetière mérovingien du Maltrat à Vouciennes," *Revue archéologique* sixth series 15 (1940), pp. 210–215, 221–234.

72. Henri Gaillard de Semainville, *Les cimetières mérovingens de la Côte chalonnaise et de la Côte maçonnaise*, Revue archéologique de l'Est et du Centre-Est, third supplement (Dijon: Les presses de l'imprimerie universitaire, 1980), pp. 164–167, 173–174.

73. Édouard Salin, *La civilisation mérovingienne d'après les sépultures, les textes et le laboratoire* 2 (Paris: Éditions A. et J. Picard et Cie., 1952), pp. 202–212.

142 CREATING COMMUNITY WITH FOOD AND DRINK

74. Alain Simmer, *La nécropole mérovingienne d'Ennery (Moselle): Fouilles d'Emile Delort (1941)*, Mémoires de l'AFAM 4 (Rouen: AFAM, 1993), pp. 103–105. I thank Guy Halsall for drawing my attention to this citation.

75. Emile Socley, "Rapport sur plusieurs greniers funéraires découverts dans un cimetière, de la période mérovingienne, à Noiron-sous-Gévry (Côte-d'Or)," *Bulletin de la Société préhistorique française* 9 (1912), pp. 308–323; Emile Socley, "Les greniers funéraires de Noiron-sous-Gevry (Côte-d'Or)," *Bulletin de la Société préhistorique française* 9 (1912), pp. 745–762; Salin, *La civilisation mérovingienne* 4, pp. 37–42.

76. In the identification of cases of charcoal remains (*charbon de bois*), great caution is necessary due to their resemblance to decomposed organic material. Bailey K. Young, *Quatre cimetières mérovingiens de l'Est de la France: Lavoye, Dieue-sur-Meuse, Mezières-Manchester et Mazerny*, BAR International Series 208 (Oxford: BAR, 1984), pp. 123–125. Alain Simmer notes that 17 percent of the sepulchers at Audun-le-Tiche (Moselle) bear remains of ritual conflagration. Alain Simmer, *Le cimetière mérovingien d'Audun-le-Tiche (Moselle)*, AFAM, Mémoire 2 (Paris: Éditions Errance, 1988), p. 139.

77. Young, *Quatre cimetières*, pp. 123–125.

78. In Anglo-Saxon England, by contrast, David Wilson has noted no correlation between the presence of charcoal in a sepulcher and the age or sex of the interred individual. Wilson, *Anglo-Saxon Paganism*, pp. 123–130.

79. Young, "Merovingian Funeral Rites," pp. 124–126. For a different interpretation, see: Lotte Hedeager, *Iron Age Societies: From Tribe to State in Northern Europe, 500 BC to AD 700*, translated John Hines (Oxford: Blackwell Publishers, 1992), pp. 32, 80–81.

80. Demolon and Verhaeghe, "La céramique," p. 388.

Notes to the Epilogue

1. Gregory of Tours, *Liber vitae patrum* 19.1, edited by Bruno Krusch, in MGH: SRM 1.2 (Hanover: Impensis bibliopolii Hahniani, 1885), pp. 286–287.

2. Raymond Van Dam, *Saints and their Miracles in Late Antique Gaul* (Princeton: Princeton University Press, 1993), pp. 101–102.

3. Gregory of Tours, *Liber vitae patrum* 19.3, edited by Krusch, in MGH: SRM 1.2, pp. 288–289.

4. Venantius Fortunatus, *De vita sanctae Radegundis* 1.17, 1.20, 1.24, edited by Bruno Krusch, in MGH: SRM 2, new edition (Hanover: Impensis bibliopolii Hahniani, 1956), pp. 370–372; Judith George, *Venantius Fortunatus: A Latin Poet in Merovingian Gaul* (Oxford: Clarendon Press, 1992), pp. 161–168.

5. John Kitchen, *Saints' Lives and the Rhetoric of Gender: Male and Female in Merovingian Hagiography* (Oxford: Oxford University Press, 1998), pp. 101–109.

NOTES 143

6. Gregory of Tours, *Liber in gloria confessorum* 24, edited by Bruno Krusch, in MGH: SRM 1.2, pp. 313–314.
7. Bruno Krusch, ed., *Vita Rusticulae sive Marciae abbatissae Arelatensis* 16, 19, 26, 27, in MGH: SRM 4 (Hanover: Impensis bibliopolii Hahniani, 1902), pp. 346–347, 350–351.
8. Conrad Leyser, *Authority and Asceticism from Augustine to Gregory the Great* (Oxford: Oxford University Press, 2000), pp. 88–94.

SELECT BIBLIOGRAPHY

Primary Sources

Ambrose of Milan, *De virginibus libri tres,* edited by Egnatius Cazzaniga. In Corpus scriptorum latinorum Pravianum. Turin: In aedibus Io. Bapt. Paraviae et sociorum, 1948.

Anthimus, *De observatione ciborum ad Theodoricum regem francorum epistola,* edited and translated by Eduard Liechtenhan. Corpus medicorum latinorum 8.1. Berlin: In aedibus academiae scientiarum,1963.

Atsma, Hartmut, and Jean Vezin, eds. *Testament d'Erminethrude.* In *ChLA* 14.592, 72–75. Dietikon-Zurich: URS GrafVerlag, 1985.

Augustine of Hippo, *Confessionum libri XIII,* edited by Lucas Verheijen. CCSL 27. Turnhout: Typographi Brepols editores pontificii, 1981.

———, *De utilitate ieiunii,* edited by S. D. Ruegg. In CCSL 13.2, 225–241. Turnhout: Typographi Brepols editores pontificii, 1969.

———, *Fragmenta sermonum* 190, edited by Jacques-Paul Migne. In PL 39, 2100–2101. Paris: Apud editorem in via dicta d'Amboise, 1847.

———, *Le Lettere,* edited by Luigi Carrozzi. In *Opera di Sant'Agostino* 22. Rome: Nuova biblioteca agostiniana, Citta' nuova editrice, 1971.

———, *Opera omnia,* edited by Jacques-Paul Migne. In PL 33. Paris: Apud editorem in via dicta d'Amboise, 1845.

Aurelian of Arles, *Regula ad monachos,* edited by Jacques-Paul Migne. In PL 68, 386–398. Paris: Apud editorem in via dicta d'Amboise, 1847.

———, *Regula ad virgines,* edited by Jacques-Paul Migne. In PL 68, 397–408. Paris: Apud editorem in via dicta d'Amboise, 1847.

Avitus of Vienne, *Epistolarum ad diversos libri tres,* edited by Rudolf Peiper, 35–103. In MGH: AA 6.2. Berlin: Apud Weidmannos, 1883.

———, *Poematum libri VI,* edited by Rudolf Peiper. In MGH: AA 6.2, 197–294. Berlin: Apud Weidmannos, 1883.

Baudonivia, *De vita sanctae Radegundis libri II* 2, edited by Bruno Krusch. In MGH: SRM 2, new edition, 377–395. Hanover: Impensis bibliopolii Hahniani, 1956.

Benedict of Nursia, *Regula,* edited by Rudolph Hanslik. CSEL 75, revised edition. Vienna: Hoelder-Pichler-Tempsky, 1977.

Bieler, Ludwig, ed. and trans. *The Irish Penitentials.* Scriptores latini Hiberniae 5. Dublin: The Dublin Institute for Advanced Studies, 1963.

146   CREATING COMMUNITY WITH FOOD AND DRINK

Boretius, Alfred, ed. *Capitularia regum Francorum.* MGH: Leges 2, Capitularia 1. Hanover: Impensis bibliopolii Hahniani, 1883.

Caesarius of Arles, *Ad regularum virginum,* edited by Germain Morin. In *Sanctus Caesarius episcopus Arelatensis, Opera omnia* 2, 99–129. Brugges: Jos. van der Meersch, 1942.

―――, *Regula monachorum,* edited by Germain Morin. In *Sanctus Caesarius episcopus Arelatensis, Opera omnia* 2, 149–155. Brugges: Jos. van der Meersch, 1942.

―――, *Sanctae sorori Caesariae abbatissae,* edited by Germain Morin. In *Sanctus Caesarius episcopus Arelatensis, Opera omnia* 2, 134–144. Brugges: Jos. van der Meersch, 1942.

―――, *Sermones,* edited by Germain Morin. CCSL 103–104, revised edition. Turnhout: Typographi Brepols editores pontificii, 1953.

Cassiodorus, *Institutiones,* edited by R. A. B. Mynors. Oxford: Clarendon Press, 1937.

―――, *Variarum libri duodecim,* edited by Theodor Mommsen. MGH: AA 12, 1–385. Berlin: Apud Weidmannos, 1894.

Columbanus, *Paenitentiale,* edited and translated by G. S. M. Walker. In *Sanctus Columbanus, Opera,* 169–181. Scriptores latini Hiberniae 2. Dublin: The Dublin Institute for Advanced Studies, 1957.

―――, *Regula coenobialis,* edited and translated by G. S. M. Walker. In *Sanctus Columbanus, Opera,* 142–169. Scriptores latini Hiberniae 2. Dublin: The Dublin Institute for Advanced Studies, 1957.

de Clercq, Charles, ed. *Concilia Galliae a.511-a.695.* CCSL 148A. Turnhout: Typographi Brepols editores pontificii, 1963.

de Vogüé, Adalbert. "La régle de Donat pour l'abbesse Gauthstrude." *Benedictina* 25 (1978), 219–313.

Desiderius of Cahors, *Epistulae,* edited by Wilhelm Arndt. In CCSL 117, 309–342. Turnhout: Typographi Brepols editores pontificii, 1967.

Eckhardt, Karl August. *Pactus legis salicae.* MGH: Leges 4.1. Hanover: Impensis bibliopolii Hahniani, 1962.

Eligius of Noyon, *Praedicatio de supremo iudicio,* edited by Bruno Krusch. In MGH: SRM 4, 749–761. Hanover: Impensis bibliopolii Hahniani, 1902.

Ferreolus of Uzès, *Regula ad monachos,* edited by Jacques-Paul Migne. In PL 66, 959–976. Paris: Apud J.-P. Migne, editorem, 1866.

Finsterwalder, Paul Willem, ed. *Die Canones Theodori Cantuariensis und ihre Überlieferungsformen.* Weimar: Hermann Böhlaus Nachfolger, Hof-Buchdruckerei GmbH, 1929.

Fructuosus of Braga, *Regula monachorum,* edited by Jacques-Paul Migne. In PL 87, reprint edition, 1097–1110. Turnhout: Brepols, 1982.

Galen, *On the Powers of Food,* translated by Mark Grant. In *Galen on Food and Diet,* 68–190. London: Routledge, 2000.

Gregory of Tours, *De virtutibus sancti Martini episcopi,* edited by Bruno Krusch. In MGH: SRM 1.2, 134–211. Hanover: Impensis bibliopolii Hahniani, 1885.

―――, *Liber de virtutibus sancti Juliani,* edited by Bruno Krusch. In MGH: SRM 1.2, 112–134. Hanover: Impensis bibliopolii Hahniani, 1885.

BIBLIOGRAPHY

———, *Liber in gloria confessorum,* edited by Bruno Krusch. In MGH SRM 1.2, 294–370. Hanover: Impensis bibliopolii Hahniani, 1885.

———, *Liber in gloria martyrum,* edited by Bruno Krusch. In MGH: SRM 1.2, 34–111. Hanover: Impensis bibliopolii Hahniani, 1885.

———, *Liber vitae patrum,* edited by Bruno Krusch. In MGH SRM 1.2, 211–294. Hanover: Impensis bibliopolii Hahniani, 1885.

———, *Libri historiarum X,* edited by Bruno Krusch. MGH SRM 1.1, revised edition. Hanover: Impensis bibliopolii Hahniani, 1951.

Gregory the Great, *Dialogi,* edited and translated by Adalbert de Vogüé. SC 260. Paris: Les Éditions du CERF, 1979.

———, *Registrum epistolarum libri VIII-XIV,* edited by Dag Norberg. CCSL 140A. Turnhout: Typographi Brepols editores pontificii, 1982.

Gundlach, Wilhelm, ed. *Epistolae aevi merovingicae collectae.* In MGH: Epistolae 1, 434–468. Berlin: Apud Weidmannos, 1892.

Jerome, *Adversus Jovinianum,* edited by Jacques-Paul Migne. In PL 23, reprint edition, 221–353. Turnhout: Brepols, 1983.

———, *Epistulae,* edited by Isidore Hilberg. CSEL 54 and 56, revised edition. Vienna: Verlag der Österreichischen Akademie der Wissenschaften, 1996.

John Cassian, *De institutis coenobiorum,* edited by Michael Petschenig. CSEL 17. Vienna: F. Tempsky, 1888.

Jonas of Bobbio, *Vitae Columbani abbatis discipulorumque eius, libri II,* edited by Bruno Krusch. In MGH: SRG 37, 1–294. Hanover: Impensis bibliopolii Hahniani, 1905.

———, *Vita Vedastis episcopi Atrebatensis,* edited by Bruno Krusch. In MGH: SRG 37, 295–320. Hanover: Impensis bibliopolii Hahniani, 1905.

Krusch, Bruno, ed. *Passio Praeiecti episcopi et martyris Arverni.* In MGH: SRM 5, 212–248. Hanover: Impensis bibliopolii Hahniani, 1910.

———, ed. *Vita Carileffi abbatis Anisolensis.* In MGH: SRM 3, 386–394. Hanover: Impensis bibliopolii Hahniani, 1896.

———, ed. *Vita Eligii episcopi Noviomagensis.* In MGH: SRM 4, 634–742. Hanover: Impensis bibliopolii Hahniani, 1902.

———, ed. *Vita Genovefae virginis Parisiensis.* In MGH: SRM 3, 204–238. Hanover: Impensis bibliopolii Hahniani, 1896.

———, ed. *Vita Iuniani confessoris Commodoliacensis.* In MGH: SRM 3, 376–379. Hanover: Impensis bibliopolii Hahniani, 1896.

———, ed. *Vita Rusticulae sive Marciae abbatissae Arelatensis.* In MGH: SRM 4, 337–351. Hanover: Impensis bibliopolii Hahniani, 1902.

———, ed. *Vita Sadalbergae abbatissae Laudunensis.* In MGH SRM 5, 40–66. Hanover: Impensis bibliopolii Hahniani, 1910.

———, ed. *Vita sanctae Balthildis.* In MGH: SRM 2, new edition, 475–508. Hanover: Impensis bibliopolii Hahniani, 1956.

———, ed. *Vita sanctae Chrothildis.* In MGH: SRM 2, 341–348. Hanover: Impensis bibliopolii Hahniani, 1888.

———, ed. *Vitae Caesarii episcopi Arelatensis libri duo.* In MGH: SRM 3, 433–501. Hanover: Impensis bibliopolii Hahniani, 1896.

148   CREATING COMMUNITY WITH FOOD AND DRINK

Leander of Seville, *Liber de institutione virginum et contemptu mundi ad Florentinam sororem,* edited by Jacques-Paul Migne. In PL 72, 871–894. Paris: Paul Garnier fratres, Editores, 1878.

Levillain, Léon. *Examen critique des chartes mérovingiennes et carolingiennes de l'abbaye de Corbie.* Mémoires et documents publiés par la Société de l'École des chartes 5. Paris: A. Picard et Fils, Éditeurs, 1902.

Levison, Wilhelm, ed. *Visio Baronti monachi Longoretensis.* In MGH: SRM 5, 368–394. Hanover: Impensis bibliopolii Hahniani, 1888.

——, ed. *Vita Anstrudis abbatissae Laudunensis.* In MGH: SRM 6, 64–78. Hanover: Impensis bibliopolii Hahniani, 1913.

——, ed. *Vita Audoini episcopi Rotomagensis.* In MGH: SRM 5, 536–567. Hanover: Impensis bibliopolii Hahniani, 1910.

Lowe, E. A., ed. *The Bobbio Missal: A Gallican Mass-Book (Ms. Paris. Lat. 13246)* 2. Henry Bradshaw Society 58. London: Harrison and Sons, Ltd., 1920.

MacKinney, Loren C. "An Unpublished Treatise on Medicine and Magic from the Age of Charlemagne." *Speculum* 18 (1943), 494–496.

Marcellus, *De medicamentis liber,* edited by Max Niedermann, translated by Julia Kollesch and Diethard Nickel. Corpus medicorum latinorum 5. Berlin: Akademie Verlag, 1968.

Martin of Braga, *Capitula ex orientalium patrum synodis ordinata atque collecta,* edited by Claude W. Barlow. In *Martinus episcopus Bracarensis, Opera omnia,* 123–144. Papers and Monographs of the American Academy in Rome 12. New Haven: Yale University Press, 1950.

Martine, François, ed. and trans. *Vita sancti Lupicini abbatis.* In *Vie des pères de Jura,* 308–363. SC 142. Paris: Les Éditions du CERF, 1968.

——, ed. and trans. *Vita S. Romani.* In *Vie des pères de Jura,* 24–307. SC 142. Paris: Les Éditions du CERF, 1968.

McCarthy, Maria Caritas, trans. *The Rule for Nuns of Caesarius of Arles: A Translation with a Critical Introduction.* Catholic University of America, Studies in Mediaeval History, new series 16. Washington, D.C.: Catholic University of America, 1960.

McNamara, Jo Ann and John E. Halborg, trans. *Sainted Women of the Dark Ages.* Durham: Duke University Press, 1992.

Migne, Jacques-Paul, ed. *Regula cuiusdam patris ad virgines.* In PL 88, 1051–1070. Paris: J.-P. Migne editorem, 1862.

Mohlberg, Leo Cunibert, ed. *Missale Gothicum: Das Gallikanische Sakramentar (Cod. Vatican. Regin. Lat. 317) des VII.-VIII. Jahrhunderts,* Codices liturgici e Vaticanis praesertim delecti phototypice expressi. Augsburg: Dr. Benno Filser Verlag GmbH, 1929.

——, Leo Eizenhöfer, and Petrus Siffrin, eds. *Liber sacramentorum romanae aeclesiae ordinis anni circuli (Cod. Vat. Reg. Lat. 316/ Paris Bibl. Nat. 7193, 41/56),* third edition. Rerum ecclesiasticarum documenta series maior, fontes 4. Rome: Casa editrice Herder, 1981.

Munier, C., ed. *Concilia Galliae a.314-a.506.* CCSL 148. Turnhout: Typographi Brepols editores pontificii, 1963.

Pardessus, Jean-Marie, ed. *Charta qua Leodebodus, abbas Sancti Aniani plurima dona confert monasteriis Sancti Aniani et Sancti Petri Floriacensis (Ann. 667).* In *Diplomata:*

BIBLIOGRAPHY

Chartae, epistolae, leges aliaque instrumenta ad res Gallo-Francicas spectantia 2.358, reprint edition, 142–145. Aalen: Scientia Verlag, 1969.

Petronius, *Satyricon,* translated by Michael Heseltine, revised by E. H. Warmington. Cambridge: Harvard University Press, 1975.

Rau, R., ed. *Briefe des Bonifatius, Willibalds Leben des Bonifatius, nebst einigen zeitgenössichen Dokumenten.* Ausgewählte Quellen zur deutschen Geschichte des Mittelalters 4b. Darmstadt: Wissenschaftliche Buchgesellschaft, 1968.

Schmitz, H. J., ed. *Die Bussbücher und die Bussdisciplin der Kirche* 1. Mainz: Verlag von Fanz Kirchheim, 1883.

Shea, George W. *The Poems of Alcimus Ecdicius Avitus: Translation and Introduction.* Medieval and Renaissance Texts and Studies 172. Tempe: Medieval and Renaissance Texts and Studies, 1997.

Sidonius Apollinaris, *Epistulae,* edited by Christian Luetjohann. MGH: AA 8. Berlin: Apud Weidmannos, 1887.

Sulpicius Severus, *Dialogi,* edited by Karl Halm. In CSEL 1, 152–223. Vienna: Apud C. Geroldi filium, 1866.

————, *Vita sancti Martini,* edited by Karl Halm. In CSEL 1, 107–137. Vienna: Apud C. Geroldi filium, 1866.

Venantius Fortunatus, *De vita sanctae Radegundis libri II* 1, edited by Bruno Krusch. In MGH: SRM 2, new edition, 364–376. Hanover: Impensis bibliopolii Hahniani, 1956.

————. *Opera poetica,* edited by Friedrich Leo. MGH: AA 4.1. Berlin: Apud Weidmannos, 1881.

————. *Personal and Political Poems,* translated by Judith George. Translated Texts for Historians 23. Liverpool: Liverpool University Press, 1995.

————, *Vita sancti Germani,* edited by Bruno Krusch. In MGH: AA 4.2, 11–27. Berlin: Apud Weidmannos, 1885.

————, *Vita sancti Marcelli,* edited by Bruno Krusch. In MGH: AA 4.2, 49–54. Berlin: Apud Weidmannos, 1885.

————, *Vita sancti Martini,* edited by Bruno Krusch. In MGH: AA 4.2, 293–370. Berlin: Apud Weidmannos, 1885.

————, *Vita sancti Paterni,* edited by Bruno Krusch, in MGH: AA 4.2, 33–37. Berlin: Apud Weidmannos, 1885.

Wasserschleben, Hermann, ed. *Die irische Kanonensammlung,* second edition. Leipzig: Verlag von Bernhard Tauchnitz, 1895.

Wlaschky, M. "*Sapientia artis medicinae:* Ein frühmittelalterliches Kompendium der Medizin." *Kyklos* 1 (1928), 103–113.

Zeumer, Karl, ed. *Leges Visigothorum.* MGH: Leges 1. Hanover: Impensis bibliopolii Hahniani.

————, ed. *Marculfi formulae.* In MGH: Formulae 1, 32–112. Hanover: Impensis bibliopolii Hahniani, 1886.

Secondary Sources

Aigrain, René. "Le voyage de Sainte Radegonde à Arles." *Bulletin philologique et historique* (1926–1927), 119–127.

150 CREATING COMMUNITY WITH FOOD AND DRINK

Althoff, Gerd. "Der frieden-, bündnis- und gemeinschaftstiftende Charakter des Mahles im früheren Mittelalter." In *Essen und Trinken im Mittelalter und Neuzeit: Vorträge eines interdisziplinären Symposions vom 10.–13. Juni an der Justus-Liebig-Universität Gießen,* edited by Irmgard Bitsch, Trude Ehlert and Xenja von Ertzdorff, 13–25. Sigmaringen: Jan Thorbecke Verlag, 1987.

Amory, Patrick. *People and Identity in Ostrogothic Italy 489–554.* Cambridge: Cambridge University Press, 1997.

Amundsen, Darrel W. "Visigothic Medical Legislation." *Bulletin of the History of Medicine* 40 (1971), 553–569.

Angenendt, Arnold. "Theologie und Liturgie der mittelalterlichen Toten-Memoria." In *Memoria: Der geschichtliche Zeugniswert des liturgischen Gedenkens im Mittelalter,* edited by Karl Schmid and Joachim Wollasch, 79–199. Münstersche Gedenkens im Mittelalter-Schriften 48. Munich: Wilhelm Fink Verlag, 1984.

Arbesmann, Rudolph. "Fasting and Prophecy in Pagan and Christian Antiquity." *Traditio* 7 (1949), 1–71.

Audollent, August. *Les tombes gallo-romaines à l'inhumation des Martres-de-Veyre (Puy-de-Dôme).* Mémoires pres. par div. savants à l'Académie des Inscriptions 13. Paris: Imprimerie nationale, 1923.

Baader, Gerhard. "Early Medieval Latin Adaptations of Byzantine Medicine in Western Europe." In *Symposium on Byzantine Medicine,* edited by John Scarborough, 251–259. Dumbarton Oaks Papers 38. Washington, D.C.: Dumbarton Oaks Research Library and Collection, 1984.

———. "Die Entwicklung der medizinischen Fachsprache in der Antike und im frühen Mittelalter." In *Medizin im mittelalterlichen Abendland,* edited by Gerhard Baader and Gundolf Keil, 417–442. Wege der Forschung 363. Darmstadt: Wissenschaftliche Buchgesellschaft, 1982.

———. "Gesellschaft, Wirtschaft und ärztlicher Stand im frühen und hohen Mittelalter." *Medizin-historisches Journal* 14 (1979), 176–185.

Baratte, François. "Remarques préliminaires à un inventaire de la vaisselle d'argent trouvée en Gaule." In his *Argenterie romaine et byzantine. Actes de la table ronde, Paris 11–13 octobre 1983,* 85–95. Paris: De Boccard, 1988.

Barnish, S. J. B. "Introduction." In *The Variae of Magnus Aurelius Cassiodorus Senator,* ix–liii. Translated Texts for Historians 12. Liverpool: Liverpool University Press, 1992.

Barth, Fredrik. "Towards Greater Naturalism in Conceptualizing Societies." In *Conceptualizing Society,* edited by Adam Kuper, 17–33. London: Routledge, 1982.

Bataille, Georges. "The Notion of Expenditure." In *Visions of Excess: Selected Writings, 1927–1939,* edited and translated by Allan Stoekl, 116–129. Theory and History of Literature 14. Minneapolis: University of Minnesota Press, 1985.

Behm-Blancke, Günter. "Trankgaben und Trinkzeremonien im Totenkult der Völkerwanderungszeit." *Alt-Thüringen* 16 (1979), 171–227.

Benoit, Fernand. "Topographie monastique d'Arles au VIᵉ siècle." In *Études mérovingiennes: Actes des journées de Poitiers 1ᵉʳ–3 mai 1952,* 13–17. Poitiers: Éditions A. et J. Picard, 1953.

BIBLIOGRAPHY

Bergengruen, Alexander. *Adel und Grundherrschaft im Merowingerreich.* Vierteljahrschrift für Sozial- und Wirtschaftsgeschichte, Beihefte 41. Wiesbaden: Franz Steiner Verlag GmbH, 1958.

Biarne, J. "Les temps du moine d'après les premières règles monastiques d'Occident (IVᵉ-VIᵉ siècles)." In *Les temps chrétien de la fin de l'antiquité au moyen âge IIIᵉ-XIIIᵉ siècles,* 99–128. Colloques internationaux du CNRS 604. Paris: Éditions du CNRS, 1984.

Biraben, J.-N. and Jacques Le Goff. "The Plague in the Early Middle Ages." In *Biology of Man in History: Selections from the "Annales: Économies, sociétés, civilisations,"* edited by Robert Forster and Orest Ranum, 48–80. Baltimore: Johns Hopkins University Press, 1975.

Bitel, Lisa M. *Land of Women: Tales of Sex and Gender from Early Ireland.* Ithaca: Cornell University Press, 1996.

Böckenhoff, Karl. *Speisesatzungen mosaischer Art in mittelalterlichen Kirchenrechtsquellen des Morgen- und Abendlandes.* Münster: Druck und Verlag der Aschendorffschen Buchhandlung, 1907.

Bonnassie, Pierre. "Consommation d'aliments immondes et cannibalisme de survie dans l'Occident du haut moyen âge." *Annales ESC* 44 (1989), 1035–1056.

Boulanger, C. *Le cimetière franco-mérovingien et carolingien de Marchélepot (Somme): Étude sur l'origine de l'art barbare.* Paris: Imprimerie nationale, 1909.

Bradley, Keith. "The Roman Family at Dinner." In *Meals in a Social Context: Aspects of the Communal Meal in the Hellenistic World,* edited by Inge Nielsen and Hanne Sigismund Nielsen, 36–55. Åhrus Studies in Mediterranean Antiquity 1. Åhrus: Åhrus University Press, 1998.

Brennan, Brian. "St. Radegund and the Early Development of her Cult at Poitiers." *Journal of Religious History* 13 (1985), 340–354.

Brothwell, Don and Patricia Brothwell. *Food in Antiquity: A Survey of the Diet of Early Peoples,* expanded edition. Baltimore: The Johns Hopkins University Press, 1969.

Brown, Peter. *The Body and Society: Men, Women and Sexual Renunciation in Early Christianity.* New York: Columbia University Press, 1988.

———. *The Cult of Saints: Its Rise and Function in Latin Christianity.* Chicago: University of Chicago Press, 1981.

———. "The Decline of the Empire of God: Amnesty, Penance and the Afterlife from Late Antiquity to the Middle Ages." In *Last Things: Death and the Apocalypse in the Middle Ages,* edited by Caroline Walker Bynum and Paul Freedman, 41–59; 277–283. Philadelphia: University of Pennsylvania Press, 2000.

———. "*Gloriosus obitus:* The End of the Ancient Other World." In *The Limits of Ancient Christianity: Essays on Late Antique Thought and Culture in Honor of R. A. Markus,* edited by William E. Klingshirn and Mark Vessey, 289–314. Ann Arbor: University of Michigan, 1999.

———. *Power and Persuasion in Late Antiquity: Towards a Christian Empire.* Madison: University of Wisconsin Press, 1992.

———. "Relics and Social Status in the Age of Gregory of Tours." In his *Society and the Holy in Late Antiquity,* 222–250. London: Faber & Faber, Ltd., 1982.

152 CREATING COMMUNITY WITH FOOD AND DRINK

————. "The Rise and Function of the Holy Man in Late Antiquity." In his *Society and the Holy in Late Antiquity*, 103–152. Berkeley: University of California Press, 1982.

————. *The Rise of Western Christendom: Triumph and Diversity A.D. 200–1000*. Malden: Blackwell Publishers, 1996.

————. "Sorcery, Demons, and the Rise of Christianity from Late Antiquity into the Middle Ages." In *Witchcraft: Confessions and Accusations*, edited by Mary Douglas, 17–45. London: Tavistock Publications, 1970.

————. "Vers la naissance du purgatoire: Amnistie et pénitence dans le christianisme occidental de l'Antiquité tardive au haut Moyen Age." *Annales: Histoire, sciences sociales* 6 (1997), 1247–1261.

Bullough, Donald. *Friendship, Neighbours and Fellow Drinkers: Aspects of Community Conflict in the Early Medieval West*. Chadwick Lecture 1990. Cambridge: Department of Anglo-Saxon, Norse and Celtic, 1991.

————. "Social and Economic Structure and Topography of the Early Medieval City." In *Topografia urbana et vita cittadina nell'alto medioevo in Occidente, 26 aprile–1 maggio 1973* 1, 351–399. Settimane di studio del Centro italiano di studi sull'alto medioevo 21. Spoleto: Presso la sede del Centro, 1974.

Burns, Thomas S. *A History of the Ostrogoths*. Bloomington: Indiana University Press, 1984.

Bynum, Caroline Walker. "Fast, Feast and Flesh: The Religious Significance of Food to Medieval Women." In *Food and Culture: A Reader*, edited by Carole Counihan and Penny van Esterik, 138–158. New York: Routledge, 1997.

————. *Holy Feast and Holy Fast: The Religious Significance of Food to Medieval Women*. Berkeley: University of California Press, 1987.

Cameron, Averil. "Social Language and its Private Deployment," in *East and West: Modes of Communication. Proceedings of the First Plenary Conference at Merida*, edited by Evangelos Chrysos and Ian Wood, 111–125. TRW 5. Leiden: E. J. Brill, 1999.

Châtelet, Madeleine, Patrice Georges and Paschal Rohmer. *Erstein "beim Limersheimerweg" (Bas-Rhin): Une nécropole mérovingienne du 6ᵉ–7ᵉ siècle*, unpublished preliminary report. Strasbourg: Service régionale d'archéologie d'Alsace, 2000.

Chavasse, Antoine. *Étude sur l'onction des infirmes dans l'Église latine du IIIᵉ au XIᵉ siècle* 1, doctoral dissertation. Lyons: La Faculté de théologie de Lyon, 1942.

————. *Le sacramentaire gélasien (Vaticanus Reginensis 316)*. Bibliothèque de théologie, series 4, vol. 1. Paris: Desclée et Co., 1958.

Clark, Elizabeth A. "The Lady Vanishes: Dilemmas of a Feminist Historian after the 'Linguistic Turn.'" *Church History* 67 (1998), 1–31.

Claude, Dietrich. *Untersuchungen zu Handel und Verkehr der vor- und frühgeschichtlichen Zeit im Mittel- und Nordeuropa, 2: Der Handel im westlichen Mittelmeer während des Frühmittelalters*. Abhandlungen der Akademie der Wissenschaften in Göttingen, philologisch-historische Klasse, third series, vol. 144. Göttingen: Vandenhoeck & Ruprecht, 1985.

Coates, Simon. "Regendering Radegund? Fortunatus, Baudonivia and the Problem of Female Sanctity in Merovingian Gaul." In *Gender and Christian Religion:*

BIBLIOGRAPHY 153

Papers Read at the 1996 Summer Meeting and the 1997 Winter Meeting of the Ecclesiastical History Society, edited by R. N. Swanson, 37–50. Studies in Church History 34. Woodbridge: The Boydell Press, 1998.

———. "Venantius Fortunatus and the Image of Episcopal Authority in Late Antique and Early Merovingian Gaul." *English Historical Review* 115 (2000), 1109–1137.

Colardelle, Michel. *Sépulture et traditions funéraires du Ve au VIIIe siècle après J.-C. dans les campagnes des Alpes françaises du Nord (Drôme, Isère, Savoie, Haute-Savoie).* Grenoble: Publications de la Société alpine du documentation et de recherche en archéologie historique, 1993.

Collins, Roger. *Early Medieval Europe 300–1000,* second edition. New York: St. Martin's Press, 1999.

Connerton, Paul. *How Societies Remember.* Cambridge: Cambridge University Press, 1989.

Constable, Giles. *Letters and Letter Collections.* Typologie des sources du moyen âge Occidental 17. Turnhout: Éditions Brepols, 1976.

Coon, Lynda L. *Sacred Fictions: Holy Women and Hagiography in Late Antiquity.* Philadelphia: University of Pennsylvania Press, 1997.

Cooper, Kate. *The Virgin and the Bride: Idealized Womanhood in Late Antiquity.* Cambridge: Harvard University Press, 1996.

———and Conrad Leyser. "The Gender of Grace: Impotence, Servitude and Manliness in the Fifth-Century West." *Gender & History* 12 (2000), 536–551.

Corbier, Mireille. "The Ambiguous Status of Meat in Ancient Rome." *Food and Foodways* 3 (1989), 233–264.

———. "The Broad Bean and the Moray: Social Hierarchies and Food in Rome." In *Food: A Culinary History from Antiquity to the Present,* edited by Jean-Louis Flandrin and Massimo Montanari, 128–140. New York: Columbia University Press, 1999.

Coudanne, Louise, "Baudonivie, moniale de Sainte-Croix et biographe de Sainte Radegonde." In *Études mérovingiennes: Actes des journées de Poitiers 1er–3 mai 1952,* 45–49. Poitiers: Éditions A. et J. Picard, 1953.

Coupry, Jacques. "Circonscription d'Aquitaine." *Gallia* 29 (1971), 333–367.

Cramer, Peter. *Baptism and Change in the Early Middle Ages c.200-c.1150.* Cambridge: Cambridge University Press, 1993.

Cumont, Franz. *Lux perpetua.* Paris: Librairie Orientaliste Paul Geuthner, 1949.

Davidson, Hilda Ellis. *The Lost Beliefs of Northern Europe.* London: Routledge, 1993.

de Clercq, Charles. *La législation religieuse franque de Clovis à Charlemagne. Études sur les actes de conciles et les capitulaires, les statuts diocésaines et les règles monastiques 507–814.* Louvain: Bibliothèque de l'Université, 1936.

Delamain, Philippe. *Le cimetière d'Herpes (Fouilles et collection Ph. Delamain).* Angoulême: Chez L. Coquemard, 1892.

Delaruelle, Étienne. "Sainte Radegonde, son type de sainteté et la chrétienté de son temps." In *Études mérovingiennes: Actes des journées de Poitiers 1er–3 mai 1952,* 65–74. Poitiers: Éditions A. et J. Picard, 1953.

Demolon, Pierre and Frans Verhaeghe, "La céramique de Veme au Xeme siècle dans le Nord de la France et la Flandre belge: État de la question." In *Travaux du* groupe de recherches et d'études sur la céramique dans le Nord-Pas-de-Calais. Actes du colloque d'Outreau (10–12 avril 1992), edited by Daniel Piton, 385–407. Arras: Groupe de recherches et d'études sur la céramique dans le Nord, 1993.

de Nie, Giselle. *Views from a Many-Windowed Tower: Studies of Imagination in the Works of Gregory of Tours.* Studies in Classical Antiquity 7. Amsterdam: Rodopi, 1987.

Deroux, Carl. "Des traces inconnues de la *Dietétique* d'Anthime dans un manuscrit du Vatican (Reg. Lat. 1004)." *Latomus* 33 (1974), 680–687.

Dierkens, Alain. "Superstitions, christianisme et paganisme à la fin de l'époque mérovingienne: A propos de l'*Indiculus superstitionum et paganiarum.*" In *Magie, sorcellerie, parapsychologie,* edited by Hervé Hasquin, 9–26. Laicité série recherches 5. Brussels: Éditions de l'Université de Bruxelles, 1984.

Doppelfeld, Otto. "Die Domgrabung XI. Das fränkische Frauengrab." *Kölner Domblatt* 16–17 (1959), 41–78.

———. "Die Domgrabung XII. Totenbett und Stuhl des Knabengrabes." *Kölner Domblatt* 18–19 (1960), 85–106.

Douglas, Mary. "Deciphering a Meal." In *Food and Culture: A Reader,* edited by Carole Counihan and Penny van Esterik, 36–54. New York: Routledge, 1997.

———. *Natural Symbols: Explorations in Cosmology.* London: Pantheon Books, 1970.

———. *Purity and Danger: An Analysis of the Concepts of Pollution and Taboo.* New York: Praeger, 1966.

———. "Sacred Contagion." In *Reading Leviticus: A Conversation with Mary Douglas,* edited by John F.A. Sawyer, 86–106. Journal for the Study of the Old Testament, Supplement Series 227. Sheffield: Sheffield Academic Press Ltd., 1996.

Drew, Katherine Fischer. "Marcellus Empiricus." in *Lexikon des Mittelalters* 6, 221–222. Munich: Artemis Verlag, 1993.

Effros, Bonnie. "Appearance and Ideology: Creating Distinctions between Merovingian Clerics and Lay Persons." In *Encountering Medieval Dress and Textiles: Objects, Texts and Images,* edited by Janet Snyder and Désirée Koslin. New York: Palgrave Macmillan, forthcoming.

———. "Beyond Cemetery Walls: Early Medieval Funerary Topography and Christian Salvation," *EME* 6(1997), 1–23.

———. *Caring for Body and Soul: Burial and the Afterlife in the Merovingian World.* University Park: Pennsylvania State University Press, 2002.

———. "Images of Sanctity: Contrasting Descriptions of Radegund by Venantius Fortunatus and Gregory of Tours." *UCLA Historical Journal* 10 (1990), 38–58.

———. *Merovingian Mortuary Archaeology and the Making of the Early Middle Ages.* Berkeley: University of California Press, in press.

———. "Monuments and Memory: Repossessing Ancient Remains in Early Medieval Gaul." In *Topographies of Power in the Early Middle Ages,* edited by Mayke de Jong and Frans Theuws., 93–118. TRW 6. Leiden: E. J. Brill, 2001.

———. "Skeletal Sex and Gender in Merovingian Mortuary Archaeology." *Antiquity* 74 (2000), 632–639.

———. "Symbolic Expressions of Sanctity: Gertrude of Nivelles in the Context of Merovingian Mortuary Custom." *Viator* 27 (1996), 1–10.

BIBLIOGRAPHY

Elm, Susanna. *"Virgins of God": The Making of Asceticism in Late Antiquity*. Oxford: Clarendon Press, 1994.

Enright, Michael J. *Lady with a Mead Cup: Ritual, Prophesy and Lordship in the European Warband from La Tène to the Viking Age*. Dublin: Four Courts Press, 1996.

Ewig, Eugen. *Die Merowinger und das Frankenreich*. Urban-Taschenbücher 392. Stuttgart: Kohlhammer, 1988.

Fentress, James and Chris Wickham. *Social Memory*. Oxford: Basil Blackwell, 1992.

Février, Paul-Albert. "A propos du répas funéraire: Culte et sociabilité." *Cahiers archéologiques* 26 (1977), 29–45.

———. "La tombe chrétienne et l'Au-delà." In *Le temps chrétien de la fin de l'antiquité au moyen âge IIIe-XIIIe siècles, Paris, 9–12 mars 1981*, 163–183. Colloques internationaux du CNRS 604. Paris: Éditions du CNRS, 1984.

Finot, André. "Les médecins des rois mérovingiens et carlovingiens." *Histoire des sciences médicales* 4 (1970), 41–48.

Fischer, Klaus-Dietrich. "Zur Entwicklung des ärztlichen Standes im römischen Kaisserriech." *Medizin-historisches Journal* 14(1979), 165–175.

Flandrin, Jean-Louis and Massimo Montanri, eds. *Food: A Culinary History from Antiquity to the Present*. New York: Columbia University Press, 1999.

Flemming, Rebecca. *Medicine and the Making of Roman Women: Gender, Nature and Authority from Celsus to Galen*. Oxford: Oxford University Press, 2000.

Flint, Valerie I. J. "The Early Medieval 'Medicus,' the Saint—and the Enchanter." *Social History of Medicine* 2 (1989), 127–145.

———. *The Rise of Magic in Early Medieval Europe*. Princeton: Princeton University Press, 1991.

Folz, Robert. "Zur Frage der heiligen Könige: Heiligkeit und Nachleben in der Geschichte des burgundischen Königtums," *Deutsches Archiv für Erforschung des Mittelalters* 14 (1958), 317–344.

Fontaine, Jacques. "Hagiographie et politique, de Sulpice Sévère à Venance Fortunat." *Revue historique écclesiastique en France* 62 (1976), 113–140.

Fouracre, Paul. "Merovingian History and Merovingian Hagiography." *Past and Present* 127 (1990), 3–38.

———. "The Work of Audoenus of Rouen and Eligius of Noyon in Extending Episcopal Influence from the Town to the Country in Seventh-Century Neustria." In *The Church in Town and Countryside: Papers Read at the Seventeenth Summer Meeting and Eighteenth Winter Meeting of the Ecclesiastical History Society*, edited by Derek Baker, 77–91. Studies in Church History 16. Oxford: Basil Blackwell, 1979.

Fritze, Wolfgang. "Die fränkische Schwurfreundschaft der Merowingerzeit: Ihr Wesen und ihre politische Funktion." *Zeitschrift der Savigny-Stiftung für Rechtsgeschichte,* germanistische Abteilung 71 (1954), 74–125.

Gäbe, Sabine. "Radegundis: Sancta, Regina, Ancilla. Zum Heiligskeitideal der Radegundisviten von Fortunat und Baudonivia." *Francia* 16 (1989), 1–30.

Gaillard de Semainville, Henri. *Les cimetières mérovingens de la Côte chalonnaise et de la Côte maçônnaise*. Revue archéologique de l'Est et du Centre-Est, third supplement. Dijon: Les presses de l'imprimerie universitaire, 1980.

Garine, Igor L. de. "Food, Tradition and Prestige." In *Food, Man and Society,* edited by Dwain N. Walcher, Norman Kretchmer and Henry L. Barnett, 150–173. New York: Plenum Press, 1976.

Gauthier, Nancy. "Le réseau de pouvoirs de l'évêque dans la Gaule du haut moyen-âge." In *Towns and their Territories between Late Antiquity and the Early Middle Ages,* edited by Gian Pietro Brogiolo, Nancy Gauthier and Neil Christie, 173–207. TRW 9. Leiden: E. J. Brill, 2000.

———. "La topographie chrétienne entre idéologie et pragmatisme." In *The Idea and Ideal of the Town between Late Antiquity and the Early Middle Ages,* edited by Gian Pietro Brogiolo and Bryan Ward-Perkins, 195–209. TRW 4. Leiden: E. J. Brill, 1999.

Geary, Patrick J. *Before France and Germany: The Creation and Transformation of the Merovingian World.* New York: Oxford University Press, 1988.

———. "Exchange and Interaction between the Living and the Dead in Early Medieval Society." In his *Living with the Dead in the Middle Ages,* 77–92. Ithaca: Cornell University Press, 1994.

George, Judith W. *Venantius Fortunatus: A Latin Poet in Merovingian Gaul.* Oxford: Clarendon Press, 1992.

Gilchrist, Roberta. *Gender and Material Culture: The Archaeology of Religious Women.* London: Routledge, 1993.

Ginzburg, Carlo. "The Inquisitor as Anthropologist." In his *Clues, Myths and the Historical Method,* translated by John and Anne Tedeschi, 156–164. Baltimore: The Johns Hopkins University Press, 1986.

Godelier, Maurice. *Idéel et le matériel: Pensée, économies, sociétés.* Paris: Librairie Arthème Fayard, 1984.

Goetz, Hans-Werner. "'Beatus homo qui invenire amicum.' The Concept of Friendship in Early Medieval Letters of the Anglo-Saxon Tradition on the Continent (Boniface, Alcuin)." In *Friendship in Medieval Europe,* edited by Julian Haseldine, 124–136. Phoenix Mill: Sutton Publishing, 1999.

———. *Frauen im frühen Mittelalter. Frauenbild und Frauenleben im Frankenreich.* Weimar: Böhlau Verlag, 1995.

———. "Frauenbild und weibliche Lebensgestaltung im fränkischen Reich." In his *Weibliche Lebensgestaltung im frühen Mittelalter,* 7–44. Cologne: Böhlau Verlag, 1991.

———. "Heiligenkult und Geschlecht: Geschlectsspezifisches Wunderwirken in frühmittelalterliche Mirakelberichten?" *Das Mittelalter* 1 (1996), 89–111.

———. "Der kirchliche Festtag im frühmittelalterlichen Alltag." In *Feste und Feiern im Mittelalter: Paderborner Symposion des Mediävistenverbandes,* edited by Detlef Altenburg, Jörg Jarnut and Hans-Hugo Steinhoff, 53–62. Sigmaringen: Jan Thorbecke Verlag, 1991.

———. "*Nomen feminile:* Namen und Namengebung der Frauen im frühen Mittelalter." *Francia* 23 (1996), 99–134.

———. "Social and Military Institutions." In *The Cambridge Medieval History,* edited by Rosamond McKitterick, 451–480. Cambridge: Cambridge University Press, 1995.

Goffart, Walter. *The Narrators of Barbarian History (A.D. 500–800): Jordanes, Gregory of Tours, Bede and Paul the Deacon.* Princeton: Princeton University Press, 1988.

Gourevitch, Danielle. "Présence de la médecine rationelle gréco-romaine en Gaule." In *La médecine en Gaule: Villes d'eaux, sanctuaires des eaux,* edited by André Pelletier, 65–88. Paris: Picard, Éditeur, 1985.

Grant, Mark. "Introduction." In *Anthimus, De observatione ciborum,* 9–44. Blackawton: Prospect Books, 1996.

Grimm, Veronika E. *From Feasting to Fasting, the Evolution of a Sin: Attitudes to Food in Late Antiquity.* London: Routledge, 1996.

Guelphe, Walter. "L'éretisme dans le sud-ouest de la Gaule à l'époque mérovingienne." *Annales du Midi* 98 (1986), 293–315.

Gurevich, Aron I. *Categories of Medieval Culture,* translated by G. L. Campbell. London: Routledge and Kegan Paul, 1985.

———. *Medieval Popular Culture: Problems of Belief and Perception,* translated by Janos M. Bak and Paul A. Hollingsworth. Cambridge Studies in Oral and Literate Culture 14. Cambridge: Cambridge University Press, 1988.

Hagen, Ann. *A Handbook of Anglo-Saxon Food and Drink,* 2 vols. Hockwold cum Wilton: Anglo-Saxon Books, 1992–1995.

Halbwachs, Maurice. *On Collective Memory,* edited and translated by Lewis A. Coser. Chicago: University of Chicago Press, 1992.

Halsall, Guy. "Burial, Ritual and Merovingian Society." In *The Community, the Family and the Saint: Patterns of Power in Early Medieval Europe. Selected Proceedings of the International Medieval Congress, University of Leeds, 4–7 July 1994, 10–13 July 1995,* edited by Joyce Hill and Mary Swan, 325–338. Turnhout: Brepols, 1998.

———. *Settlement and Social Organization: The Merovingian Region of Metz.* Cambridge: Cambridge University Press, 1995.

———. "Violence and Society in the Early Medieval West: An Introductory Survey." In his *Violence and Society in the Early Medieval West,* 1–45. Woodbridge: Boydell & Brewer, 1998.

Hannig, Jürgen. "*Ars donandi:* Zur Ökonomie des Schenkens im früheren Mittelalter." In *Armut, Liebe, Ehre: Studien zur historische Kulturforschung,* edited by Richard van Dülmen, 11–37. Frankfurt: Fischer Taschenbuch Verlag GmbH, 1988.

Hardt, Matthias "Silbergeschirr als Gabe im Frühmittelalter." *Ethnographisch-Archäologische Zeitschrift* 37 (1996), 431–444.

———. "Silverware in Early Medieval Gift Exchange: *Imitatio Imperii* and Objects of Memory." In *Franks and Alamanni in the Merovingian Period: An Ethnographic Perspective,* edited by Ian Wood, 317–342. Studies in Historical Archaeoethnology 3. Woodbridge: Boydell, 1998.

———. "Verborgene Schätze nach schriftlichen Quellen der Völkerwanderungszeit und des frühen Mittelalters." In *Archäologisches Zellwerk: Beiträge zur Kulturgeschichte in Europa und Asien. Festschrift für Helmut Roth zum 60. Geburtstag,* edited by Ernst Pohl, Udo Recker and Claudia Theune, 255–266. Rahden: Verlag Marie Leidorf GmbH, 2001.

Harl, K. W. "Sacrifice and Pagan Belief in Fifth- and Sixth-Century Byzantium." *Past and Present* 128 (1990), 7–27.

158 CREATING COMMUNITY WITH FOOD AND DRINK

Harmening, Dieter. *Superstitio: Überlieferungs- und theoriegeschichtliche Untersuchungen zur kirchlich-theologischen Aberglaubensliteratur des Mittelalters.* Berlin: Erich Schmidt Verlag, 1979.

Harries, Jill. "Christianity and the City in Gaul." In *The City in Late Antiquity,* edited by John Rich, 77–98. Leicester-Nottingham Studies in Ancient Society 3. London: Routledge, 1992.

Harrison, Dick. *The Age of Abbesses and Queens: Gender and Political Culture in Early Medieval Europe.* Lund: Nordic Academic Press, 1998.

Hastorf, Christine A. "Gender, Space and Prehistory." In *Engendering Archaeology: Women and Prehistory,* edited by Joan M. Gero and Margaret W. Conkey, 132–159. Oxford: Basil Blackwell, 1991.

Hauck, Karl. "Rituelle Speisegemeinschaft im 10. und 11. Jahrhundert." *Studium generale* 3 (1950), 611–621.

Heather, Peter. *The Goths.* Oxford: Blackwell Publishers, 1996.

Hedeager, Lotte. *Iron-Age Societies: From Tribe to State in Northern Europe, 500 BC to AD 700,* translated by John Hines. Oxford: Blackwell, 1992.

Heinzelmann, Martin. *Gregor von Tours (538–594): 'Zehn Bücher Geschichte.' Historiographie und Gesellschaftskonzept im 6. Jahrhundert.* Darmstadt: Wissenschaftliche Buchgesellschaft, 1994.

———and Joseph-Claude Poulin. "Genovefa." In *Lexikon des Mittelalters* 4, 1237. Munich: Artemis Verlag, 1989.

Hellmuth, Leopold. *Gastfreundschaft und Gastrecht bei den Germanen.* Österreichische Akademie der Wissenschaften, philosophisch-historische Klasse, Sitzungsberichte 440. Vienna: Verlag der Österreichischen Akademie der Wissenschaften, 1984.

Hen, Yitzhak. *Culture and Religion in Merovingian Gaul, A.D. 481–751.* Leiden: E. J. Brill, 1995.

Henisch, Bridget A. *Fast and Feast: Food in Medieval Society.* University Park: Pennsylvania State University Press, 1976.

Hochstetler, Donald. "The Meaning of Monastic Cloister for Women According to Caesarius of Arles." In *Religion, Culture, and Society in the Early Middle Ages. Studies in Honor of Richard E. Sullivan,* edited by Thomas F. X. Noble and John J. Contreni, 27–40. Kalamazoo: Medieval Institute Publications, 1987.

Homeyer. "Der Dreißigste." In *Abhandlungen der Königlichen Akademie der Wissenschaften zu Berlin, 1864,* 87–120. Philologische und historische Abhandlungen. Berlin: Königliche Akademie der Wissenschaften, 1865.

Horden, Peregrine. "The Death of Ascetics: Sickness and Monasticism in the Early Byzantine East." In *Monks, Hermits and the Ascetic Tradition: Papers Read at the 1984 Summer Meeting and the 1985 Winter Meeting of the Ecclesiastical History Society,* edited by W. J. Sheils, 41–52. Studies in Church History 22. Oxford: Ecclesiastical History Society, 1985.

Hulin, L. Carless. "The Diffusion of Religious Symbols with Complex Societies." In *The Meaning of Things: Material Culture and Symbolic Expression,* edited by Ian Hodder, 90–96. One World Archaeology 6. London: Unwin Hyman, 1989.

Hunter, David. G. "Clerical Celibacy and the Veiling of Virgins: New Boundaries in Late Ancient Christianity." In *The Limits of Ancient Christianity: Essays on Late An-*

tique Thought and Culture in Honor of R. A. Markus, edited by William E. Klingshirn and Mark Vessey, 139–152. Ann Arbor: University of Michigan Press, 1999.

Iossifides, A. M. "Wine: Life's Blood and Spiritual Essence in a Greek Orthodox Convent." In *Alcohol, Gender and Culture,* edited by Dimitra Gefou-Madianou, 80–100. London: Routledge, 1992.

Jacob, Jean-Paul and Jean-Régis Mirbeau Gauvin. "Du don au mort à la redemption: Évolution du dépôt funéraire du Bas-Empire à l'apparition du don *pro anima.*" *Revue d'histoire du droit* 48 (1980), 307–327.

James, Edward. *The Merovingian Archaeology of South-West Gaul* 1. BAR Supplementary Series 25(i). Oxford: BAR, 1977.

———. *The Franks.* Oxford: Basil Blackwell, 1988.

———. "A Sense of Wonder: Gregory of Tours, Medicine and Science." In *The Culture of Christendom: Essays in Medieval History in Commemoration of Denis L. T. Bethell,* edited by Mark Anthony Meyer, 45–60. London: The Hambledon Press, 1993.

Janes, Dominic. "Treasure Bequest: Death and Gift in the Early Middle Ages." In *The Community, the Family and the Saint: Patterns of Power in Early Medieval Europe. Selected Proceedings of the International Medieval Congress, University of Leeds, 4–7 July 1994, 10–13 July 1995,* edited by Joyce Hill and Mary Swan, 363–377. Turnhout: Brepols, 1998.

Janssen, Walter. "Essen und Trinken im frühen und höhen Mittelalter aus archäologischer Sicht." In *Liber castellorum: 40 Variaties op het Thema Kasteel,* edited by T. J. Hoekstra, H. L. Janssen and I. W. L. Moerman, 324–337. Zutphen: De Walburg Pers, 1981.

Jarnut, Jörg. "Konsumvorschriften im Früh- und Hochmittelalter." In *Haushalt und Familie in Mittelalter und früher Neutzeit: Vorträge eines interdisziplinären Symposions vom 6.–9. Juni 1990 an der Rheinischen Friedrich Wilhelms-Universität Bonn,* edited by Trude Ehlert, 119–128. Sigmaringen: Jan Thorbecke Verlag, 1991.

Judic, Bruno. "Les 'manières de table' de Grégoire le Grand: Les cuillers envoyées de Lérins à Rome." *Le moyen âge* 106 (2000), 49–62.

Kaiser, Reinhold. *Das römische Erbe und das Merowingerreich,* revised edition. Enzyklopädie deutscher Geschichte 26. Munich: R. Oldenbourg Verlag, 1997.

Kerth, Klaus, Arno Rettner and Eva Stauch. "Die tierischen Speisebeigaben von zwei merowingerzeitlichen Gräberfeldern in Unterfranken." *AK* 24 (1995), 441–455.

Kieckhefer, Richard. *Magic in the Middle Ages.* Cambridge: Cambridge University Press, 1989.

———. "The Specific Rationality of Medieval Magic." *American Historical Review* 99(1994), 813–836.

Kitchen, John. *Saints' Lives and the Rhetoric of Gender: Male and Female in Merovingian Hagiography.* New York: Oxford University Press, 1998.

Klingshirn, William E. *Caesarius of Arles: The Making of a Christian Community in Late Antique Gaul.* Cambridge: Cambridge University Press, 1994.

Kopytoff, Igor. "The Cultural Biography of Things: Commoditization as Process." In *The Social Life of Things: Commodities in Cultural Perspective,* edited by Arjun Appadurai, 64–91. Cambridge: Cambridge University Press, 1986.

160 CREATING COMMUNITY WITH FOOD AND DRINK

Kötting, Bernhard. "Die Tradition der Grabkirche." In *Memoria: Der geschichtliche Zeugniswert des liturgischen Gedenkens im Mittelalter,* edited by Karl Schmid and Joachim Wollasch, 69–78. Münstersche Gedenkens im Mittelalter-Schriften 48. Munich: Wilhelm Fink Verlag, 1984.

Krautheimer, Richard. "Mensa-coemiterium-martyrium." In his *Studies in Early Christian, Medieval and Renaissance Art,* 35–58. New York: New York University Press, 1969.

Kroll, Jerome and Bernard Bachrach. "Sin and the Etiology of Disease in Pre-Crusade Europe." *Journal of the History of Medicine and Allied Sciences* 41 (1986), 395–414.

Krüger, Karl Heinrich. *Königsgrabkirchen der Franken, Angelsachsen und Langobarden bis zur Mitte des 8. Jahrhunderts.* Münstersche Mittelalter-Schriften 4. Munich: Wilhelm Fink Verlag, 1971.

Kyll, Nikolaus. *Tod, Grab, Begräbnisplatz, Totenfeier: Zur Geschichte ihres Brauchtums im Trierer Lande und in Luxemburg unter besonderer Berücksichtigung des Visitationshandbuches des Regino von Prüm (+915).* Rheinisches Archiv 81. Bonn: Ludwig Röhrscheid Verlag, 1972.

Lambot, D.C. "Le prototype des monastères cloîtrés de femmes: L'abbaye Saint-Jean d'Arles (VIe siècle)." *Revue liturgique et monastique* 23 (1937–1938), 169–174.

Laporte, Jean-Pierre. "Pour une nouvelle datation du testament d'Ermenthrude." *Francia* 14 (1986), 574–577.

Laurioux, Bruno. "Cuisiner à l'antique: Apicius au moyen âge." *Médiévale* 26 (1994), 17–38.

Lauwers, M. "'Religion populaire,' culture folklorique, mentalités. Notes pour une anthropologie culturelle du moyen âge." *Revue d'histoire ecclésiastique* 82 (1987), 221–258.

Lebecq, Stéphane. "The Role of Monasteries in the Systems of Production and Exchange of the Frankish World between the Seventh and the Beginning of the Ninth Centuries." In *The Long Eighth Century,* edited by Inge Lyse Hansen and Chris Wickham, 121–148. TRW 11. Leiden: E. J. Brill, 2000.

le Jan, Régine. "Convents, Violence and Competition for Power in Seventh-Century Francia." In *Topographies of Power in the Early Middle Ages,* edited by Mayke de Jong and Frans Theuws, 243–269. TRW 6. Leiden: E. J. Brill, 2001.

Leyser, Conrad. *Authority and Asceticism from Augustine to Gregory the Great.* Oxford; Clarendon Press, 2000.

———. "Masculinity in Flux: Nocturnal Emission and the Limits of Celibacy in the Early Middle Ages." In *Masculinity in Medieval Europe,* edited by Dawn M. Hadley, 103–120. London: Longman, 1999.

———. "'This Sainted Isle': Panegyric, Nostalgia, and the Invention of Lerinian Monasticism," in *The Limits of Ancient Christianity: Essays on Late Antique Thought and Culture in Honor of R. A. Markus,* edited by William E. Klingshirn and Mark Vessey, 188–206. Ann Arbor: University of Michigan Press, 1999.

Lifshitz, Felice. "Is Mother Superior? Towards a History of Feminine Amtscharisma." In *Medieval Mothering,* edited by John Carmi Parsons and Bonnie Wheeler, 117–138. New York: Garland Publishing, Inc., 1996.

BIBLIOGRAPHY 161

Lindsay, Hugh. "Eating with the Dead: The Roman Funerary Banquet." In *Meals in Context: Aspects of the Communal Meal in the Hellenistic World,* edited by Inge Nielsen and Hanne Sigismund Nielsen, 67–80. Åhrus Studies in Mediterranean Antiquity 1. Åhrus: Åhrus University Press, 1998.

Loseby, Simon T. "Arles in Late Antiquity: *Gallula Roma Arelas* and *Urbs Genesii.*" In *Towns in Transition: Urban Evolution in Late Antiquity and the Early Middle Ages,* edited by Neil Christie and Simon T. Loseby, 45–70. Aldershot: Scolar Press, 1996.

———. "Gregory's Cities: Urban Functions in Sixth-Century Gaul." In *Franks and Alamanni in the Merovingian Period: An Ethnographic Perspective,* edited by Ian Wood, 239–284. Studies in Archaeoethnology 3. Woodbridge: The Boydell Press, 1998.

———. "Marseilles and the Pirenne Thesis, I: Gregory of Tours, the Merovingian Kings, and 'un grand port.'" In *The Sixth Century: Production, Distribution and Demand,* edited by Richard Hodges and William Bowden, 203–229. TRW 3. Leiden: E. J. Brill, 1998.

———. "Marseilles and the Pirenne Thesis, II: 'Ville morte.'" In *The Long Eighth Century,* edited by Inge Lyse Hansen and Chris Wickham, 167–193. TRW 11. Leiden: E. J. Brill, 2000.

MacKinney, Loren C. "Medical Ethics and Etiquette in the Early Middle Ages: The Persistence of Hippocratic Ideals." *Bulletin of the History of Medicine* 26 (1952), 1–31.

MacMullen, Ramsay. *Christianity and Paganism in the Fourth to Eighth Centuries.* New Haven: Yale University Press, 1997.

Mann, Michael. *The Sources of Social Power,* 1: *A History from the Beginning to A.D. 1760.* Cambridge: Cambridge University Press, 1986.

Markus, Robert A. *The End of Ancient Christianity.* Cambridge: Cambridge University Press, 1990.

———. "From Caesarius to Boniface: Christianity and Paganism in Gaul." In *Le septième siècle: Changements et continuités. Actes du Colloque bilatéral franco-britannique tenu au Warburg Institute les 8–9 juillet 1988,* edited by Jacques Fontaine and J. N. Hillgarth, 154–172. London: The Warburg Institute, University of London, 1992.

———. *Gregory the Great and his World.* Cambridge: Cambridge University Press, 1997.

Masai, François. "La 'Vita patrum Iurensium' et les débuts du monachisme à Saint-Maurice-d'Agaune." In *Festschrift Bernhard Bischoff zu seinem 65. Geburtstag,* edited by Johanne Autenrieth and Franz Brunhölzl, 43–69. Stuttgart: Anton Hierseman, 1971.

Mathisen, Ralph W. "Barbarian Bishops and the Churches 'in barbaricis gentibus' during Late Antiquity." *Speculum* 72 (1997), 664–697.

———. "Crossing the Supernatural Frontier in Western Late Antiquity." In *Shifting Frontiers in Late Antiquity,* edited by Ralph W. Mathisen and Hagith S. Sivan, 309–320. Aldershot: Ashgate Publishing Limited, 1996.

———. *Roman Aristocrats in Barbarian Gaul: Strategies for Survival in an Age of Transition.* Austin: University of Texas Press, 1993.

162   CREATING COMMUNITY WITH FOOD AND DRINK

Mauss, Marcel. *The Gift: Forms and Functions of Exchange in Archaic Societies,* translated by Ian Cunnison. New York: W. W. Norton & Company, Inc., 1967.

McGowan, Andrew. *Ascetic Eucharists: Food and Drink in Early Christian Ritual Meals.* Oxford: Clarendon Press, 1999.

McNamara, Jo Ann. "*Imitatio Helenae:* Sainthood as an Attribute of Queenship." In *Saints: Studies in Hagiography,* edited by Sandro Sticca, 51–80. Medieval & Renaissance Texts & Studies 141. Binghamton: SUNY Center for Medieval and Early Renaissance Studies, 1996.

———. "A Legacy of Miracles: Hagiography and Nunneries in Merovingian Gaul." In *Women of the Medieval World: Essays in Honor of John Mundy,* edited by Julius Kirshner and Suzanne Wemple, 36–53. Oxford: Basil Blackwell, 1985.

———. "The Need to Give: Suffering and Female Sanctity in the Early Middle Ages." In *Images of Sanctity in Medieval Europe,* edited by Renate Blumenfeld-Kosinski and Timea Szell, 199–221. Ithaca: Cornell University Press, 1991.

Meens, Rob. "Pollution in the Early Middle Ages: The Case of the Food Regulations in the Penitentials." *EME* 4 (1995), 1–19.

Metz, René. "Les vièrges chrétiennes en Gaule au IVᵉ siècle." In *Saint Martin et son temps: Memorial au XVIᵉ centenaire des débuts du monachisme en Gaule 361–1961,* 109–132. Studia anselmiana 46. Rome: Herder, 1961.

Molland, Einar. "*Ut sapiens medicus:* Medical Vocabulary in St. Benedict's *Regula monachorum.*" *Studia monastica* 6 (1964), 273–298.

Momigliano, Arnaldo. "Popular Religious Beliefs and the Late Roman Historians." In *Popular Belief and Practice: Papers Read at the Ninth Summer Meeting and Tenth Winter Meeting of the Ecclesiastical History Society,* edited by G. J. Cuming and Derek Baker, 1–18. Studies in Church History 8. Cambridge: Cambridge University Press, 1972.

Montanari, Massimo. *The Culture of Food,* translated by Carl Ipsen. Oxford: Blackwell, 1994.

Moreira, Isabel. *Dreams, Visions and Spiritual Authority in Merovingian Gaul.* Ithaca: Cornell University Press, 2000.

———. "*Provisatrix optima:* St. Radegund of Poitiers' Relic Petitions to the East." *Journal of Medieval History* 19 (1993), 285–305.

Moreland, John. "Concepts of the Early Medieval Economy." In *The Long Eighth Century,* edited by Inge Lyse Hansen and Chris Wickham, 1–34. TRW 11. Leiden: E. J. Brill, 2000.

Moreau, Frédéric. "Les fouilles de Nampteuil-sous-Muret (Aisne) et fin de celles d'Aiguisy." In *Album Caranda: Sépultures gauloises, gallo-romaines et mérovingiennes.* Saint-Quentin: Imprimerie typographie et lithographique Charles Poette, 1886.

———. "Sépultures mérovingiennes: Nouvelles fouilles d'Arcy-Sainte-Restitue (Aisne)." In *Album Caranda: Sépultures gauloises, gallo-romaines et mérovingiennes.* Saint-Quentin: Imprimerie typographie et lithographique Charles Poette, 1885.

Morin, Germain. "Problèmes relatifs à la règle de S. Césaire d'Arles pour les moniales." *Revue bénédictine* 44(1932), 5–20.

Morris, Richard. *The Church in British Archaeology.* CBA Research Report 47. London: CBA, 1983.

BIBLIOGRAPHY

Naumann-Steckner, Friederike. "Death on the Rhine: Changing Burial Customs in Cologne, 3rd to 7th Century." In *The Transformation of the Roman World AD 400–900,* edited by Leslie Webster and Michelle Brown, 143–158. London: British Museum Press, 1997.

Nelson, Janet L. "Monks, Secular Men and Masculinity, c.900." In *Masculinity in Medieval Europe,* edited by Dawn M. Hadley, 121–142. London: Longman, 1999.

———. "Queens as Jezebels: Brunhild and Balthild in Merovingian History." In her *Politics and Ritual in Early Medieval Europe,* 1–48. London: Hambledon Press, 1986.

Noble, Thomas F. X. "The Transformation of the Roman World: Reflections on Five Years of Work." In *East and West: Modes of Communication. Proceedings of the First Plenary Conference at Merida,* edited by Evangelos Chrysos and Ian Wood, 259–277. TRW 5. Leiden: E. J. Brill, 1999.

Nonn, Ulrich. "Erminethrud-Eine vornehme neustrische Dame um 700." *HJ* 102 (1982), 135–143.

Norberg, Dag. "Remarques sur les lettres de Saint Didier de Cahors." In *Classical, Medieval and Renaissance Studies in Honor of Berthold Louis Ullman* 1, edited by Charles Henderson, 277–281. Rome: Edizioni di storia e letteratura, 1964.

Oexle, Judith. "Merowingerzeitliche Pferdebestattungen—Opfer oder Beigaben?" *FS* 18 (1984), 122–172.

Oexle, Otto Gerhard. "Mahl und Spende im mittelalterlichen Totenkult." *FS* 18 (1984), 401–420.

Park, Katharine. "Medicine and Society in Medieval Europe, 500–1500." In *Medicine in Society: Historical Essays,* edited by Andrew Wear, 59–90. Cambridge: Cambridge University Press, 1992.

Paxton, Frederick S. "Anointing the Sick and the Dying in Christian Antiquity and the Early Medieval West." In *Health, Disease and Healing in Medieval Culture,* edited by Sheila Campbell, Bert Hall and David Klausner, 93–102. New York: St. Martin's Press, 1992.

———. *Christianizing Death: The Creation of a Ritual Process in Early Medieval Europe.* Ithaca: Cornell University Press, 1990.

———. "Liturgy and Healing in an Early Medieval Saint's Cult: The Mass *in honore sancti Sigismundi* for the Cure of Fevers." *Traditio* 49 (1994), 23–43.

———. "Power and the Power to Heal: The Cult of St. Sigismund of Burgundy." *EME* 2 (1993), 95–110.

———. "Sickness, Death and Dying: The Legacy of Barbarian Europe in Ritual and Practice." In *Minorities and Barbarians in Medieval Life and Thought,* edited by Susan J. Ridyard and Robert G. Benson, 223–233. Sewanee: University of the South Press, 1996.

Pearson, Kathy L. "Nutrition and the Early-Medieval Diet." *Speculum* 72 (1997), 1–32.

Percival, John. "Villas and Monasteries in Late Roman Gaul." *Journal of Ecclesiastical History* 48 (1997), 1–45.

Périn, Patrick. "Les Ardennes à l'époque mérovingienne: Étude archéologique." *Études ardennaises* 50 (1967), 3–46.

Petersen, Joan M. "Dead or Alive? The Holy Man as Healer in East and West in the Late Sixth Century." *Journal of Medieval History* 9 (1983), 91–98.

164 CREATING COMMUNITY WITH FOOD AND DRINK

Peyroux, Catherine. "Gertrude's *furor*: Reading Anger in an Early Medieval Saint's *Life*." In *Anger's Past: The Social Uses of an Emotion in the Middle Ages*, edited by Barbara H. Rosenwein, 36–55. Ithaca: Cornell University Press, 1998.

Pietri, Charles. "L'espace chrétien dans la cité: Le *vicus christianorum* et l'espace chrétien de la cité arverne (Clermont)." *Revue d'histoire de l'église de France* 66 (1980), 177–209.

Pietri, Luce. "Les sépultures privilégiées en Gaule d'après les sources littéraires." In *L'inhumation privilégiée du IVe au VIIIe siècle en Occident: Actes du colloque tenu à Créteil les 16–18 mars 1984*, edited by Yvette Duval and Jean-Charles Picard, 133–142. Paris: De Boccard, 1986.

Pilet, Christian. *La nécropole de Frénouville: Étude d'une population de la fin du IIIe à la fin du VIIe siècle* 1. BAR International series 83(i). Oxford: BAR, 1980.

Pirling, Renate. "Ein fränkisches Fürstengrab aus Krefeld-Gellep." *Germania* 42 (1964), 188–216.

Pohl, Walter. "Telling the Difference: Signs of Ethnic Identity." In *Strategies of Distinction: The Construction of Ethnic Communities, 300–700*, edited by Walter Pohl and Helmut Reimitz, 17–69. TRW 2. Leiden: E. J. Brill, 1998.

Prinz, Friedrich. *Frühes Mönchtum im Frankenreich: Kultur und Gesellschaft in Gallien, den Rheinlanden und Bayern am Beispiel der monastischen Entwicklung (4. bis 8. Jahrhundert)*, second edition. Munich: R. Oldenbourg Verlag, 1988.

Reynolds, Burnam W. "*Familia sancti Martini: Domus ecclesiae* on Earth as It Is in Heaven." *Journal of Medieval History* 11 (1985), 137–143.

Riché, Pierre. "Note d'hagiographie mérovingienne: La vita S. Rusticulae." *Analecta bollandiana* 72 (1954), 369–377.

Richter, Michael. *The Formation of the Medieval West: Studies in the Oral Culture of the Barbarians*. Dublin: Four Courts Press, 1994.

Riddle, John M. "Pharmacy." In *Late Antiquity: A Guide to the Postclassical World*, edited by G. W. Bowersock, Peter Brown and Oleg Grabar, 641–642. Cambridge: Harvard University Press, 1999.

———. "Theory and Practice in Medieval Medicine." *Viator* 5 (1974), 157–184.

Rose, Valentin. "Die Diätetik des Anthimus an Theuderich König der Franken." In his *Anecdota graeca et graecolatina: Mitteilungen aus Handschriften zur Geschichte der griechischen Wissenschaft* 2, reprint edition, 41–102. Amsterdam: Verlag Adolf M. Hakkert, 1963.

Rousselle, Aline. "Abstinence et continence dans les monastères de Gaule méridionale à la fin de l'antiquité et au début du moyen age: Étude d'un régime alimentaire et de sa fonction." In *Hommage à André Dupont (1987–1972): Études médiévales languedociennes*, 239–254. Montpellier: Féderation historique du Languedoc méditerranéen et du Roussillon, 1974.

———. *Croire et guérir: La foi en Gaule dans l'antiquité tardive*. Paris: Librarie Arthème Fayard, 1990.

———. "La sage-femme et le thaumaturge dans la Gaule tardive: Les femmes ne font pas de miracles." In *La médecine en Gaule: Villes d'eaux, sanctuaires des eaux*, edited by André Pelletier, 241–251. Paris: Picard, Éditeur, 1985.

Salin, Édouard. *La civilisation mérovingienne d'après les sépultures, les textes et le laboratoire*, vols. 2 and 4. Paris: Éditions A. et J. Picard, 1952–1959.

BIBLIOGRAPHY 165

Sartory, G. "In der Arena der Askese. Fasten im frühen Christentum." In *Speisen, Schlemmen, Fasten. Eine Kulturgeschichte des Essens,* edited by Uwe Schultz, 71–82. Frankfurt: Insel, 1993.

Scheibelreiter, Georg. "Königstöchter im Kloster: Radegund (+587) und der Nonnenaufstand von Poitiers (589)." *Mitteilungen des Instituts für österreichische Geschichtsforschung* 87 (1979), 1–37.

Scheurer, Ferdinand and Anatole Lablotier. *Fouilles du cimetière barbare de Bourogne.* Paris: Berger-Levrault, Éditeurs, 1914.

Schmidt-Wiegand, Ruth. "Spuren paganer religiosität in den frühmittelalterlichen Leges." In *Iconologia sacra: Mythos, Bildkunst und Dichtung in der Religions- und Sozialgeschichte Alteuropas. Festschrift für Karl Hauck zum 75. Geburtstag,* edited by Hagen Keller and Nikolaus Staubach, 249–262. Berlin: Walter de Gruyter, 1994.

Schmitt, Jean-Claude. "'Religion populaire' et culture folklorique." *Annales ESC* 31 (1976), 941–953.

Schnapp, Alain. *The Discovery of the Past: The Origins of Archaeology.* London: British Museum Press, 1996.

Schönfeld, Walther. "Die Xenodochien in Italien und Frankreich im frühen Mittelalter." In *Zeitschrift der Savigny-Stiftung für Rechtsgeschichte,* kanonistische Abteilung 12 (1922), 1–54.

Schulenberg, Jane Tibbetts. "Female Sanctity: Public and Private Roles, ca.500–1100." In *Women and Power in the Middle Ages,* edited by Mary Erler and Maryanne Kowaleski, 102–125. Athens: University of Georgia Press, 1988.

Schulze, Mechtild. "Diskussionsbeitrag zur Interpretations früh- und hochmittelalterlicher Flußfunde." *FS* 18 (1984), 222–248.

Scuvée, Frédéric. *Le cimetière barbare de Réville (Manche) (VIe-VIIe siècles).* Caen: Caron et Cie, 1973.

Shanzer, Danuta. "Bishops, Letters, Fast, Food and Feast in Later Roman Gaul." In *Revisiting Late Roman Gaul,* edited by Ralph Mathisen and Danuta Shanzer, 217–236. London: Ashgate, 2001.

———. "Two Clocks and a Wedding: Theodoric's Diplomatic Relations with the Burgundians." *Romanobarbarica* 14 (1996–1997), 225–258.

Simmer, Alain. *Le cimetière mérovingien d'Audun-le-Tiche (Moselle).* Mémoires de l'AFAM 2. Paris: Éditions Errance, 1988.

———. *La nécropole mérovingienne d'Ennery (Moselle): Fouilles d'Emile Delort (1941).* Mémoires de l'AFAM 4. Rouen: AFAM, 1993.

Smith, Julia M. H. "Did Women Have a Transformation of the Roman World?" *Gender & History* 12 (2000), 552–571.

Smith, Jonathan Z. *To Take Place: Toward Theory in Ritual.* Chicago: University of Chicago Press, 1987.

Socley, Emile. "Les greniers funéraires de Noiron-sous-Gevry (Côte-d'Or)." *Bulletin de la Société préhistorique française* 9 (1912), 745–762.

———. "Rapport sur plusieurs greniers funéraires découverts dans un cimetière, de la période mérovingienne, à Noiron-sous-Gévry (Côte-d'Or)." *Bulletin de la Société préhistorique française* 9 (1912), 308–323.

166 CREATING COMMUNITY WITH FOOD AND DRINK

Stancliffe, C. E. "From Town to Country: The Christianisation of the Touraine 370–600." In *The Church in Town and Countryside: Papers Read at the Seventeenth Summer Meeting and Eighteenth Winter Meeting of the Ecclesiastical History Society*, edited by Derek Baker, 43–59. Studies in Church History 16. Oxford: Basil Blackwell, 1979.

Theissen, Gerd. *The Social Setting of Pauline Christianity: Essays on Corinth*, edited and translated by John Schütz. Philadelphia: Fortress Press, 1975.

Thelamon, Françoise. "Ascèse et sociabilité. Les conduites alimentaires des moines d'Egypte au IVᵉ siècle." *Revue des études augustiniennes* 38 (1992), 295–321.

Thiérot, Amaury and Raymond Lantier. "Le cimetière mérovingien du Maltrat à Vouciennes." *Revue archéologique* sixth series 15 (1940), 210–246.

Thomas, Louis-Vincent. *Rites de mort. Pour la paix des vivants*. Paris: Fayard, 1985.

Van Dam, Raymond. *Leadership and Community in Late Antique Gaul* (Berkeley: University of California Press, 1985.

———. *Saints and their Miracles in Late Antique Gaul*. Princeton: Princeton University Press, 1993.

van Uytfanghe, Marc. *Stylisation biblique et condition humaine dans l'hagiographie mérovingienne (650–750)*. Verhandelingen van de Koninklijke Academie voor Wetenschnappen, Letteren en Schone Kunsten van België, Klasse der Letteren 49, vol.120. Brussels: Paleis der Academiën, 1987.

Veyne, Paul. *Bread and Circuses: Historical Sociology and Political Pluralism*, abridged with an introduction by Oswyn Murray, translated by Brian Pearce. London: Penguin Books, 1990.

Vierck, Hayo. "Hallenfreude: Archäologische Spuren frühmittelalterlicher Trinkgelage und mögliche Wege zur ihrer Deutung." In *Feste und Feiern im Mittelalter: Paderborner Symposion des Mediävistenverbandes*, edited by Detlef Altenburg, Jörg Jarnut and Hans-Hugo Steinhoff, 115–122. Sigmaringen: Jan Thorbecke Verlag, 1991.

Wallace-Hadrill, J. M. *The Long-Haired Kings*. Medieval Academy of America Reprints for Teaching. Toronto: University of Toronto Press, 1982.

Ward, Benedicta. "Pelagia: Beauty Riding by." In her *Harlots of the Desert: A Study of Repentance in Early Monastic Sources*, 57–75. Kalamazoo: Cistercian Publications, Inc., 1987.

Weiner, Annette B. *Inalienable Possessions: The Paradox of Keeping-While-Giving*. Berkeley: University of California Press, 1992.

Wemple, Suzanne Fonay. *Women in Frankish Society: Marriage and the Cloister 500 to 900*. Philadelphia: University of Pennsylvania Press, 1985.

Whatley, E. Gordon. "An Early Literary Quotation from the *Inventio S. Crucis*: A Note on Baudonivia's *Vita S. Radegundis* (BHL 7049)." *Analecta bollandiana* 111 (1993), 81–91.

Wilson, David. *Anglo-Saxon Paganism*. London: Routledge, 1992.

Wittern, Susanne. *Frauen, Heiligkeit und Macht. Lateinische Frauenviten aus dem 4. bis 7. Jahrhundert*. Ergebnisse der Frauenforschung 33. Stuttgart:Verlag J.B. Metzler, 1994.

Wolfram, Herwig. *The Roman Empire and its Germanic Peoples*, translated by Thomas Dunlap. Berkeley: University of California Press, 1997.

Wood, Ian. "Administration, Law and Culture in Merovingian Gaul," in *The Uses of Literacy in Early Medieval Europe*, edited by Rosamond McKitterick, 63–81. Cambridge: Cambridge University Press, 1990.

———. "Early Merovingian Devotion in Town and Country." In *The Church in Town and Countryside: Papers Read at the Seventeenth Summer Meeting and the Eighteenth Winter Meeting of the Ecclesiastical History Society*, edited by Derek Baker, 61–76. Studies in Church History 16. Oxford: Basil Blackwell, 1979.

———. "The Frontiers of Western Europe: Developments East of the Rhine in the Sixth Century." In *The Sixth Century: Production, Distribution and Demand*, edited by Richard Hodges and William Bowden, 231–253. TRW 3. Leiden: E. J. Brill, 1998.

———. "Letter and Letter-Collections from Antiquity to the Early Middle Ages: The Prose Works of Avitus of Vienne." In *The Culture of Christendom: Essays in Medieval History in Commemoration of Denis L. T. Bethell*, edited by Marc Anthony Meyer, 29–43. London: The Hambledon Press, 1993.

———. *The Merovingian Kingdoms 450–751*. London: Longmans, 1994.

———. *The Missionary Life: Saints and the Evangelisation of Europe 400–1050*. Harlow: Longman, 2001.

———. "A Prelude to Columbanus: The Monastic Achievement in the Burgundian Territories." In *Columbanus and Merovingian Monasticism*, edited by H. B. Clarke and Mary Brennan, 3–32. BAR International Series 113. Oxford: BAR, 1981.

———. "Topographies of Holy Power in Sixth-Century Gaul." In *Topographies of Power in the Early Middle Ages*, edited by Mayke de Jong and Frans Theuws, 137–154. TRW 6. Leiden: E. J. Brill, 2001.

———. "The Use and Abuse of Latin Hagiography in the Early Medieval West," in *East and West: Modes of Communication. Proceedings of the First Plenary Conference at Merida*, edited by Evangelos Chrysos and Ian Wood, 93–109. TRW 5. Leiden: E. J. Brill, 1999.

Young, Bailey K. "Merovingian Funeral Rites and the Evolution of Christianity: A Study in the Historical Interpretation of Archaeological Material." Ph.D. diss. University of Pennsylvania, 1975.

———. "Paganisme, christianisation et rites funéraires mérovingiens." *AM* 7 (1977), 5–81.

———. "Pratiques funéraires et mentalités païennes." In *Clovis: Histoire et mémoire. Le baptême de Clovis, l'événement*, edited by Michel Rouche, 15–42. Paris: Presses de l'Université de Paris-Sorbonne, 1997.

———. *Quatre cimetières mérovingiens de l'Est de la France: Lavoye, Dieue-sur-Meuse, Mezières-Manchester et Mazerny*. BAR International Series 208. Oxford: BAR, 1984.

———. "Quelques réflexions sur les sépultures privilégiées, leur contexte et leur évolution surtout dans la Gaule de l'Est." In *L'inhumation privilégiée du IVe au VIIIe siècle en Occident: Actes du colloque tenu à Créteil les 16–18 mars 1984*, edited by Yvette Duval and Jean-Charles Picard, 69–88. Paris: De Boccard, 1986.

INDEX

Aaron the Presbyter, 131 n. 35
Abraham, 26, 108 n. 70
abstinence from food and drink, *see* fasting
Acts, Book of, 18–9
Adam, 42
adventus ceremony, 52
Adversus Jovinianum, 59
Aemilianus, 31
agape, 74
Agaune, shrine of, 61
Agde, Council of, 17, 35, 57
Agnes, 12, 47, 49–50
Agrestius, 20
ale, *see* beer
Alemannic population, 9
alms, *see* charity
Ambrose of Milan, 43, 75
amicitia, see friendship
amulets, 6, 57, 129 n. 19, 129 n. 21
Anglo-Saxon burial customs, 142 n. 78
anointing of the sick, 58, 131 n. 34, 133 n. 55
Anstrude, 6
Anthimus, 7, 63–6, 134 n. 73
Apicius, 7, 30, 64
archiater, 56, 63
Arcy-Sainte-Restitue, cemetery of, 72
Arians, interactions with Catholics, 17–18, 65
Aristotle, 62
Arles
    Council of, 47
    monastery of Saint-Jean, 44–5, 49
armament
    clerical lack of, 32, 39–40
    deposition of, 89–90
    symbolic role of, 5, 26, 28–9
Attalus, 65
Audollent, Auguste, 69
Audouen of Rouen, 11, 26
Augustine of Hippo, 12, 29, 31, 36, 41, 43,
    45, 62, 74–5
Aurelian of Arles, *Rules* of, 46
Austrechild, 56–7
Auxerre, 112 n. 118

Avitianus, 106 n. 56
Avitus of Vienne, 19, 26, 39, 42, 108 n. 83

Balthild, 59
banquets, see feasting
Barontus, 59, 78–9, 132 n. 44
Baudonivia, 48–52, 125 n. 83
Bayerische Landesamt für Denkmalpflege,
    88
beer, 4, 9, 16, 64, 66, 80, 117 n. 63
Benedict of Nursia, 21, 43
    Rule of, 29–30, 46, 58
Benignus, 78
bishops' role in towns, 34–6
Blaesilla, 41, 45
boars, castrated, 11
Bobbio Missal, 21
Bordeaux
    church of Saint-Seurin, 82
    Council of, 26
Boulanger, C., 81
Bourogne, cemetery of, 84
Brunhild, 11, 33, 78, 133 n. 61
Bullough, Donald, 10
Burgundofara, 53, 127 n. 105
Bynum, Caroline Walker, 48

Caelius Aurelianus, 58
Caesaria II of Arles, 49
Caesaria of Arles, 44–5
Caesarius of Arles
    charity of, 22
    on feasting, 6–7, 18, 27, 40–1, 44–8,
        52–4, 102 n. 5
    on moderation, 31, 43–5
    on physicians, 57–8, 76–7
    Rule for Monks of, 45
    Rule for Virgins of, 16, 41, 43–8, 50,
        52–3, 122 n. 36
    Recapitulatio of, 46
Caluppa, 31
Cana, wedding at, 15, 94
Canones hibernenses, 14

170 CREATING COMMUNITY WITH FOOD AND DRINK

captives, redemption of, 22
Carilephus, 32
Caristia, 76
caritas, 28
carmen funebris, 77
carmina diabolica, 73
Cassiodorus, 58, 63
celestial medicine, 131 n. 43, 131 n. 44, 131
    n. 45
ceramic vessels, *see also* organic residues
    deposits in graves, 69–72, 74, 77, 81–5
    production and provenance of, 80, 82, 90
    symbolic potential of, 23, 110 n. 101
Chaldaeans, 108 n. 70
charity, in form of food for poor, 35–6,
    75–6, 93
Charon's obol, 82. *See also* paganism
Chartres, 93
Chelles, monastery of, 59, 112 n. 118
Childebert, 32, 77, 103 n. 19
Chilperic, 27, 56
Chilperic II, 30
Chlothar II, 26
Chlotild, 16, 48
claustration
    for nuns, 40, 42–4, 121 n. 30, 122 n. 38,
        122 n. 39, 126 n. 95
    for monks, 46
Clement of Alexandria, 29, 41
clerical interaction with lay nobility, 27–8,
    33–4, 36–7
Clichy, Council of, 10
Clovis, 65
Cocytus river, 82
Cologne
    cathedral of, 80
    church of St. Severinus, 79–80
Columbanus, 9, 12–13, 20, 33–4, 40, 53,
    102 n. 4, 127 n. 105
    Rule of, 20, 29–30, 46
    penitential of, 10
Concilium germanicum, 79
Condat, monastery of, 29
Confessions, 36, 75
Constantinople, 7, 52, 56, 63
convivia, see feasts
Corbie, monastery of, 30, 64, 109 n. 89
Corinthians, Letters to the, 10, 19
corporal punishment, 17, 20, 77, 110 n. 92
councils, *see individual locations*
cross, making the sign of, 6, 9, 15–16,
    18–21, 33, 61, 110 n. 92, 110 n. 94
Cynics, 12

de Nie, Giselle, 15
De institutione virginum et contemptu mundi, 47

De institutis coenobiorum, 44–5
De materia medica, 55, 129 n. 22
De medicamentis, 55
De observatione ciborum, 7, 63–4, 6
Delamain, Philippe, 83, 86
desert saints, 12, 14, 16, 40
Desiderius of Bordeaux, 57, 130 n. 25
Desiderius of Cahors, 26
Dialogues, 21
Dierkens, Alain, 141 n. 56
dietary regimens, 63–4, 95
digestion, process of, 135 n. 78, 135 n. 79
Dioscorides, 55, 58, 129 n. 22
Donatus of Besançon, *Rule* of, 20, 46–7
drunken behavior and dancing
    condemnation of, 15, 18, 27–8, 76–7, 103
        n. 19, 114 n. 30, 114 n. 31, 137 n. 21
    punishment for, 10, 18

Easter feast, 28
Echternach, monastery of, 64
Eden, Garden of, 19, 42
Eligius of Noyon, 11, 26, 58, 77
Ennery, cemetery of, 89
Enright, Michael J., 107 n. 62
Époisses, villa of, 33
Erminethrudis, 23
Eucharist, 3–4, 13–15, 17, 21–2, 48, 58, 74,
    106 n. 49
    on behalf of the dead, 77–8, 91 106 n.
        49
Euchstochium, 133 n. 64
Eufronius of Tours, 52
Eumerus of Nantes, 58
Eustasius, 20
Eve, 42
evergetism, 12
ex voto offerings, 78
excommunication, 17, 95
exorcism
    of vessels, 24
    of water, salt, and oil, 21

Faremoutiers, monastery of, 53
fasting
    to curb female proclivities, 7, 16, 41,
        48–9, 62
    for good health, 62, 66
    moderation for monks, 29–32, 62
    moderation for nuns, 43, 45, 47, 49–50,
        62, 125 n. 81, 134 n. 75
    in penance, 5, 10, 13
    as purificatory rite, 5, 62
    as source of authority, 2–3, 5–6, 41,
        93–4, 125 n. 77
Faustus of Riez, 29

INDEX

171

feasting, *see also* fasting, food, funerary
  feasting, hospitality
  clerical support for, 6, 8, 11–14, 24–5,
    27–9, 32–6
  imagery of, 126 n. 90, 136 n. 3
  pagan antecedents of, 8–9, 18
  partial prohibition against for nuns, 29,
    45–6, 50, 123 n. 52, 123 n. 53
  symbolic role of, 3–4, 16–17, 66
Feralia, 76
Ferreolus of Uzès, 42
Finsterwalder, Paul Willem, 109 n. 89
fish, 3, 31, 42, 115 n. 46
Flavia, 46
Flood, punishment of, 19
Florentina, 47
Florentius of Tricastina, 53
food and drink
  deposited in graves, 16–17, 69–71,
    74–5, 77, 79–80, 82, 85, 87–8, 90,
    138 n. 27, 138 n. 33
  distribution of, 14, 27
  offerings of at graves, 87, 90
  offerings of at Mass, 78
  opposition to waste of, 10
  shortages of, 16, 107 n. 60
  unclean, 10, 19–20
forbidden fruit, 42
Fos, port of, 30
Framoaldus, 78–9
Fredegar, 1
Frénouville, cemetery of, 127 n. 1
friendship, 5–6, 25–6, 28
Fructuosus of Braga, *Rule* of, 30
Fulda, monastery of, 109 n. 89
funerary feasting, 3, 8, 15–17, 34, 67, 69–74,
    91, 95
  archaeological evidence for, 80, 89
  clerical condemnation of, 73, 75–7,
    79–80, 87, 90, 138 n. 29
  methodological problems regarding, 78
  among priests, 76
funerary fires, archaeological traces of, 80,
    88–9, 142 n. 76
Furia, 41, 120 n. 9
Fuscina, 39

Gaius Petronius, 71
Galen, 7, 58, 62, 64
Gallus of Clermont, 34
garum, 21–2, 30
Gauthstrude of Jussamoutiers, 46
Gelasian sacramentary, 18, 21
gender distinctions, 2, 16, 43–9, 97 n. 2, 98
    n. 11, 98 n. 15, 122 n. 38, 122 n. 39
  archaeological evidence of, 80, 85, 90–1

Genesis, Book of, 26
Genovefa, 15, 21–2, 43, 48
Gertrude of Nivelles, 2, 48
glass vessels
  chronology and distribution of, 82, 90
  deposition of in graves, 69, 74, 77, 82,
    84, 86–7
  miracles involving, 23
Glory of the Martyrs, 18
gluttony, punishment for, 18, 28, 42
Goetz, Hans-Werner, 5, 98 n. 15, 123 n. 42
graves, care for, 77–9, 138 n. 35
Gregory I, 11, 15, 21, 31, 78
Gregory of Langres, 65
Gregory of Tours, 1, 47–8, 50, 52, 76–8, 117
    n. 58, 131 n. 39
  on feasting, 6, 17, 27, 34
  on miracles, 15, 23, 30–1, 33, 110 n.
    101, 132 n. 48
  on physicians, 56–7, 59–60, 130 n. 25
Guntramn, 27, 57

Hauck, Karl, 12
healing, *see* amulets, herbs, holy oil,
    physicians, relics, saints
Helena, model for female behavior, 50
Helipidius of Lyons, 56
Hen, Yitzhak, 112 n. 118
Henisch, Bridget Ann, 106 n. 47
herbs and herbal remedies, 6, 55, 61
heretics, exclusion of, 17–18
Hermes, cemetery of, 89
hermits, 31–2
herniary brace, 127 n. 1
Herpes, cemetery of, 83, 86
Hippocrates, 58, 62
hoards, 22
Hochstetler, Donald, 122 n. 38
Holy Cross, relic of, 50, 52
holy oil, 6–7, 15, 58, 130 n. 34
Honoratus, *Rule* of, 43, 45
horses and other animals, deposition of,
    87–8
hospitality, 5, 14, 25–7, 32, 35–6, 39, 95. *See
    also* feasting
  by abbesses and nuns, 39–40, 42, 45–8,
    50–1
  by bishops and monks, 29, 102 n. 3, 119
    n. 90
  churches as places of plenty, 11–12, 16,
    23–4
humours, 62–4, 95, 134 n. 70

idols, 78
illness as punishment for sins, 60, 132 n. 48
Indiculus superstitionum et paganiarum, 79

172 CREATING COMMUNITY WITH FOOD AND DRINK

infirmaries in monasteries, 58
Ingenuus, 23
intra muros, monasteries located, 47
Irenaeus of Lyons, 12
Irish penitentials, 20, 109 n. 85

Jerome, 29, 31, 41, 45, 59, 62, 120 n. 9, 130
 n. 37, 133 n. 64
Jesus, as provider of food, 14–5, 51, 94
Jews, 17, 59, 131 n. 39
John Cassian, 12, 29, 41, 44–5, 126 n. 88
John of Ephesus, 130 n. 35
Jonas of Bobbio, 9, 21, 33–4
Julian of Brioude, relics of, 34–5
Junianus, 59
Jura fathers, *Life* of, 29
Justin II, 52

Kashrut, 19, 109 n. 85
knives, deposition of in graves, 85, 87
Krefeld-Gellep, cemetery of, 82

Lablotier, Anatole, 84
Lambot, D.C., 122 n. 39
Lantier, Raymond, 88
Last Supper, 15, 94
last testaments, *see* wills
lay healers, 6–7
le Jan, Régine, 119 n. 5
Leander of Seville, 47
Lenten fasting, 27
Leo, 65
Leodebodus, 23
leprosy, 60, 132 n. 46
Lérins, monastery of, 31, 43, 45
Les Andelys, monastery of, 16
Leubovera, 50
Leunast, 59
Leviticus, Book of, 19
Liber in gloria confessorum, 23
Liber historiae Francorum, 1
Life of the Fathers, 30, 33
Lot, 14
Luke, Gospel according to, 39
Lupicinus, 12, 29, 31
Luxueil, monastery of, 20, 127 n. 105
luxury vessels, 22–3
Lyons, Council of, 13

MacKinney, Loren, 134 n. 73
Mâcon, Council of, 20, 26, 36
magic
 in healing, 57, 61, 130 n. 24
 versus miracles, 15
Mainz, 109 n. 89
maleficium, see magic

malpractice, 56–57, 129 n. 14, 129 n. 15
Mamertus of Vienne, 12, 35
Manes, 74
Marcellina, 43
Marcellus of Bordeaux, 55, 129 n. 12
Marcellus of Paris, 77
Marchélepot, cemetery of, 81
Marileif, 56
Maroveus of Poitiers, 50, 52
Marseilles
 nunnery in, 44
 port of, 30
Martha and Mary, 39
Martin of Braga, 77
Martin of Tours, 15, 26, 30, 33, 48–9, 93, 130 n.
 25
Martius, 31
Martres-de-Veyre, cemetery of, 69
martyria, see saints, graves of
masculinity, expression of, 6, 26, 28–9,
 39–40
Masses
 for dead, 74, 77–9, 138 n. 33, 139
 n. 37
 restrictions on celebration of, 35
matricularii, 35
Matthew, Gospel according to, 19
Mazerny, cemetery of, 89
McCarthy, Maria Caritas, 126 n. 88
mead, 64
medical practice, 55, 130 n. 22, 130 n. 35.
 See also individual texts, physicians
 ancient medicine, 7
 archaeological evidence for, 128 n. 1
 dangers of, 56–7
 decline of, 55–6, 62–3
 manuscripts related to, 7
Melania the Younger, 45
Misere mei Deus, 79
Missale Gothicum, 59
Monegund, 41, 61, 93
Monica, 75
Montanari, Massimo, 40, 117 n. 63
Moreau, Frédéric, 70, 72
Morley, cemetery of, 89
Moses, 108 n. 70

Nampteuil-sous-Muret, cemetery of, 70
Natural History, 55
Noiron-sous-Gevry, cemetery of, 89
novemdial sacrificium, 74
Numbers, Book of, 109 n. 85

Oexle, Judith, 88
organic residues found in vessels, 82–3,
 85–6, 90

INDEX

Orléans, Council of, 10, 13, 35, 43, 47, 109
    n. 91

Pactus legis salicae, 11
Paedagogus, 29, 41
paganism, *see also* amulets, drunken
    behavior and dancing, sacrifices
    alleged survivals from, 12, 75–7, 85, 106
      n. 47, 107 n. 69
    continued practice of, 10–11, 82, 102 n.
      4, 107 n. 61
    feasting, 4–5
    healing practices of, 6–7, 78, 133 n. 56
    interruption of rites, 9–11, 14
Paradise, 19, 108 n. 83
Parentalia, 74–6, 78, 87, 91
Paris, Council of, 77
Passio Praeiecti, 27–8
Paternus, 30
Patiens of Lyons, 36
Patroclus, 30–1, 117 n. 58
Paul of Tarsus, 10, 19
Paula, 133 n. 64
Pelagia of Antioch, 41
pharaoh, 108 n. 70
phylacteries, *see* amulets
physicians, 7, 55–8, 63–4, 95, 130 n. 30. *See*
    also medical practice
    clerical disdain for, 59, 130 n. 37, 132
      n. 43
Pilet, Christian, 128 n. 1
pilgrimage, 93
Pliny the Elder, 6, 55, 130 n. 22
plunder, 6
poison, 20–1
Poitiers, monastery of Sainte-Croix, 44,
    47–51, 122 n. 36, 132 n. 46
Polemius Silvius, calendar of, 76
Portianus, 33
potlatch, 104 n. 25
Projectus of Issoire, 27–8
prayers, *see also* Eucharist, Masses
    at meals, 18, 110 n. 94
    for the dead, 17, 23
pseudo-Augustinian writings, 75
purgatorial suffering, 13, 78–9
purity and pollution, 5, 11, 18–23, 95, 109
    n. 85

Radegund of Poitiers, 12, 41, 44, 47–52,
    93–4, 132 n. 46
Ravenna, 63, 65–6
recipes for cooking, 4, 18, 30, 62
Regino of Prüm, 73
Regula cuiusdam patris ad virgines, 53, 127
    n. 105

relics, *see also* saints
    consumption of, 53
    healing by, 6–7, 33, 57, 59–61, 66, 93–5
    burial with, 48
Remigius of Reims, shroud of, 61
Reovalis, 56
Réville, cemetery of, 80
Riddle, John, 62
Rogations, 12–13, 35
Rules, episcopal enforcement of, 47–8. *See*
    also under names of authors.
rustici, 78
Rusticula of Arles, 41–2, 94
Rusticus of Toulouse, 31

Sabinus of Canossa, 21
sacrifices, 10–11, 17, 19, 78, 109 n. 91
    consumption of by Christians, 18–19
Sadalberga, 16
Saint-Cyran-en-Brenne, monastery of, 59
Saint-Denis, monastery of, 15
St. Peter, feast day of, 76
St. Ricquier, monastery of, 109 n. 89
saints, *see also* relics
    burial of, 73, 74
    feast days of, 112 n. 118
    graves of, 75, 78
    healing by, 53
Salin, Édouard, 88
Salvius of Albi, 62
Samson, cemetery of, 89
Sapientia artis medicinae, 63, 134 n. 71, 134
    n. 77
Satyricon, 71
Scheibelreiter, Georg, 47
Scholastica, 43
serpents, 33, 42, 77
Sidonius Apollinaris, 34, 36, 76
Sigibert, 52
Sigismund, relics of, 61
Sigivald, 33
Sigrada, 6
Simmer, Alain, 142 n. 76
slavery, 1–2, 65
Sodom and Gomorrah, 14
Sophia, 52
sorcery, *see* magic
spices, 30, 64
spoons, 72
Sulpicius Severus, 15, 30, 42, 49

terra sigillata, 74
Theodore of Canterbury, penitential of,
    14–15, 20, 109 n. 89
Theodore of Marseilles, 27
Theodoric, 7, 56, 63–6

174   CREATING COMMUNITY WITH FOOD AND DRINK

Theodosius II, 55
Theudebert, 65
Theuderic, 7, 33–4, 63–6
Thiérot, Amaury, 88
Timothy, Letters to, 10, 49
Tobias, 108 n. 70
Toledo, Council, 76–7
Tours, Council, 76, 109 n. 91, *see also*
      Gregory of Tours, Martin of Tours
treasure hoard, 12
Trimalchio, 71

unction, *see* anointing of the sick

Vaast of Arras, 9, 13
van Uytfanghe, Marc, 102 n. 3
Variae, 63
vegetarianism, 12–13, 23, 31, 49, 117 n. 58,
      105 n. 32, 106 n. 48
Venantius Fortunatus, 15, 26, 28, 30–1, 36,
      41, 62, 77
    on Radegund, 12, 47–52, 126 n. 90
Vienne, 12
Vilicus of Metz, 36
Vinitharius, 30, 64
violence, vulnerability of churches to, 119
    n. 5
Visio Baronti, 78–9

Vita Audoini, 26
Vita Columbani, 9
Vita Genovefae, 21–2
Vita sancti Paterni, 30
Vita Vedastis, 9
Vivarium, monastery of, 58
Vouciennes, cemetery of, 88

Waldebert, 16, 127 n. 105
warbands, 107 n. 62
weaponry, *see* armament
Weiner, Annette, 6
Wenigumstadt, cemetery of, 88
wills, 22–23
wine, 3–4, *see also* Eucharist
    imported from Gaza, 78
    spontaneous generation of, 15–16, 51
women, absence of in sources, 1–2
Wood, Ian, 102 n. 4
wooden cooking vessels, 23, 112 n. 117
Würzburg, 109 n. 89

xenodochia, 35, 42

Young, Bailey, 82, 85, 89

Zeno, 63
Zeuzuleben, cemetery of, 88